On Freedom, Love, and Power

JACQUES ELLUL

Compiled, edited, and translated by Willem H. Vanderburg

One of the most important and original thinkers of the twentieth century, Jacques Ellul (1912–1994) was a noted sociologist, historian, law professor, and self-described 'Christian anarchist.' During the Second World War, he was active in the French Resistance, and his efforts to rescue Jews from the Holocaust earned him international recognition. Ellul taught at the University of Bordeaux, and wrote and published extensively on the relationship between technology and culture, the tenets of the Christian faith, and the principles of human freedom and responsibility. This book, which makes available for the first time a transcription of a series of seminars given by Ellul in 1974, refines and clarifies some of his most controversial insights on the Jewish and Christian Bibles and their relevance to contemporary society.

In this work, Jacques Ellul reaches out to those who struggle with the dilemmas of our age by examining those posed to us by the Jewish and Christian scriptures. The results of his enquiry are surprising and enlightening. Genesis has nothing to do with the controversies over evolution versus creation. Job's search for answers to his questions has unexpected results. The distinction between the kingdom of heaven and the kingdom of God sheds light on what Christianity ought to be, and the gospel of John in its opening verses calls attention to overlooked connections and revelations.

In this examination of the spiritual roots of our civilization, Ellul's message stands out above the confusion of voices ranging from the new scientific atheism to the evangelical right. He does not ignore disciplines such as philosophy, theology, or religious studies, but rather transcends them. He accomplishes this through his critical awareness of the 'cultural glasses' through which we read the 'old stories' of the Jewish and Christian Bibles. Based on his sociological and historical analyses of the role science and *technique* have played and continue to play in society, Ellul recognizes that we, like those who came before us, have ended up serving the system we have built to serve us. While challenging the orthodoxies of Christianity, Judaism, and modern science, *On Freedom, Love, and Power* offers a deeply spiritual meditation, one that is in dialogue with the very lives we live and the world we inhabit.

WILLEM H. VANDERBURG is the director of the Centre for Technology and Social Development at the University of Toronto. He was a NATO postdoctoral fellow under Jacques Ellul from 1973 to 1978 at the University of Bordeaux.

JACQUES ELLUL

On Freedom, Love, and Power

Compiled, Edited, and Translated
by Willem H. Vanderburg

UNIVERSITY OF TORONTO PRESS
Toronto Buffalo London

© University of Toronto Press Incorporated 2010
Toronto Buffalo London
www.utppublishing.com
Printed in Canada

ISBN 978-1-4426-4220-1 (cloth)
ISBN 978-1-4426-1117-7 (paper)

Library and Archives Canada Cataloguing in Publication

Ellul, Jacques
Freedom, love, and power / Jacques Ellul; compiled, edited, and translated
by Willem H. Vanderburg.

Includes bibliographical references and index.
ISBN 978-1-4426-4220-1 (bound).   ISBN 978-1-4426-1117-7 (pbk.)

1. Bible – Criticism, interpretation, etc. – History – 20th century
I. Vanderburg, Willem H   II. Title.

BS511.E45 2010   220.6   C2010-903920-3

This book has been published with the help of a grant from the Canadian
Federation for the Humanities and Social Sciences, through the Aid to
Scholarly Publications Program, using funds provided by the Social
Sciences and Humanities Research Council of Canada.

University of Toronto Press acknowledges the financial assistance
to its publishing program of the Canada Council for the Arts and the
Ontario Arts Council.

Canada Council   Conseil des Arts
for the Arts   du Canada

ONTARIO ARTS COUNCIL
CONSEIL DES ARTS DE L'ONTARIO

University of Toronto Press acknowledges the financial support of the
Government of Canada through the Canada Book Fund for its publishing
activities.

Contents

Introduction   vii

**PART ONE: FREEDOM FROM MORALITY AND RELIGION
(GENESIS 1–3)**   1

1 Introductory Remarks to Genesis 1–3   3

2 The First Creation Account   17

3 The Second Creation Account   40

4 The Break between God and Humanity   61

5 The Consequences of the Break between God and Humanity   77

**PART TWO: THE LOVE THAT SEEKS US OUT
(JOB 32–42)**   99

6 Introduction   101

7 Elihu (Chapters 32–37)   105

8 God's Appearance (Chapters 38–39)   118

9 The Two Beasts (Chapters 40–41)   126

10 Job's Conversion (Chapter 42)   135

11 Reconciliation (Chapter 42)   140

**PART THREE: THE CULMINATION OF JUDAISM:
THE KINGDOM OF LOVE**   147

12 Introduction   149

13 The First Three Parables (Matthew 13:1–43)   160

14 The Second Set of Parables (Matthew 13:44–50)   169

15 The Parable of the Debtors (Matthew 18:23–35)   174

16 The Parable of the Labourers' Wages (Matthew 20:1–16)   180

17 The Parable of the Wedding Feast (Matthew 22:1–14)   188

18 The Parables of the Virgins and the Talents (Matthew 25:1–30)   196

19 The Remaining References to the Kingdom of Heaven   204

**PART FOUR: IT WAS ALL THERE IN THE BEGINNING
(JOHN 1:1–2)**   211

20 Love within the Beginning   213

Epilogue: History and Reconciliation   219

Index   235

Introduction

It is a chilly fall evening in 1974. After pulling a cord that operates a real bell perched on a wall, the gate is opened, we are welcomed and escorted down a path, up some stairs into a vestibule, via which we enter a large dining room. A small number of people are informally talking together. When it is time to start our meeting, we seat ourselves in a semicircle around a dining room table, behind which Jacques Ellul has taken his place. Most of us know him from the University of Bordeaux where he is a professor, and most of us have been invited because we have approached him with deeply existential questions. We are a rather mixed group, coming from Protestant, Catholic, Jewish, and Agnostic backgrounds in roughly equal numbers. The purpose of our gathering is to read the Bible together. Jacques Ellul begins by reading the text from a translation that is carefully chosen to reflect the Hebrew or Greek text as closely as the French language permits. A general discussion follows, on which Jacques Ellul builds a formal explanation of what the text means. After another discussion we tackle the next block of text, generally completing two or three of these cycles per session. Unable to take notes because of blindness, I have been given permission to record the formal presentation.

To my amazement, what unfolds in these sessions is a message unlike any I have ever heard in churches I have attended in four different countries. I know that I am far from the only one who has had this experience. For example, when I was asked to organize a symposium to mark Jacques Ellul's death in 1994, I was surprised to learn that all but one of the university professors I had invited to speak had become Christians through the reading of his work; but for all of them it made for a very uneasy relationship with organized religion. I must also confess that if I were reading this book and reached the above phrase 'to read the Bible together,' I would have probably closed it and put it back on the shelf because it brings back too many frustrating and painful experiences. This kind of reaction led Jacques Ellul to wonder if this is an age in which God is silent. Christian churches seem to be concentrating on maintaining or improving their real estate or aimlessly drifting on the currents of one philosophical or theological fashion after another, leaving their members bewildered and frustrated (if they bother to stick around at all). I can therefore safely say that if churches meet your needs, this book is not for you. However, if occasional visits leave you frustrated, if you left a long time ago, or if you wonder what goes on in these buildings on a Sunday morning, then this book may be for you.

Part 1 of this book brings some good news in the message that the God to whom we are introduced in the first few chapters of Genesis has nothing to do with the god(s) of religion, morality, and magic. Of course, it is not easy to disentangle this good news from the religious baggage we bring to making sense of these texts but, at least in principle, it clears the terrain for something that is entirely different. It has nothing to do with what every human community, society, and civilization has to do out of necessity: the creation of a culture as a way of making sense of and living in the world, which includes deep spiritual roots and points of orientation in reality. This is the religious stuff of being human; but the hope, consolation, and purpose it provides is achieved at the expense of our freedom.

In part 2, a discussion of the book of Job raises the issues of human suffering and who or what is responsible for it. Again, all the usual answers eloquently represented in the discussions between Job and his friends are swept aside to make room for a very different perspective. God is not the spectator who from afar watches the forces of good and evil battle it out at the expense of humanity, and who is therefore directly or indirectly responsible for our mess. Again, our preconceptions are swept aside. Our conceptions of why there is evil in the world and our holding God at least partly accountable for it, are transformed by a love that seeks us out and that prepares us for reconciliation.

In part 3, the distinction between the parables of the kingdom of heaven and those of the kingdom of God in the gospel of Matthew defines a Christianity that is deeply rooted in the Jewish Bible. The ways of the kingdom of heaven, based on freedom, love, and non-power, are the opposite of those of our civilization. These seek to endlessly increase the power of our science and technology. These ways systematically strain the interdependence of everything in human life and the world, making them uneconomic, socially non-viable, and environmentally unsustainable. As a result, our ways constitute a massive assault on all life.

In part 4, we come back to the message of Genesis, filled out with the ultimate love story as a way of freedom that must not be shackled once more by religion, morality, and magic.

I have taken the liberty to add a brief and inadequate summary of Jacques Ellul's study of the book of Revelation which, more than any other book in the Christian Bible, has been used to create more nonsense and more aberrations than all the others combined. I did this because it so beautifully recaps the ultimate love story as the good news in an age in which many are in desperate need of real hope, real faith, and real love.

By this time I can well imagine that my reader must be getting very impatient with me. How can I be so arrogant as to imply that one person gets it and most others do not, even though they read the same Bible? There are several explanations that can perhaps make this somewhat plausible. Jacques Ellul did not grow up in a church. It is likely, therefore, that as a historian and sociologist he would have regarded the Christian message merely out of professional interest as a significant influence on Western civilization in the past. Its present relevance has been severely undercut by churches claiming that Jesus is the answer without having any idea as to what the questions (of our age) are. All this changed following an intervention of God in his life, although he burned the manuscript of its account before he died. However, I believe there is another reason that sets Jacques Ellul's attempt at making sense of this message apart from the efforts of most historians, philosophers, and theologians, trapped as most of them are in our highly peculiar way of dividing up the task of knowing and dealing with the world by means of disciplines and specialties. These disciplinary silos completely disregard what science and technology have rediscovered in a tragic way, namely, that everything in human life in the world is related to everything else and that disregarding this interconnectedness explains a great deal of our suffering and hopelessness. Hence, I hardly think it an accident that an intervention occurred in the life of Jacques Ellul, as opposed to someone else's life. I will not dwell on what someone has already pointed out, namely, that as a sociologist and historian he accurately predicted almost all the important developments resulting from the permeation of civilization by science and technology during the second half of the twentieth century.

It is in relation to this understanding of what is happening to human life and society that Jacques Ellul seeks to discover what a Christian presence in this time might have been. As a result, his perspective is very different from that of disciplines such as religious studies, philosophy, or theology. This has far-reaching consequences, as I will seek to explain.

We are all born into a particular culture; and it is highly probable that our moral and religious convictions remain those of our own culture. For example, I was born in the Netherlands where, at that time, over eighty per cent of the population would attend a Protestant or Catholic service on Sunday morning. Like most young people, I took on the moral and religious beliefs of my home and community. However, I am entirely convinced that had I been born in a different society and civilization, my beliefs would likely have been very different. The fact of the matter is that I did not search all over the world to see which set of beliefs was more true than all others, and yet I live as if mine are. It is highly likely that, had I been born into a culture shaped by traditions such as Judaism, Islam, or Buddhism, I would have lived them in the same way.

Acknowledging this is not a first step on the path to cultural relativism. On the contrary, it is simply a recognition that, socio-culturally and historically, our moral and religious beliefs have protected us (be it in very different ways) from having our lives and communities come unravelled. Our cultures include absolutized elements that help cover over an abyss of relativism, nihilism, and *anomie*. It is this situation that we must confront.

When anyone reads a Jewish or Christian Bible, he or she reads it in a particular language, and thus within a culture. This includes an ensemble of interrelated meanings and values anchored in deeply unconscious collective commitments. These constitute the means that any reader relies on in order to make sense of the text. Such culture-based symbolization places the text in relation to everything else we know and live, which accommodates it to our ways and our world. Such an accommodation transforms the meaning of a text, particularly when it has been translated from a language distant from our own, such as Hebrew. Superimposed on this is another problem. What happens if the text concerns a revelation from beyond our ways and our world? About the God who reveals himself, we are specifically told that his ways are not our ways. How can we symbolize something that is entirely 'other' in our (cultural) terms?

A simple analogy may help to illustrate the point. A person has visited a new place, and upon her return she wishes to paint one particularly beautiful scene. Since it was a bright sunny day, she was wearing sunglasses, and she must now try to imagine what the colours would have been like without them. To help this process along, she looks at a few scenes out of her windows with and without these sunglasses to see how they affect her colour perception. In the same vein, we know that different cultures have organized the world of colour somewhat differently. Hence, a part of growing up in a particular culture involves something analogous to putting on a particular kind of sunglasses that deal with the world of colour in a way that is unique to that culture, except that they cannot be taken off. A non-cultural vantage point of the world of colour thus becomes impossible. Moreover, a culture organizes much more than the world of colour. It teaches us to make sense of and purposefully live in our world by 'putting on' an ensemble of meanings, values, and commitments through which we live our lives.

All this occurs because every daily-life experience grows the organization of the brain-mind by means of neural and synaptic changes. Such changes symbolize that experience, making it possible to live it in the context of all previously symbolized experiences. The organization of the brain-mind thus sustains the living of our lives. The importance of this becomes painfully obvious when we encounter people with a short-term memory loss or moderately advanced Alzheimer's disease. They can experience only separate moments connected by the life lived before the onset of the disease. On the level of a group or society, this symbolization is fundamental in creating, adapting, and evolving a way of life and in the making of their history. The rise and fall of civilizations are reflections of how well a symbolically created culture provides meaning, direction, and purpose for the lives of its members.

Because our entire life is built on these meanings, values, and commitments, we can never entirely give them up. We live as if the reality we have come to know and live is reality itself, minus some details yet to be discovered and lived. In this way, the unknown is no longer threatening and cannot upset our life, which has been woven together from countless relationships within an ultimately unknowable reality. In other words, we have extrapolated what we know and live to include, in principle, all of reality, thereby leaving no place for anything that is radically 'other.' This absolutization of what we know and live includes whatever, in the experience of our community, is so important and valuable that it has made us and our world who and what we are. What simply is

the greatest good we have experienced becomes the absolute good, beyond which nothing more important and valuable can be lived or im-
agined. The only way we can gain some awareness of our deep spiritual
roots and reference points comes from comparing different cultures, or
from comparing the same culture during different epochs in the history
of its people. Such comparisons reveal the spiritual dimension of our
collective cultural journeys. All this is well known in disciplines such as
cultural anthropology, the sociology of religion, and depth psychology.
In a sense, the metaconsciously created absolutes, commonly referred to
as myths, constitute the 'cultural DNA' that orients and supports our
lives in an ultimately unknowable reality.

So what happens when we try to make sense of a God whose ways are
not our ways and who calls us to be holy, that is, to be set apart from the
world by learning his ways? How can we make sense of something that
is entirely 'other' and has no corresponding meaning, value, and commitment in our culture? What are we to make of a revelation that designates our meanings and values, and our commitments to our way of life
and culture, as a service of idols which turn us into their slaves? Does this
revelation still hold for contemporary scientific, rational, and secular cultures? Even if we accept what is being revealed, we are in no position to
take off our 'cultural glasses.' This puts believers in this revelation into a
terrible predicament. We can hardly put off our (cultural) old nature and
give up everything that has provided meaning, direction, and purpose
for our lives. It would plunge us into absolute *anomie* (or meaninglessness), which we well know drives people to depression, despair, and suicide. It is one thing to talk about dying to our old nature, being reborn,
and putting on a new nature, but how does one actually live this?

This dilemma can be avoided by uncritically symbolizing what we are
reading and by accommodating it to our culture and way of life. The
revelation is then turned into a morality, religion, and philosophical-
theological system taken to be superior to all those created by cultures
throughout human history, including our own. Believers tend to become
trapped in self-justification and the judgment of others with this morality
and religion and in the extreme, aspire to create a Christian society with
Christian institutions. The problem is that this would transform the revelation into the exact opposite of what it reveals itself to be, namely, an
anti-morality, an anti-religion, and an anti-metaphysics. Jacques Ellul re-
peatedly shows this, beginning with his explanation of the first three
chapters of Genesis.

The above-mentioned way of resolving radical conflicts has been documented in what is supposed to the most objective, controlled, rational, and self-critical human knowing, namely, science. Considerable distortions occur, however, when what is observed threatens the knowledge and beliefs of the observer because it is radically 'other.' Especially in the social sciences, we usually forget that any field observation is as much an experiment on how the observer will react. To exclude this behaviour is to ignore the well-known reactions most of us have when facing these kinds of situations, as documented in social science theories. There is a powerful but unconscious tendency to reinterpret what is being observed, to the point of distorting it in order to create a better fit between what is observed and what the observer brings to the task, thereby reducing tension and anxiety. For example, if a cultural anthropologist observes a phenomenon that is deeply troubling to his ways and beliefs, the interpretation is almost always detrimental to the people and culture being observed. An unintentional and unconscious element of self-justification has taken over. This makes it next to impossible to treat these people as fellow human beings, in the sense that had the cultural anthropologist grown up in that culture he almost certainly would have observed things very differently. If all this can happen in science, it can also happen in the reading of the Bible.

In our reading of the Bible, we must be aware that it is existentially impossible to confront the ultimate clash between what is revealed to us and the cultural ensemble of meanings, values, and commitments that we necessarily use to make sense of what we read. We must realize that God's ways are entirely other than anything a human culture and civilization can create, live, or imagine. Hence, we must be alert to a likely distortion of the text in order to protect ourselves from *anomie*. To the extent that we dare to live in the knowledge that we are loved by God, to that extent we can face our condition of being enslaved to and rooted in myth. However, to affirm this is one thing, and to live it quite another. The history of the Jewish people and that of the Christian church show that the most common way of resolving the clash between what they read and what they read *with* has been the turning of the revelation into its exact opposite: a morality and a religion, in order to satisfy the necessities that human life in the world imposes on a culture. On the intellectual plane, Christian theologies and philosophies have been typical of their time, place, and culture, in ways that become embarrassingly clear only with hindsight.

If Judaism and Christianity merely contribute additional moralities and religions to the many already created by humanity through its diverse cultures, we will obey the necessities of a community having to justify itself, and its members being compelled to judge others and themselves. We must not confuse the necessity of every culture having to create a morality and a religion with the calling of being a transforming salt or yeast. This involves bearing witness to God's unconditional love, how this love gives us permission to taste our freedom, and how even a small taste of this freedom can enhance our ability to love. In an age of scientific knowing and technological doing, which greatly strengthen the power of the state and the transnational corporation (now constituting the majority of the world's hundred largest economies), this is not an easy matter. Do we not believe that, in principle, science knows everything, and hence that it is without limits? We are thereby creating a myth out of a human endeavour by endowing it with god-like qualities in the domain of human knowing. Do we not believe that anything short of the latest technological doing will damn us to underdevelopment and backwardness? Because we have grown up and spent our entire lives within an essentially urban-industrial-information life-milieu, in which almost every activity directly or indirectly depends on one technology or another, our experiences and our lives appear to be symbolized in the organization of our brain-minds in a way that puts us into an existential situation in which we can no longer imagine who we would be, how we would live, and what our world would be like without science and technology. Science and technology have made us and our world who and what we are. Not only are the state and the transnational corporation the primary loci of this power, they are the very condition for having it. Who can tell us what we cannot know scientifically or what we cannot do technologically? If very few of us can answer this question, are we not in the position described by Abraham Maslow to the effect that, if your only tool is a hammer, all your problems look like nails? Are we not then enslaved by myths in our knowing and doing; and even though these have taken on a secular form, does this in any way alter the human condition? If we regard this as merely science- and technology-'bashing,' how is this different from claiming that the thermostat on the wall is 'bashing' the furnace? Without our secular myths, we would be plunged into an existentially unlivable situation, because what we have declared as being very good, and even the greatest good we know, is making us economically poorer, socially less viable, and environmentally unsustainable. Even comprehensively self-interested behaviour would do better.

It is here that I believe the life and work of Jacques Ellul make a land-mark contribution. As noted, he did not grow up with the theological tutelage of a Jewish synagogue or a Christian church. I believe this is very important, because theology has accepted a discipline-based mode of scholarship based on the assumption that each discipline can advance our understanding of human life in the world relatively autonomously from other disciplines. Most theologians thus have little or no critical awareness of the ensemble of meanings, values, and commitments through which they do their work. As a result, theologians may be ill-prepared for the above problems, working as they do with the illusion of objectivity and detachment from cultural vantage points and roots.

Starting out as a historian of legal institutions, Jacques Ellul soon rec-ognized that these institutions could not be abstracted from the entire institutional framework of a society and culture without a substantial loss of understanding and a distortion of the subject matter. This put him at odds with his own discipline, which had always proceeded as if legal institutions could be understood by themselves. Underneath his social and historical analyses lies the strong conviction that there is something indivisible about human life and society. He also learned this while attempting to make sense of his world, troubled as it was by the Great Depression and the rise of Fascism. It was not possible to understand the economic aspects of these developments apart from all the others, and vice versa. During an interview for the Canadian Broadcasting Corporation in the summer of 1979, he expressed this as the need to 'think globally,' that is, the need to respect the interconnect-edness of human life in the world. Implied in this concept is an ac-knowledgement of the limitations of discipline-based scholarship.

Jacques Ellul thus found himself in the company of most of the great thinkers of the nineteenth and early twentieth centuries who studied any particular category of phenomena (such as economic, social, political, legal, moral, or religious) against the background of all the others. With some of these thinkers he also shared the conviction that slavery was not an acceptable form of human life. Hence, any theoretical activity at-tempting to reduce the unintelligible complexity of our lives and our world to an intelligible complexity should pay particular attention to those aspects that threaten human freedom. For Karl Marx, capitalism enslaved rich and poor alike. As a result, this socio-economic order had to be transformed to set humanity free. (This had nothing in common with what was done in the name of Marx by totalitarian regimes.) In the twentieth century, this socio-economic order became increasingly dom-inated by a new phenomenon, which Max Weber called rationality. He warned that it was locking humanity into an iron cage. Still later, and independently from Weber, who was virtually unknown in France at that time), Jacques Ellul examined the rise of what may be regarded as a much more evolved form of this rationality, which he called *technique*. He showed that, sociologically and historically, the influence people had on the evolution of this human creation was far less decisive than the influence it had on individual and collective human life during the second half of the twentieth century. Once again, our freedom was threatened.

Human life based on *technique* is in many aspects the opposite of human life based on culture, which, by means of symbolization, seeks to make sense of and evolve everything in relation to everything else. Simply put, *technique* represents the widespread use of a scientific and discipline-based approach to knowing accompanied by a similar technical approach to doing. The resulting intellectual and professional division of labour restricts practitioners to their domains of specialization. What they know about human life, society, and the biosphere is limited to what their domains receive from the world for improvement, and after these improvements have been made, to what is returned to the world. The transformation of these 'inputs' into 'outputs' is improved in terms of those aspects commensurate with the domains of specialization of the practitioners. The criteria for deciding what constitutes an improvement cannot be related to what is better for human life, society, and the biosphere, because this transcends the domains of specialization. Improving something must be based on what the practitioners know, with the result that the best they can do is to obtain the greatest possible 'outputs' from the 'inputs' as measured by criteria such as efficiency, productivity, and profitability. This technical approach explains the successes and failures of our civilization: we succeed brilliantly at improving the performance of everything and fail spectacularly at ensuring that all these improvements fit into and are compatible with human life, society, and the biosphere. Once again, we have ended up serving what we created to serve us.

The previously mentioned intervention in his life made Jacques Ellul realize that his global thinking and appreciation of the interconnectedness of human life in the world lacked one decisive element that would change everything, namely, God being with humanity in the world. As he struggled to work this out, he soon learned that he could count on very little help from clergy and theologians.

Jacques Ellul was keenly aware of his culture and history, which he brought to the reading of the Bible, and of the irreconcilable opposition between the two. His understanding of human life in the world could not be assimilated into his understanding of the biblical message, nor could that message be assimilated into his understanding of human life. Each one transformed the other in a process in which both played an essential role. For example: the matter of human freedom cannot be understood apart from how, as people of our time, place, and culture, we are constrained by the necessity of rooting and orienting ourselves by myths; and it would be equally impossible to expose these roots and not be plunged into despair, were it not for the assurance of liberation and freedom founded on God's unconditional love. The Bible puts it plainly: the revelation is the light that helps us find another way in our daily-life activities. It poses questions about where we are and where we are going, in order to have us take responsibility and find another way. As we struggle with these questions, we discover new things about ourselves and our world, which sends us back to the light in order to make sense of them.

The best analogy I can think of is the accounts of people who have had a so-called near-death experience. One common element in these accounts is the reliving of a person's life, but with one crucial difference. It reveals a much richer understanding of how these people affected others in their lives and how this understanding affected them in turn. In most instances, this experience unveils a profound harm done to others and oneself; and knowing this would be unbearable were it not for the fact that all this happens in the enveloping presence of a loving light. In other words, our enslavement to the myths of our culture makes it next to impossible to live a moment of our life with an adequate knowledge of what is really happening. When we accept and begin to live the assurance that we are loved and liberated from all slavery, we can begin to probe this darkness – not by applying a new theoretical insight, but by finding a new way for our lives. It must be remembered that freedom is a prerequisite for commitment and love. For example, a slave cannot commit himself to another person because his master could sell him the next day. That new freedom would be surrendered if the gospel of liberation and love were turned into a Christian morality and religion. Nor can there be any question of surrendering to a theological system that has all the right answers. This would turn human life into enslavement to this system, including the principles and world views embedded in it. Instead, God's freedom restores the commandments to their original purpose, that of creating a sphere of freedom and love that not only fulfils them but creates the possibility of going further in love. In all this we must never forget that this enslavement protected us, and to a lesser degree continues to protect us, from fully recognizing what we are doing to others and ourselves, which could only drive us to despair. Our servitude can only be faced in the presence of faith, hope, and love.

I have suggested that near-death experiences may provide a useful explanatory analogy of what is going on during our lives. It helps us to understand salvation (being loved), sin (being enslaved), and judgment (the separation of wheat from tares, or what is unto life and what is unto death). The latter is also compared to the purification of gold, where a fire makes the impurities come to the surface so that they can be removed. It is as if God were a surgeon removing the cancer from our bodies so that we might live. This is what human history looks like when illuminated with the light of the revelation. Without that light human history appears as Shakespeare's 'tale told by an idiot, full of sound and fury, signifying nothing.'

Christianity has frequently turned the relationship between freedom (as a prerequisite for relationships of love) and sin (enslavement) upside down. It is only after we know we have been liberated that we can have some awareness of what it is to be alienated. This is a consequence of, and not a step leading up to, God's love, forgiveness, and new life. To the extent that we learn to live by this love, pardon, and freedom, to that extent will we become aware of our alienation. It can never be the other way around.

All this has profound implications for the present-day schism between conservative and liberal Christianity. There can be no question of a *Sola Scriptura*. By this I do not mean that the revelation is not an indivisible whole, so that each text must be understood in the context of all the others. What I mean is that the Bible cannot be read from a vantage point of enslavement; and if the inevitable distortion of the text is to be minimized, we must understand that our lives are lived in the world by means of a particular culture. In other words, theology must never become a discipline. It must instead be shaped by a dialogue between the Bible and our understanding of our lives and the world. Otherwise we make the conservative error of focusing primarily on the light of that revelation; and our eyes now being accustomed to that light, we will be unable to see in the dark (world) where we live our lives. Or, conversely, we become trapped in the liberal error, where compassion for our fellow human beings and the suffering of the world accustoms our eyes to the dark, with the result that the light of the revelation blinds us. What we need to do is to hold the light in one hand in such a way that it does not blind us but illuminates the way ahead. Yes, it leaves only one hand to reach for others in need, but if we faithfully bear the light we may announce their liberation from slavery.

In sum, I believe the work of Jacques Ellul, seen as a dialogue between his 'social and historical' and his 'biblical' studies, reunites the 'vertical' and the 'horizontal' dimensions of the revelation. In this way, it could restore the Christian community to its task of being a transformative presence in the world, likened to salt in food or yeast in bread dough. His social and historical writings help us understand how *technique* has disconnected us from the earth in order to reconnect us in unsustainable and unjust ways. He has also shown how *technique* does not liberate us from the moralities and religions of the past, but instead connects us to new secular gods that are potentially even more alienating and dangerous. Of course, no one heeded the warning when there was a window of opportunity to intervene in a transformative way. As *technique* has now become our life-milieu and system, resulting from an all-out enslavement to efficiency, transformative interventions have become much more difficult, at least for some time to come. This is all the more reason to live by faith, hope, and love, so as to be the transformative force that alters our course away from the destruction of ourselves and our planet. It is walking with the revelation as 'a lamp unto our feet' during this period of human history that constitutes the gift Jacques Ellul has left us. We have been liberated to enable us to live by the love of our God and our neighbour, and thus to have no need to dishonour, to steal, to covet, to lie, and everything else that once came with the condition of enslavement. Today we are called to work this out in a so-called secular age dominated by science, *technique*, the transnational, and the state and their all-pervasive integration propaganda.

A brief note as to how this book came into being. Parts 1 and 3 were recorded as described at the beginning of this Introduction. Parts 2 and 4 were recorded by Dr Frank Brugerolle in sessions Jacques Ellul held for the Pessac-Mérignac parish of the Église Réformée in France. I am deeply grateful to him for making copies of these and other studies, and to Burney Médard, who personally carried these copies to our meeting at a U.S. airport, from which I took them home. To help create the freedom for all participants to speak their minds, I stopped my tape recorder whenever someone asked a question, and continued recording when Jacques Ellul answered them. For this reason, I have inserted into the text the phrase 'In response to your questions: ...' This phrase introduces those answers which the reader may find helpful, and which can be understood without knowing the questions. I have also followed this approach in parts 2 and 4 because the recordings were carried out with a single microphone; and although the questions from the congregation were recorded, they were usually inaudible. Unfortunately, the recordings of the first part of the book of Job were lost; and because of illness, Jacques Ellul did not complete part 4, which originally was to include the first five verses of the gospel of John as well as some later parts (which were recorded).

Working with these fragments has confronted the readers of the first draft and myself with the inadequacy and occasional borderline dishonesty of many Bible translations. Particularly when the translated text is rearranged or made to sound literary without the courtesy of warning the reader that the original Hebrew literally means something else, this is more than a little frustrating. In the sessions I recorded, Jacques Ellul's dining-room table was always covered with texts in the original Hebrew or Greek and translations such as those of his friend André Chouraqui, which attempted to keep the French as close as possible to the original texts. I know of no English equivalents.

I am grateful to Calvin Seerveld and Al Wolters, who kindly provided me with transliterations of the Hebrew words. As a check on my translation, a first draft of my conversion of these spoken sessions (or parts thereof) into a readable text was informally read and commented on by a number of friends, after which I reworked the text. My anonymous reviewers passed on some excellent suggestions for some additional footnotes. My sincere thanks to you all. Dominique, Jean, and Yves Ellul have been very supportive of this project. I also wish to thank Virgil Duff and Margaret Burgess, of the University of Toronto Press, who have been most helpful. Last but not least, I would not have been able to complete this task without the assistance of my wife Rita, who is my eyes on the world.

With a small portion of the estate of my parents, Beverly and Gary Vanderburg, I have been able to bring this book to the attention of people in a position to pass on the message to many others in different communities. My parents' lives were deeply marked by the intolerance of the institutional church, and I wish they had lived to see this book come to completion.

In conclusion, I wish to make it very clear that this text does not represent a literal translation of the recorded presentations. To the best of my ability, I have translated the spoken words as closely as possible to produce a readable written text. It has been a labour of love in memory of Jacques Ellul who, like no one before or after in any institutional church, has helped me to understand this ultimate love story.

Willem H. Vanderburg

PART ONE

Freedom from Morality and Religion (Genesis 1–3)

1 Introductory Remarks to Genesis 1–3

Inspiration

Any attempt to understand the first few chapters of Genesis immediately confronts us with a number of problems. For starters, there are two creation stories: there is the account arranged in seven days, followed by another that begins with the origin of the heavens and the earth as created by God. The two accounts do not agree, as is evident from the many contradictions commentators have pointed out. I will mention only one, which is typical. The first account tells us that at first there was only water over which God's Spirit moved; while the second account begins with land, with water in the form of rain coming later. There are also contradictions between these two accounts and what we know scientifically.

Another problem stems from the two accounts being contained in the Pentateuch, commonly referred to as the five books of Moses. However, Moses could not have been the author of these accounts for the linguistic reason that Moses probably did not speak the Hebrew found in the text, since it is of a later time. Following the discovery of the Babylonian and Egyptian creation stories in the late nineteenth century, commentators observed that the Genesis accounts not only resembled these but that they were likely inspired by the Babylonian story. Such claims probably reveal an anti-biblical stance, just as earlier there had been a pro-biblical stance. A last problem, even more obvious than the others, is how human beings could know anything about what had happened before they were created. It is this last question that should be addressed first because it raises the issue of how the text was inspired.

From the fourth century on, Christian theologians have replied to this question, with an astounding ease and radical simplicity, that human beings knew what had happened before they were created because they were directly inspired by God. In other words, the Holy Spirit spoke and the biblical authors wrote it down. It should be noted that there has never been an equivalent Jewish interpretation. The difficulty of the doctrine of direct inspiration is that it leaves no room for contradictions in the text, and it is true that for centuries commentators simply did not see them. I am not suggesting that this is voluntary, but that in reading a text there may be things you simply do not see, as if the unconscious creates a blackout. People lived with the theory of the infallibility of the Bible, with the consequence that there could be no errors.

There was another theological current, which I believe to be the correct one.[1] It held that the Bible itself is not compatible with infallible inspiration. God never mechanizes human beings, to reduce biblical authors to a kind of dictaphone. On the contrary, the God revealed in the Bible is, first and foremost, the One who liberates people.[2] He does not set people free from alienation only to enslave them again to other things. This is fundamental for the interpretation of any text. For example, from this perspective it is impossible to interpret the Ten Commandments as imperatives imposed by God on people as a kind of external will. The intent is the exact opposite, namely, to permit human beings to live.[3] If the God of the Bible is the One who liberates, human beings are not crushed, terrorized, or mechanically manipulated. When God speaks, human beings are put into a situation of responsibility and decision as opposed to a situation with new constraints. God questions

---

1 Jacques Ellul's 'Innocent Notes on "The Hermeneutic Question,"' in Marva Dawn's *Sources and Trajectories* (Grand Rapids, MI: Eerdmans, 1997), may assist the reader to understand how to read the Bible. Perhaps the best overall reference for the reader is part 3 of *What I Believe*, trans. Geoffrey W. Bromiley (Grand Rapids, MI: Eerdmans, 1989).

2 See Jacques Ellul, *The Ethics of Freedom*, trans. Geoffrey W. Bromiley (Grand Rapids, MI: Eerdmans, 1976) for a detailed discussion of freedom. It is perhaps Ellul's major topic in attempting to understand Judaism and Christianity.

3 The reader may find it helpful to consult Jacques Ellul's ideas about the impossibility of a Christian ethic and its necessity with regard to morality. See Jacques Ellul, *To Will and To Do*, trans. C. Edward Hopkin (Philadelphia: Pilgrim Press, 1969). Christians have often misunderstood this aspect of Christianity. See Jacques Ellul, *The Subversion of Christianity*, trans. Geoffrey W. Bromiley (Grand Rapids, MI: Eerdmans, 1986), especially chapter 4, which deals with the issues of morality and male–female relations, and ties them together.

people and places them before a decision. As far as the Bible is concerned, this seems undeniable to me. Hence, when God reveals himself to people, they do not become dictaphones. They hear and respond as the people they are with their means, their knowledge, their language, and their culture. If they are poor spellers they will make spelling mistakes; and I say this in recognition of how important this can be in Hebrew, where the text regularly plays with spelling. Hence, if a biblical author made a spelling mistake the results can be very serious. Of course, they were surrounded by other people who reflected on these texts and who heard in them a word from God. In other words, instead of dictaphones we see human authors who used their culture and all its means, and who therefore would make the 'intellectual errors' of their culture and time. For example, it has often been acknowledged that from a scientific perspective Jesus did not know any more than the people of his time. In the same way, those who worked on the first two chapters of Genesis shared with the people of their culture and time an ensemble of beliefs, which are not necessary in order to understand the Word of God.

According to this understanding of biblical inspiration, there cannot be a single account. Consider the hypothesis of infallible inspiration once more. It implies that God chooses a person, tells him or her everything, and that would be the end of it. There would be no need to add anything. This is not the way the Old Testament unfolds. It is a kind of lengthy account with new beginnings, a great deal of journeying, and even starts over from time to time. It is not progressive because there are also regressions. What we find is human beings who, one after another, heard certain things from God and who transcribed what they thought they heard using what they knew. That is why there are successive revelations that follow and renew one another. No revelation is the last one, and none is better than the preceding one. I would say that each time the Word is looked at from a different angle or vantage point, as it were. Furthermore, we encounter writings which unfold in the course of a history, and this is fundamental. This God of the Old Testament is neither the God of philosophy nor of metaphysics, but a God who enters into the history of people, who follows in people's paths and who is therefore a historical God. In other words, it is not (as some theological interpretations hold) that God makes people ascend to where he is, as it were, to reveal himself; but on the contrary (as other interpretations hold), a God who descends to where people are, and who enters into history. These two orientations are also found in Jewish thought.

Because different texts involve different perspectives and vantage points via which people understand the revealed Word, they must be compared with each other if we are to get at their meaning. No single text can be exhaustive. All this is further confirmed by the fact that God never reveals a metaphysics, a philosophy, or a system. One of the biggest mistakes has been the transformation of the Bible into a metaphysics. It is the problem of all catechisms, which are at the same time true and false. For example, when children are taught that God is eternal, unchangeable, and so on, they learn things the Bible never says. I would even say that the Bible says the opposite. For example, when theological metaphysics asserts that God cannot suffer because he is God, the whole Bible tells you the exact opposite. It is understandable that catechisms say these kinds of things, but they construct a metaphysics that is foreign to the Bible. Similarly, the creation account of six days has been transformed into a metaphysics of the creation, but the text is about something else entirely.

The Meaning of the Text

The question of the meaning of the text is central, and I will deal with it via three aspects. First, there is the meaning of the text itself. In addition, the text has a kind of existential orientation that provides us with a meaning rather than a factual account. Finally, each element must be interpreted in relation to the others.

Concerning the first aspect, I have argued that no single text in the Bible can be understood on its own. It cannot be taken literally or as being exhaustive. It must not be separated from the others, since it is but one illumination and does not stand by itself. Hence, there can be several meanings. Commentators have generally distinguished three kinds. First, there is the literal sense of the text. There is also the spiritual meaning, which is the meaning it has from the perspective of God's revelation. For example, the use of the term 'the heavens' does not refer to the sky and outer space, nor to a kind of cover above us where God would live. The spiritual meaning of 'the heavens' is the abode of God. For lack of a human term to symbolize this abode, the Bible utilizes the term 'sky' in the singular for what we experience, and 'the heavens' for the abode of God. This spiritual meaning of 'the heavens' is rather significant because it means that God's abode was created, like the earth. In other words, there is no spiritual domain that is eternal, with God and the heavenly host. The 'world' of God is created just like ours, each with its own 'people.' Finally, there is the esoteric meaning, which is hidden. For example, the Jewish Kabbala has developed this by giving each Hebrew letter a number, and the numbers are then manipulated to search for hidden meanings in the text. With the aid of computers, this opens up almost limitless possibilities, especially since in Hebrew there are only consonants. The vowels are added in order to pronounce the words. With the same consonants different vowels may be added, giving different words. For example, the name for God used in the second chapter of Genesis is YHWH, which can be vocalized as Yahweh or Jehovah. Here it creates no difficulties, because the name of God is unpronounceable in any case. However, for many words it can lead to the possibility of clever plays on words. The Kabbala has explored this to great length; but I believe that, although interesting, it is ultimately false.

Christian theologians have also developed esoteric meanings. For example, from the fourth to the tenth century they created something similar to the Kabbala by affirming that this symbolizes that, and so on. The text is then transposed into something else. In the Song of Songs 'the beloved' can be taken to be the soul, or the Church, or for that matter anything else. In this way these theologians came up with symbolic interpretations that leave the door wide open.

In contemporary Protestantism there exists the Christocentric meaning, which holds that all texts are a prophecy about Jesus Christ; and you then have to search for these traces in all the texts of the Old Testament, for example. This is not wrong. There is the remarkable work of Wilhelm Vischer entitled *The First Prophets of Jesus Christ in the Old Testament*,[4] but it is hardly exhaustive.

There is the claim of some historians, scientists, rationalists, and positivists that these biblical texts have no meaning for us. They are literary or historical texts, like all others. What this means is that when, for example, you read the first chapter of Genesis it can only tell you how the Jews in the eighth century before Jesus Christ expressed themselves and how they thought on a purely literary and cultural level. The above approaches are hardly exhaustive; and to keep things in perspective, I like to cite a rabbinical saying that each text has seventy-seven meanings plus the only true one, which only God knows. Hence, there is plenty of scope for playing with meanings.

---

4 Wilhelm Vischer, *The Witness of the Old Testament to Christ*, trans. A.B. Crabtree (London: Lutterworth Press, 1949).

All this leaves us with two possibilities. Discouraged by all these possible meanings, should we attempt to reduce everything to a few simple truths? This has frequently been the position some Christians were driven to while under attack from historians or positivists. It goes something like this. All right, we are willing to abandon the first two chapters of Genesis, since they are so full of errors that little remains that is true. Only three or four general ideas can be saved, such as there being a moment that was the point of departure for everything, that men and women were created each in relation to the other, or that God subordinated the world to people so that when we exercise our supremacy we conform to God's original design. This is more or less all that Father Chaine retains in his 700-page commentary on the book of Genesis.[5] This represents one possibility of reducing everything to the extreme.

The other possibility (which is my position) is that the text is infinitely richer and has infinitely more substance, as I will try to show. However, if there is a plurality of meanings enhanced by vocalizing the Hebrew, is it possible to read into these texts anything we like? Seeing scores of interpretations, some people have come to this conclusion. I do not believe this is justified, provided that you do not separate the texts. If you do separate one piece from the rest, or one text from the rest, then indeed you can give it almost any meaning you like. However, if you respect the integrality and general orientation of the text by interpreting it within the broader context of the entire text, then the number of possible interpretations becomes greatly constrained. This is why I cannot accept approaches such as that of the Kabbala or of symbolic interpretation, because they completely ignore the overall thrust of the revelation. Hence there are diverse meanings, but not every meaning is possible. For example, in the Old Testament it is possible to discern various developments or thrusts in relation to which each text must be compared and measured. All too often we read a text with a prejudgment or an orientation that is not of the text itself. For example, especially for the first two chapters of Genesis, everything has been distorted, beginning with the infusion of Greek philosophy toward the end of the third century via the theologians. The problem is that Greek philosophy asks questions to which the Bible does not in the least seek to reply. The Greeks were interested in the origin of the world, but I will seek to show that the first two chapters of Genesis have no interest in

---

5   J. Chaine, *Le livre de la Genèse* (Paris: Cerf, 1949).

this subject whatsoever. Once theologians began to think along the lines of Greek philosophy, they began to interpret the first two chapters of Genesis as an answer to the origin of the world. In other words, they began to read these texts as answers to philosophical or metaphysical questions, resulting in a complete distortion of what these texts are all about, which has nothing to do with the origin of the world.

Similar problems began to occur when Greek concepts, such as objective knowledge, were adopted. This concept is entirely foreign to Jewish thought. Hence, we need to take certain precautions. We need to know how to read a particular text. For example, it is impossible to read a medieval text the way we read a contemporary novel. They are rooted in completely different contexts.

I will now turn to the second question, namely, that the texts are there to provide a meaning. Once again, we encounter a common misunderstanding with regard to science. Since the sixteenth century, theologians and scientists have confused truth with reality, as it were.[6] Most

---

6   The distinction between reality and truth is absolutely fundamental in the thought of Jacques Ellul. He most fully develops it in his book *The Humiliation of the Word* (Grand Rapids, MI: Eerdmans, 1985). It is his only work in which he develops his sociological/historical insights and his Christian insights on the Bible in alternating chapters.

For now, it may be helpful if the reader recognizes that God's creation is seen differently through the lenses of different cultures and at different times. What a particular community experiences is often very different from and even incompatible with what all the others experience. A distinction must therefore be made between the reality as it is known and lived by a community during a certain time in its historical journey, and the reality that lies beyond, which constitutes the unknown. As a result, any community would be open to the risks of relativism, nihilism, and *anomie* unless it were protected against them. Such protection comes from every community having learned to live the reality it knows as reality itself, minus some details yet to be discovered. The unknown is no longer a threat because it has been transformed into more of what is already known and lived. The members of any community can thus go about their lives with the full confidence that the reality they know and live is reality itself. Whatever is 'wholly other' has been eliminated from their universe, and this accomplished by what in cultural anthropology, the sociology and history of religion, and depth psychology has been referred to as 'myth.' Such an 'absolutization' of the reality as it is known and lived by the community includes whatever is most valuable and essential, to the point that life and the world would be unimaginable without it. This entity is usually referred to as the central myth or the sacred. The sacred and myths constitute, for a culture and its way of life, a design for living in reality. On the biological level, they are comparable to DNA as the 'blueprint' for noncultural life.

In his book *The New Demons* (New York: Seabury, 1975), Ellul shows that so-called secular mass societies are also possessed by myths, although these have taken on a

theologians assumed that God created the reality of this world, and that therefore God gave us knowledge of this reality. Nothing is more foreign to the Bible. Nor do the 'historical' books furnish us with a scientific history, that is, the kind of account that would result if we studied that history. They could have provided us with the facts, but that did not interest the authors because they had other things in mind which they considered to be more important. Of course, they could not have established the facts regarding the reality of creation for lack of a scientific approach and tradition. But, more fundamentally, that is not what preoccupied them. The theologians were the first to confuse truth and reality by thinking that the truth as revealed was reality. The scientists followed suit but in the opposite direction, by thinking that the reality they studied was the truth. The Bible deals with something entirely

---

secular form. A literal translation of the title of the French original would be 'The Newly Possessed.' For a study of the role cultures played in human life prior to industrialization, which I believe to be implicit in the work of Jacques Ellul, the reader is referred to my book *The Growth of Minds and Cultures* (Toronto: University of Toronto Press, 1985), which I prepared while working with him in France and for which he wrote the introduction.

The Jewish Bible/Christian Old Testament has a great deal to say about every culture creating its gods and the risks this entails when a people puts its trust in something that can never deliver on its expectations. The cultural creations of such gods and the religions associated with them must be distinguished from the revelation received from the transcendent God of the Bible. His communicating with people introduces something into the reality they know and live, which is not a cultural creation. Ellul has developed this distinction between religion and faith in the fourth chapter of my interviews for the Canadian Broadcasting Corporation (CBC) *Perspectives on Our Age* (Toronto: House of Anansi Press, revised ed. 2004), which includes an appendix on *technique* and another on culture.

Jacques Ellul has always been careful not to read what we know into the Bible, since this revelation always transcends our understanding. His favourite joke on this subject, to the effect that every text has seventy-seven meanings plus one, is told in this book. For this reason Ellul has never equated idols with myths, and there certainly is plenty of material in the Bible suggesting that what is referred to as gods includes, but is not limited to, myths.

Israel, like all other people, relied on its culture. As a result, there was a constant tendency to transform the Revelation of the living God into a (cultural) religion. Some contemporary equivalents of this have been described by Jacques Ellul in his book *The False Presence of the Kingdom* (New York: Seabury Press, 1972). The many French examples have their current counterpart in the U.S. in a politicized evangelical/fundamentalist Christianity. The same development is occurring in Canada.

The idea that our reality is socially constructed is untenable, for the simple reason that it cannot be deconstructed without exposing our roots in reality (myths), which is existentially unbearable outside of the love of God.

different, namely meaning. When, for example, it tells us about a historical event it tells us about the meaning of that event for the people of that time, or the meaning for humanity as a whole. Its authors were not searching for historical objectivity. Faced with what they regarded as a revelation from God, they asked themselves, What is God telling us through this event? In the same vein, when we are talking about creation, the text is not trying to tell us objectively what exactly happened, but instead, what it means. In the final analysis, whether the material fact is exact or not is far less important than the meaning being transmitted.

The problem is that meaning cannot be transmitted by itself. There is no human language in the world that can transmit what Paul Ricoeur calls 'the meaning of meaning.'[7] It must be embedded or 'clothed' in something, and that something is the account. We make a terrible mistake if we read this text as an account of the facts. The account is there to transmit a meaning and nothing else. Hence if we believe that the text cannot be mistaken, it is not in relation to the facts but in relation to the meaning of what is lived. When, for example, we are told how David lived an event, we are told something about the meaning he saw in it and how he related this meaning to his God and his people.

From this perspective, the whole conflict between science and revelation, or between science and faith, has nothing to do with the opposition between the material and the spiritual. After all, the spiritual is completely embedded in the biblical accounts of the events, which are there to reveal a meaning to us.

The third and last question about meaning may be approached by asking how general or how precise the meaning should be. For example: if we say God is the meaning, this is so vague and all-encompassing that it means nothing. On the other hand, if everything in the account concurs with its meaning, the meaning of the account can be relatively precise. If the account is there to 'clothe' the meaning to be communicated, every element in the account may well be a bearer of meaning. In this respect, the structuralist approach to texts has something important to contribute. I believe structuralism is mistaken when it asserts that the entire meaning is in the structure, or rather, that there is no meaning at all. Nevertheless, it correctly points out that the structure of a text reflects a plan that interrelates all the elements in a way that makes sense. Personally, I have always been very much struck by

---

7 For an overview of Paul Ricoeur's extensive work, see Charles E. Reagan, ed., *Studies in the Philosophy of Paul Ricoeur* (Athens, OH: Ohio University Press, 1979).

the construction of biblical texts, their careful organization of all the elements, and how significant all this is. Not only does the structure provide meaning, but each and every word contributes to it, to the point that if one is changed the entire meaning may be affected. It reminds me, for example, of the change in the name of Abram to Abraham, which profoundly marks the meaning of an event in his life. What does all this mean when we encounter contradictory accounts? Scientists, as well as many exegetes, have tended to dismiss such texts. If we accept that these texts were constructed with extraordinary discipline and thought, then the real scientific question is to ask why the authors included contradictory accounts. In other words, it is not that they were unaware of these contradictions, but they deliberately included them because they meant something. From this perspective, nothing that relates to the meaning of a text is unintentional. The authors intentionally constructed the text in order to render a revelation as best as possible, which otherwise would have remained inexpressible.

If, after all, it is God who reveals, then this is inexpressible. There are simply no words or images to render God, if God is God. Hence, the biblical authors were compelled to take detours, to use images and otherwise use what was available, and to do so in the most careful and intentional manner; and even then it had to necessarily remain indirect as the only way of transmitting a part of what might be the revelation of God.

The Composition of the Text

A widely accepted historical theory of how the text of the Pentateuch came into being holds that at least three principal editors played a role. There is much to recommend this. In the first chapter of Genesis God is always called Elohim, while in the second chapter he is called Yahweh. There are also parts where God is sometimes called Elohim and sometimes Yahweh. The language and style also varies from part to part. The parts which refer to God by the name Yahweh use an older grammar. Moreover, when all the parts in which God is called Yahweh are reassembled, they constitute a coherent ensemble. The same is true for the parts in which God is called Elohim. The parts whose grammar is the most recent have a different character from the other two, in being intellectually the most rigorous (and we shall shortly see why this is the case). It seems that these texts are the work of theologians, and are usually referred to as the Priestly tradition. The Yahwist tradition has been dated around 900 B.C., the Elohist tradition around 800 B.C., and the Priestly tradition around 700 B.C.

An editor has integrated the three groups of texts into the text we have. It is thought that this was done around 600–500 B.C. Each of the 'authors' of the three parts is almost certainly not a single person but a school, each with its own unique orientation, but all appearing to have used other texts. The Yahwist tradition, which is the oldest, appears to have drawn on two things. One is a very old credo used in religious services as a sacred text around 1,000 B.C., but its origins are uncertain. This, of course, contradicts the doctrine of infallible inspiration since the Yahwists already drew on what was probably initially an oral tradition. They also used a number of accounts about their ancestors, including Abraham, Isaac, and Jacob. The editors fused all this into one continuous account, with the history of salvation as its primary orientation.

For the Yahwists, God is first and foremost the One who saves, sustains life, rights evil, heals breaks, seeks to do away with death, and generally is the God of grace. That is the central orientation of the Yahwist tradition. It is found in the second chapter of Genesis, for example.

The Elohist tradition has more northerly geographical roots, and it too has preserved certain traditions, the origins of which are once again uncertain. It is thought to have had a more popular appeal, in part because of the name used for God. Elohim is a name somewhat comparable to the one used by the Canaanites. In contrast, the name used for God in the Yahwist tradition is a sacred name which neither resembles nor compares to anything else, and of which the origin cannot be found. It is therefore supposed that the Elohist has more popular roots. The Elohist tradition has a very different orientation than the Yahwist one, as is characterized by the fact that it insists on God being distant from humanity. God is incommunicable, not directly accessible, and mediation is required.

The Priestly tradition is found in the first chapter of Genesis. If the Yahwist tradition may be characterized as pietistic and the Elohist as popular, then the priestly tradition is an intellectual one put together by professional theologians. This tradition too has its unique orientation, which it developed on the basis of Elohist texts. What is unique about this orientation is that it developed these texts with an eye on comparable accounts from the people surrounding Israel. These theologians knew the religious traditions of neighbouring people, and they utilized them in a manner that is completely opposite to what was originally thought. Initially, scholars believed that these Jews, who had come from Egypt around 1400–1300 B.C., had brought with them a variety of religious and cultural beliefs that gradually evolved and eventually produced these texts. Further research revealed that this was not at all the case. In fact, it was the exact opposite. After all, if this were the case then the oldest biblical texts should be the most comparable to Egyptian and Babylonian ones. The opposite is the case: it is the more recent biblical texts that are the more comparable ones. What these theologians did was to carefully research these other religious traditions and their texts to examine what fitted and what did not fit with what they understood the revelation to be. It is for this reason that the biblical texts turn out to be completely different from the legends, cosmogonies, and mythic accounts of their neighbours.

To illustrate my point I will read parts of a Babylonian creation story, thought by some to resemble the Genesis account.[8]

Long ago there was neither heaven nor earth. There was nothing in the world but water and the two beings that governed it. Sweet water was the domain of Apsu and salt water that of his wife Ti'amat. At that time these two domains merged, for neither rivers nor seas existed. The union of Apsu and Ti'amat gave birth to two colossal creatures, Lahmu and his wife, Lahamu. From these were born, in their turn, Anshar and Kishar. Anshar embodied everything that was above and Kishar everything that was below. From them were born Anu, the god of the heaven, who begot Ea. Ea was as wise as he was strong, much superior to his parents and all who existed before him. After Ea's birth the divine tribe multiplied rapidly, but what a noisy and rowdy bunch. The heavenly children chased each other in all directions, shouted, cried in loud voices, so much so that poor grandmother Ti'amat had frayed nerves. However, she suffered in silence and did not protest. 'They are children,' she thought, 'they behave like children, one must endure what one cannot change.' But grandfather Apsu did not agree. One day he could no longer stand their racket and sent for Mummu the dwarf, who advised and entertained him. 'Come,' he said, 'Let us go together to find Ti'amat and speak to her about all this.' And so they left to visit Ti'amat to consult one another about the children, but Apsu was not in a mood to discuss it calmly. 'Listen,' he cried, 'I cannot stand it any longer, there is not a moment of peace by day or a moment of sleep at night. We

---

8 I have been unable to locate the exact source, although I did find English translations that come very close. For this reason, I have translated the text read by Jacques Ellul.

need peace and quiet and I am going to rid myself of this whole troop of gods.' Hearing this Ti'amat could not hold back her anger. 'What are you saying?' she howled, 'Are we going to destroy what we ourselves have created? It is true that they get on our nerves. This is true of all children with regard to old people, but we just have to put up with it.'

And so this text continues for another twenty-five pages, which have little to do with a creation story. I will pick up the text beginning with Marduk. It all gets very complicated, with yet more births and children and a fight between Marduk and Ti'amat, and in the end Marduk kills Ti'amat, the primitive goddess. Marduk is busy with a new task, since for him the death of Ti'amat is only the beginning of a new order of things in which he has the upper hand. I will now read another part of the account.

Seizing the carcass of his enemy, Ti'amat, he opened it into two halves as one does with an oyster shell. He raised one half into the air to form the vault of heaven, the firmament. Then he hung from its length all the waters that were under this vault, measured them, covered them with the other half of the body of Ti'amat, and these were the foundations of the earth. He established Anu as master in the kingdom placed above the firmament. He gave to Enlil the domain between the firmament and the earth. Ea was the master of the underground waters. In this way Anu became the god of heaven, Enlil the god of the air, and Ea the god of the depths. Marduk also distributed places to the other gods and created the stars to shine in the sky. He opened a door in the east through which the sun could pass at dawn, and another in the west through which it could withdraw at dusk. And now when everything was done, the gods crowded around Marduk and complained bitterly. 'Lord Marduk,' they cried, 'you have given us domains and honours and to each of us you have assigned a task, but you have appointed no one to serve us and help us in our work. Who will take care of our homes, keep them clean, and prepare our food?' When Marduk heard these words, he thought for a long time and suddenly his face lit up. 'I know what I am going to do,' he said to himself, 'I will take water and blood and from them I will make a little puppet. His name will be Man. Man will serve the gods and will take care of their homes while the gods carry on with their affairs.'

As you see, there is in fact a point in common between the above account and that of Genesis, in that in both there is water in the beginning. Apart from this, the perspective of this text is entirely opposite to that of Genesis. They have nothing in common, especially with regard to the creation of humanity. I return to the point I made earlier: the authors of the first chapter of Genesis knew these kinds of accounts very well, and they developed their account to contest the others. The first chapter of Genesis challenges the divination of the world. Our world is not made from two pieces of a divine body. Genesis also contests any polytheism by a lack of dozens of gods. It also challenges any cosmogony involving different gods, and it contests the conception of humanity as a kind of domestic or puppet. It presents the exact opposite, namely, a humanity ruling over creation. One might question the prejudgments of those who see the texts of Genesis as deriving from these kinds of texts. Genesis certainly relates to the Babylonian text, but only to contest and challenge it as false. This is the orientation of the priestly tradition that produced the first chapter of Genesis.

2   The First Creation Account

To Begin with ...

Before we begin the study of the text, I would like to make two remarks. First, we have become accustomed to thinking that the creation story is so fundamental that the Jews put it first. Commonly referred to as the doctrine of creation, this text is thus thought of as the decisive point of departure of Jewish thought. However, the most recent studies of this thinking, which occurred between the eighth and seventh centuries B.C. (the text is thought to have been written during the seventh century), show that this is simply not the case. There was no 'problem' of creation requiring an extensive discussion. The most important given, functioning as a point of departure for Jewish thought, was the salvation of humanity and the covenant with Israel. They began with salvation, and because they learned that humanity was saved, they asked questions such as, Saved from what? Were they saved from death, from evil, or from something else? How did this whole situation develop? In other words, their train of thought went in the opposite direction to the one we are accustomed to. They did not begin with a theory of creation, to come to the recognition that because humanity is separated from God it is lost and thus in need of salvation, which in turn requires a saviour, an election, a covenant, and so on. Jewish thought developed in the opposite direction, working back from where they were. This helps to explain why the text is in fact posterior to most of the accounts in the Pentateuch (the five books of Moses).

My second remark is that we must be mindful of the purpose of this text when we seek to understand it. It is not a question of these texts explaining how the world was created. That is not its objective, and I will give you some evidence in a moment. The central theme is not a belief in creation. It is not there to provide us with information about exactly what happened, but a teaching about the God who revealed himself to Israel. This is something totally different.

To show how from the outset the authors of this text wanted to establish this perspective, let us take a look at the first two verses of chapter 1. They speak about the earth, and later in verse 10 we learn that the earth was created. In the grip of positivism, commentators in the nineteenth century concluded that the authors simply had not progressed intellectually and culturally to the point of recognizing the contradiction between the earth's already being mentioned in verse 1 and its being created in verse 10. Nevertheless, the text shows evidence of great learning and of rabbis who meticulously paid attention to each and every detail, to every 'jot and tittle,' as it is put in the New Testament. We will see that nothing in this text was left to chance. It is not in any way archaic, mythological, or primitive. Why then do these authors talk about the earth from the very beginning of the text?

The term *eretz* (usually translated as 'earth') would, for the Jews of the seventh century (when this text was written), essentially have meant the 'earth' of Israel, and that is how it would be read: the land of Israel given by God. In other words, from the outset the reader is warned that everything he or she is going to be told is very important, but it is not about the origin of the world. The text speaks about something much more limited: it is about the God of that land of Israel and his relationship with the people of Israel. God is revealed in that relationship. In sum, the reference to the land of Israel in the first verse signals to the reader that this text is not a cosmogony. It is not at all the same thing as the cosmogonies of the Babylonians (or Chaldeans) and the Egyptians. This text is a revelation of the God of Israel which shows how the relationship between God and humanity came about, and that is why the 'earth' of Israel enters the text from the outset.

I have suggested that there can be multiple translations. To give you a sense of the difficulty of interpreting a text like this one, I will read you an excerpt from a translation prepared by Fabre d'Olivet, a Hebrew scholar of the early nineteenth century. Entitled *La langue hébraique restituée*, it is one of the most beautiful I know, but it is not easy.

At-first-in-principle, he-created, Ælohîm (he caused to be, he brought forth in principle, HE-the-Gods, the-Being-of-beings), the-selfsameness-of-heavens, and-the-selfsameness-of-earth. And-the-earth was contingent-potentiality in-a-potentiality-of-being: and-darkness (a hard-making-power)-was on-the-face of-the-deep (fathomless-contingent-potentiality of being) and-the-breath of-HIM-the-Gods (a light-making-power) was-pregnantly-moving upon-the-face of-the-waters (universal passiveness).[1]

The above is an example of the multiplicity of meanings in what, at first glance, appears to be a simple text. In Hebrew you cannot separate the subject from the verb, as signified by the phrase HeElohimcreates (in Hebrew the sequence of these three words is HecreatesElohim). Literally, the phrase HetheGods reflects that Elohim is a plural and yet a singular. The phrase Beingofbeings is exactly the meaning of Elohim in Hebrew. And so the translation continues to render the depth of the meanings of the Hebrew words and phrases. This is a good translation.

For the first twenty-five verses, I will focus on Elohim as the God these texts speak about, and then on the creation. Elohim, usually translated as God, is a word that is related to many others such as El, Eloha, El'elion, and so on in Semitic languages. In the Bible there are two principal words to designate God, namely, Elohim and Yahweh. The latter is the only name of the One who has revealed himself first and foremost to Israel. We shall see later that his name is unpronounceable, and why. The other name, Elohim, is, as I have noted, related to a diversity of names used by the peoples that surrounded Israel. This is very important for the first chapter because Elohim is a generic name and, in a way, an objective name because it is not the God who personally reveals himself to Israel. For the Hebrews this was a fundamental distinction. There is the God who is distant and keeps to himself, who is Elohim, and there is the God who reveals himself to humanity, who is Yahweh. In other words, Elohim is the name humanity can give to the divine powers or forces sensed behind the whole creation. It is the God of the creation as opposed to the God of salvation.

There remains a difficulty, however: while the names of gods used by other people are always singular, Elohim is always a plural. Yet from the very outset of their religious expression, the Jews have always been monotheistic. Why then do they alone, among all the different peoples, express Elohim in the plural? This is exactly what distinguishes the Canaanite El from the Jewish Elohim. Yet the Canaanites were polytheistic and the Jews monotheistic. What makes all this even more problematic is that the verb that accompanies Elohim is always in the singular, indicating a plural singular (the Godscreates). The Jews

---

1 Antoine Fabre d'Olivet (1767–1825), *La langue hébraïque restituée* (Paris: Éditions de la Tête de Feuille, 1971), 25, 26.

manifestly encountered a single God, but they regarded this God as being so complex that within himself he was a plurality. For the Jews there is but one God, but this God is so impossible to express and encompasses so many things that he is represented as a plurality.

Christianity in general, and the Church fathers in particular, regarded this as a confirmation of God in three persons. It explains the One and the plural of the One. It is true that in the text we are examining there are indeed at least three 'elements' of divinity. We first encounter Elohimcreates and then the spirit or breath of Elohim moving the surface of the waters. The Hebrew word *ruach* means both breath and spirit. It is the same word used in the text stating that the spirit rested on Saul. This spirit already has a very definite role in the creation by establishing the relationship between Elohim and what is not God, beginning with the surface of the waters. The verb which expresses the role of the spirit is difficult to translate because there are three possible meanings. The verb means to glide like a bird, to stir or to agitate, or to brood the way a hen broods an egg. I prefer the last two translations because they articulate the kind of relationship established between the spirit and what is not God.

We are told that the earth was *tohu wabohu*, which most translations render as 'the earth was without form and void.' Although such a translation appears to make some sense of it, it really does not mean anything. The Hebrew phrase, *tohu wabohu*, has no meaning. They could have arbitrarily invented any other word and it would have made no difference. These two Hebrew words have no linguistic roots, nor do they resemble anything in the languages of the peoples that surrounded the Jews. I believe they used these two arbitrary words to indicate something that is not translatable into a human language. Rendering them as chaos or the abyss makes it into something that we have some concept of, and this is exactly what the Jews strongly refused to do. They recognized that before and beyond *tohu wabohu* there was nothing expressible by words or language. Before the creation was the indefinable *tohu wabohu*. In any case, the text is concerned with salvation, and not with the satisfaction of our scientific curiosity.

Next we encounter the abyss and the darkness over it. The former is frequently used to translate the Hebrew *tehom*, which is the plural made up from a double *tohu*. However, we can make some sense of this word because it is used in other parts of the Bible, where it designates the depths of the sea where the great fish live. This may be translated in various ways, of which 'abyss' is probably the most impressive. It is followed by something much more important, namely, the waters. This we can understand because in the entire Old Testament water plays a very definite role. It is the power of annihilation, of nothingness, which seeks to reconquer the creation and which causes everything to lose its created form. This was readily understood by the people, who were thoroughly familiar with the way unbaked clay 'melts' in water. It is the sense that God creates a form and the waters can dissolve it: this is the significance of water in the Old Testament.

It must not be concluded that water designates evil. It is a kind of negative power that tends to reduce the creation to nothing. It is an obvious polemic against the divinities of the neighbouring peoples, because water is always a positive force in Babylonian and Egyptian mythologies. In the face of Babylonian divinities or the gods of the sea, the Jews hold that for them water represents a destructive power since it threatens the creation. We are not told what went before the creation because that cannot be expressed in words. Nor are we told that God begins from zero, as it were, to make this creation.

In the third verse we encounter the first act: 'Elohim speaks,' and this is repeated throughout the creation account. It is another important revelation about God, namely, that he creates by means of his word: a word that is at the same time distinct from God and in a sense is God himself. In the Old Testament it plays a very important role, and in Hebrew there are two words for it. Usually it is *dabar*, which is very difficult to translate because it refers at the same time to the word and the action. The Hebrew absolutely does not distinguish between the two. This is why, when translating 'God speaks,' it may also be rendered as 'God acts.' In Hebrew the two are the same because what is said affects something. The word is not merely a question of words. In passing, I note that contemporary linguistic research also distinguishes between the word and words and between language and discourse, because of the power of language. In Hebrew, the word is a power that has the double effect of bringing order and establishing a relationship. Both are involved when God speaks. The other Hebrew word is the one we find in this text, namely *amar*, which is slightly different from *dabar*. It means to command or to declare. When the Old Testament tells us that God's speaking brings forth light or water, it means that God at the same time brings about something that is apart from himself and also that God transmits or gives of himself, just as people do when they speak. In other words, the Word creates and reveals at the same time. It is important to recognize (and this is fundamental for understanding the New

Testament) that we do not have one Word of God so powerful as to bring the world into being, and another Word that reveals but which is much more ambiguous and difficult to understand.[2] The two are the same Word. When God's revelation is addressed to someone, it creates a new person by arousing, evoking, and remaking this human being. Creation and revelation are the same.

It may be said, therefore, that when God speaks the whole movement of history begins, and thanks to that Word there is communication, reciprocity, and exchanges with people who also speak. This raises the question why the Jews, of all people, insisted on God's speaking. Why is Jewish religious thought set apart from all the religious thought of all other peoples? By considering it to be characteristic of God that he establishes a relationship with humanity and intervenes by his Word. I believe that this tells us that from now on a relationship is established, and that because this is a relationship of the Word it offers freedom to the listener. When we hear the Word we are not obligated to obey. There is a distance because when God speaks he creates something that is other than himself. The Word implies dialogue; and here we see the beginning of an incarnation to come. This is what the first few verses reveal about Elohim. Stretching this a lot has led to a triune God: the trinity of Elohim, the Spirit of Elohim, and the Word of Elohim. Carrying this over to the New Testament has led theologians to create the concept of God the Father, God the Word incarnate (Jesus Christ), and God the Holy Spirit. I think this is pushing the first three verses of Genesis and other texts to their limit; and I will not comment on this other than to reiterate that Elohim is a plural.

The First Five Days

We have now reached what has traditionally been called the creation. Recall that I said that the Jews had no general theory of creation, unlike the Greeks who had a theory of the cosmos that they had worked out. Nor were the Jews interested in astronomy, and they certainly knew less about it than the Chaldeans. As we will see, for the Jews the stars were simply lights hanging in the sky, and beyond this there simply was no burning question. Nor did the Jews have an objective or scientific view of

---

2 See Jacques Ellul, *The Humiliation of the Word*, trans. Joyce Main Hanks (Grand Rapids, MI: Eerdmans, 1985), for a detailed discussion of the Word, Jesus Christ, and human languages.

the world, unlike the Chaldeans who considered it as an organized house. The Jews had a temporal view of the world as an event that became in time, as opposed to a spatial view of objects filling a space. Everyone else began with space, but the Jews began with time. The conception of the world as an event that is happening, evolving, and constantly breaking out is further developed in Proverbs, Ecclesiastes, the Song of Solomon, and so on, with the result that their account of the creation was not at all what the Greeks and other people understood by it. The Jews have no conception of an original act from which everything else flows and before which nothing was. God appears in the creation as One who gives form and One who separates light from darkness, water from water, land from sea, and so on. The act of God is the act of separation, and at the same time he gives shape or form to what was formless or without form. He makes expressible and comprehensible what was *tohu wabohu*. This is absolutely fundamental, because for the Jews the question is not how the sun exists, for example, but how I as a human being relate to it, as it were, and how I can make sense of the sun. Nowhere are the Jews told how God made the sun; instead, they are told about God who makes comprehensible what was not comprehensible before. God makes it possible to say what could not be expressed. All this is related to God's creating something by means of the Word, and from then on you could say its name. God calls the light into being; he names it, and we now know what it is. There was nothing before the Word, and it is from this perspective that we must regard the creation.

It is important to note that what is usually translated as 'in the beginning' does not mean a point of departure. A better translation would be: 'within the beginning,' 'to begin with,' or 'first of all.' It is an expression that is frequently used. In the book of Chronicles, for example, the expression is often combined with the phrase 'in the days of king ...' to signify that the narration of the story of this king will now begin. It is a literary expression, not unlike an introductory phrase followed by a colon, that is, 'to begin with' followed by a colon designating that the narration will now begin.

Next comes the question of the days. In his commentary, Father Chaine[3] maintains that a day means twenty-four hours, for us as well as for the Jews. The Hebrew word, *yom*, which has been translated as 'day,' can also mean 'time.' The reason we translate it as 'day' is to match it to what follows, namely, the evening and the morning, in order to have

---

3 J. Chaine, *Le livre de la Genèse* (Paris: Cerf, 1949).

the twenty-four hour cycle. The Hebrew word means a period of time, a duration, the passing of some time, which is expressed as a whole. In Psalm 90, verse 4 there is a reference to this when it says that before God a thousand years are like a day. In Hebrew, adding several zeros to a number means an infinity; hence, what the psalm means is that an infinity of years is like a day in God's eyes. The text does not tell us that it took twenty-four hours to create this or that, but that there were stages as part of an order of creation established by God.

Another important thing to notice is that the day begins with the evening: 'And there was evening and there was morning, one day.' Here we see that in biblical thinking there is first the negative element, and at the end comes the positive element, namely, the act of God. At the beginning you have the night, and at the end the light. At the beginning you have nothingness, and at the end you have life and humanity. Again we encounter a cultural mutation of sorts since for the Greeks and Romans (and we still think the same way), the day begins with sunrise and ends with the night, which means that to the very depths of our being we are convinced that we begin with life and end with death. However, for Jewish thinking it is the opposite: you begin with death and you end with life.

Next, I would like to make a few remarks about some of the deeper meanings of the verses that follow. As noted, commentators in the grip of positivism have pointed out that there are contradictions in the creation account. For example, the light is created first; and then later, in verses fourteen and fifteen, we are told about the creation of the sun and the moon to illuminate the earth. How can you have light without a sun? The problem is that once more this was not at all what the Jewish theologians were thinking about. Their thinking was more like ours in the sense that light means time. I base this on a Jewish commentary from the first century A.D. They did not have to wait for Einstein to come up with this interpretation. From this perspective, God's first creative act is a context or framework of sorts for the world and for humanity, thereby making the movement of history possible. In passing, I will draw your attention to another polemical point directed to the Babylonian sun god, the Chaldean gods, and all celestial gods, to affirm that light and time were *created*, like everything else. For the Greeks, time has dominion over the gods: Chronos eats the gods, which is an extraordinarily pessimistic view of destiny. Not so, say the Jews, because God has created time. Similarly, for the Babylonians the light was at the origin of everything, while the Jews held that light was created.

Following the creation of time, we encounter, in the sixth verse, the creation of space. André Chouraqui[4] translates: 'a ceiling shall be in the midst of the waters.' This expanse between the waters literally means a solid blade, *reqeia*, which separates so as to arrange in a spatial order. We then have the waters above and the waters below, which is, of course, an image from the culture of that time. The waters above and below were natural occurrences observed and shared by everyone, and this poses no particular problem.

This brings us to the successive creations of the third, fourth, and fifth days. Once again, the text does not seek to tell us that this is how things happened but speaks to us about a certain order, a certain periodicity, with a comment I believe to be fundamentally important. Here differences in translation can have rather serious consequences. We all know that for centuries these texts have fuelled debates between creationism, fixism (the doctrine that species were created 'as is' and did not evolve), and evolutionism. Traditional theologians have clung to these texts to prove that Darwin was wrong, but it is they who are wrong because they have incorrectly translated these texts. The translation error has to do with the recurring phrase: plants yielding seed each *according to its kind* (or species), or the living creatures *according to their kinds*. Translations such as 'according to its kind: or 'after its kind' mean the exact opposite of the Hebrew word *lamet* which means 'with a view to ...' In other words, the Hebrew denotes the establishment of a point of departure: everything bears seed with a view towards the creation of its species. Hence, the text could perfectly well be read from the perspective of evolving. It certainly does not describe a world that, once made by God, has not changed to this day. We may now be tempted to emphasize the convergence between this text and contemporary scientific views, but this cannot yield anything of significance. To put this in perspective, I would like to point out a current convergence, from which we should not draw any conclusions. After the positivist era, when there was an irreconcilable opposition between science and the texts we are examining, we entered the era of the 'big bang' theory, which holds that the whole thing started with an incredible surge of energy. Then there was also the Gnosis of Princeton, where a group of

---

4 André Chouraqui, *La Bible* (Paris: Desclée de Brouwer, 2003); *Entête (La Genèse)* (Paris: Jean-Claude Lattès, 1992). The reader may also be interested in André Chouraqui, *Le destin d'Israel: Correspondances avec Jules Isaac, Jacques Ellul, Jacques Maritain et Marc Chagall; entretiens avec Paul Claudell* (2007).

mathematicians, physicists, and astronomers held that before anything happened there was a plan of sorts and a Word. Although all of this is fascinating, I would simply conclude from this that science evolves.[5] Not so long ago these kinds of things would have been unthinkable. Perhaps the contradictions are not as radical as people once believed.

I will conclude the study of this part of the first creation account, leading up to the creation of humanity, with two remarks. At every stage the text tells us that God says it was good. Translations to this effect are rather weak. Chouraqui translates the Hebrew literally as, 'Elohim sees: "O, here is the good."'[6] There is an astonishment of sorts on God's part at what appears, and he exclaims, 'Here is the good.' It is very interesting that during every period of time something good appears. However, the good is what God *says* and not the things in themselves. There is no good that precedes God since God does not say, 'Here is something in accordance with the good,' but instead, 'Here is the good.' It is as if he posits the good, as it were, in a particular place and way. The good is not a natural given, nor a universal given, but instead the declaration of God. It is from then on that we learn that the light is the good, and that the earth and the sea are the good, and so on. In other words, we learn that every element of the world around us has a positive connotation for God. All this is very important when we reflect on the ecological problem, for example. This world and each and

---

5 Jacques Ellul was very taken by Thomas Kuhn's *The Structure of Scientific Revolutions* (Chicago: University of Chicago Press, 2nd ed., 1970), which was not well known in France at the time I brought it to his attention. Kuhn forever transformed our thinking about science by treating it as a unique human activity open to sociological and historical analyses. He showed that the growth of scientific knowledge is not cumulative. For example, the West has had three incompatible interpretations of physical reality – the Aristotelian view, the Newtonian interpretation, and the Einsteinian perspective – before our current one(s). It is as if during a cumulative period, scientists elaborate a particular 'map' of physical reality until they discover something that cannot be fitted onto it. Such an event compels a non-cumulative redrawing of the map.

There is a certain parallel between science and culture in this respect. During cumulative periods, scientists treat the physical reality they have come to know as reality itself minus some details yet to be discovered. In other words, Kuhn's interpretation of the social organization and historical evolution of science could be taken to imply the presence of myths. This is hardly surprising since science is a human activity, and there is little to suggest that it is able to free itself from myth and avoid the threat of relativism. I believe that these are the kinds of things that were in the back of Ellul's mind when he said that science evolves.

6 André Chouraqui, *Entête (La Genèse)* (Paris: Jean-Claude Lattès, 1992).

every element of it is declared good by God; and this means that we do not have the right to do whatever we like with it. There exists a relationship between the elements of the world and the good declared by God. In Hebrew thinking there is no moral or spiritual world (which would be the world of the good and of spiritual matters) on the one hand, and a material world on the other. For the Jews the two are the same, as are matter and spirit. It is analogous to what we have said above about the Hebrew word *dabar*, which at the same time is the word and the action. The word and the spirit are also the same: they are interwoven and linked. The sky is good, morally and spiritually good, and so is the earth. Similarily, there is no separate moral life, in sharp contrast with the way we have often, and mistakenly, spiritualized things. We say that material things are not good, and we follow the Greeks in thinking that the soul, not the body, is good. For the Jews this is not at all the case: the body is very good, and the admiration of the body comes through in extraordinary texts about the human body. All this is very much related to this creation account and God's proclamation of: 'Here is the good.'

The second observation I would like to make regarding this part of the creation account relates to God's blessing the animals and all living things in verse 22. It is this blessing that makes the difference between the animals and the rest of the creation. They are declared good, like the rest of the creation, and on top of that God blesses them by speaking to them. Blessing means three things. First, it means 'to kneel,' and this is somewhat strange because you do not know who is kneeling: the one who blesses or the one who is blessed. In some texts near the end of Genesis you have the impression that the one who blesses, that is, the one who carries out the action of superiority, is the one who kneels, thereby putting himself in a position of inferiority. We are used to the opposite: the one who blesses is standing and the one who is blessed is on his knees. But this is not taken for granted in the Bible. Remember the washing of the disciples' feet by Jesus. It is the moment in the gospel of John of the greatest communion between Jesus and his disciples, and Jesus is on his knees before them. It is the same thing. Elohim blessing all living beings could well mean that Elohim bows himself before them.

Second, the Hebrew word *barak* means not only to bless but also to proclaim salvation. From the beginning, what God brings to them is that not only are they 'the good' like the rest, but in addition they are loved. The term salvation is very ambiguous but it may be understood as being loved by God. All this establishes the uniqueness of the animals.

Finally, on the sixth day, God also blesses the man and the woman. However, when they appear God does not say, 'Here is the good'; and this, as we will see, is rather important.

The Sixth Day

We will now turn to the remainder of the first creation account, which begins with the twenty-fourth verse of the first chapter and ends with the third verse of the second chapter, revealing the creation of humanity in the image of God and the seventh day. In reading the text, we notice right away that God appears to collect his thoughts; and before he creates humanity God speaks to himself. The author(s) of the text wished to mark the seriousness of this act. It is somehow not enough to have a word addressed outwardly, as it were, for it to be. God inwardly speaks to himself, because the one that is about to be created and called into existence is the one who will hear the word. It is not the same as creating the earth or the sun and so on, which are objects. When God says, 'Let us make Adam,' he speaks to himself; and the one that is coming now is the fruit of a kind of deliberation, a dialogue within God.

We are not told anything about the creation of Adam except what he is as a result of his creation. As far as the debate over his creation or evolution is concerned, I believe the poet G.K. Chesterton[7] has clarified it in an admirable fashion. With the admission that human beings were once apes (he wrote this around 1890) something rather strange has happened, in that one day the human being would draw the ape but that the ape would never draw a human being. What Chesterton says is that whether God created complete human beings, with their consciousness, intelligence, and so on, or whether human beings appeared in the course of the evolution of the animal species, their existence is equally miraculous. It ultimately comes to the same thing, whether this consciousness was the result of a mutation or whether it was present from the outset. The Old Testament is entirely silent on this matter. It speaks of other things.

What this text reveals is that people are ambiguous beings. First, this ambiguity stems from their inclusion in the order of the animals. This is why there is repetition in the text. The story of the creation of people begins once again with the animals. At first this may appear rather strange, since all the animals were created during the fifth day (verses

---

7 I have been unable to locate the exact quote.

20, 21, 22). The story appears to begin again (verses 24, 25), where again we find the birds, reptiles and other animals; and that raises the question as to why there are two accounts: one for the fifth day and one for the sixth. The answer is that human beings are included in the series of the animals. There is first the creation of the animals and then the creation of human beings, but we are reminded that people are a part of the ensemble of animals. Nevertheless, human beings are also distinct from animals. There is already a first clear element of this when the text speaks about animals: it says 'living beings with a view to their kind (or species),' with the sort of movement we have already discussed, which includes a point of departure and a development. This tells us that what follows is a diversity of the species. However, for humanity there is no further mention of it. Its creation is not a matter of species: it is not a question of races or different kinds of human beings. Compared to the diversity of animals, there are no differentiated groups of people. Humanity is a single and unique animal, while the other animals are a plurality of sorts. The difference stems from humanity being created in the image of God (or in the form, or likeness of God).

This brings me to the question of the image of God, about which libraries full of books have been written. What does the text mean when it says that Elohim created Adam (humanity) 'in our image?' What is so strange is that the word 'image' has been interpreted independently from the rest of the text. Commentators have zeroed in on this word 'image' and attempted to analyse in what way people are the image of God. In traditional Catholic theology, humanity is in the image of God either because of the existence of a free will or because of their intelligence. Sometimes, but principally in Orthodox theology, it is held that humanity is in the image of God because it is the microcosm of God the macrocosm. God is seen as the All, of which humanity is the microcosm and the reflection. For Calvin, the image of God means to be endowed with a personality: as persons they are the image of God. I believe that to sort this out, one has to stick to the text. Verse 27 clearly states: 'Elohim created humanity in his image (or in his form), in the image of Elohim he created him (or her), male and female he created them.' It cannot be more straightforward: what is the image of God in this text is that he is man and woman. That is the image of God. However, this is not first and foremost a question of sexuality, but of his being two in one. The text is intriguing: 'Elohim created humanity, Adam' (which is in the singular) 'in his form/image, in the form of Elohim he created him (or her)' (in the singular), which is followed by: 'male and female he created them' (in the plural). Because there is no punctuation, the Hebrew text could also be read as follows: 'In the image of Elohim he created him (or her) male and female. He created them.' So he creates *him* (male and female), and he creates *them* afterwards. In what way is this the image of God? Recall that Elohim is a plural singular, that is, the name Elohim is a plural which grammatically is always treated as a singular. Hence, God is several in one. Humanity is the only being created as one person separated into two forms. This, I believe, is what the text tells us.

This raises the question of what the relationship is between these two who are one. It can only be love. The relationship between man and woman is love, which expresses the fundamental relation, as Jesus puts it later, that the two will not be two but become one. Here we are faced with something complex because this love is, at the same time and in inseparable ways, a sexual and physical love and a spiritual love of the entire being. The Bible does not distinguish between these two elements. Hence, the image of God is love; and this corresponds exactly to what the text has already taught us in speaking of Elohim. God is love. When we spoke about this plurality within the unity of God, we were in effect saying that the only relationship is that of love. This confirms what we saw from the very beginning of this text. Elohim is the One who at the same time creates and reveals himself; and this establishes a relationship, that of love. I acknowledge, of course, that the word love is never mentioned. It is for these reasons that the relationship between a man and a woman is so fundamental throughout the entire Bible. I believe this is a vision of the image of God as love, and the love of a man and a woman as two in one. It is in accordance with this vision that all of humanity and all human beings should conduct themselves. I will return to this question of the image of God; and we will also see that in Hebrew Adam is a collective name. It is therefore not a question of a single man and a single woman, from which the rest of humanity has descended. Adam could be translated as 'humanity,' understood through this vision of love. It is also not a question of how many people were created, but of this ambiguous being: animal, but one that is unique and an image of God in being love.

In any case, humanity is only an image. Again, the meaning of the Hebrew word *tzelem* is difficult to interpret. It means image (or form) as translated by Chouraqui.[8] What creates the difficulty is that the Hebrew

---

8 André Chouraqui, *Entête (La Genèse)*, op. cit.

word comes from a verb of which the root means 'to obscure,' with the result that it can be equally well translated as 'shadow.' In other words, we could have just as well translated, 'Let us create humanity within our shadow (of Elohim),' since there is a play of words. In any case, we cannot translate it as 'Let us create humanity *in* our image/shadow.' Doing so would create the same misinterpretation as the one we encountered before, in the phrase incorrectly translated as 'in the beginning ...' In both cases, the same Hebrew preposition *be* means 'within' and not 'in.'

It is well known that explanations of this kind have fascinated some rabbis, who have meticulously considered every word and letter, and even the form of the letter, which sometimes is very significant. This is the case here for the form of the Hebrew word *be*; and we must also remember that the Hebrews read from right to left. The rabbis suggest, therefore, that what this means is the following. If the creation of humanity begins like that, it means that humanity is neither below (or underneath) nor above, and humanity is not in the past. The two points on the word *be* go toward love, which means that humanity turns towards love. This is what the rabbis of the third century derived from this detail. Although they were not obsessed with history the way we are, they concluded that humanity is a being launched forward as it were, which tends toward something; and consequently, there is the beginning of a history of sorts, and humanity is placed there from the moment he is created within the form. By checking commentaries of this kind, which are often extremely subtle, it is possible to avoid a great many pointless discussions. When you say that from the outset humanity was created within a movement and tending toward something, the whole debate of creation or evolution is transcended.

Finally, humanity being an image means that he-and-she cannot be thought of in themselves, independent from the One of whom he-and-she is the image. In philosophical terms, this means there cannot be a '*dasein*' as a human existence on its own. Humanity is therefore both an autonomous and a non-autonomous being, and in the same vein, perfect and imperfect. Humanity is autonomous in being free, because he-and-she is the image of God and thus necessarily free. (Freedom is a prerequisite for love). At the same time, humanity is not autonomous, because he-and-she is image. Here I return to what I mentioned before, namely, that the principal orientation of this text is to remind us of the ambiguity of humanity. Humanity is free and not free at the same time: free because humanity is an image of God, and not free because humanity is an image. Humanity is perfect and imperfect. Perfect as a completed and finished being, but also an imperfect being denoted by the creation on the sixth day. In Hebrew the symbolic meaning of the number six is an imperfection that tends toward seven, which is the number of perfection. Every number has a meaning in Hebrew. Hence being created on the sixth day signifies the imperfection of humanity.

The ambiguity of humanity is also confirmed by observing that each time God creates something during the preceding days he proclaims, 'Here is the good.' However, following the creation of humanity God does not say this, and this is the only exception. A radical difference is thus established: humanity is not the good. Humanity is not good in him-and-herself. All this fits with the thrust of the text: humanity is independent and free, and thus neither good nor evil in itself. It is true that later God proclaims that everything he made is good, but this refers to the whole of creation, within which humanity represents an indeterminate factor that establishes an openness, as it were. In other words, humanity has no destiny because God has not pronounced a word from the outside that would fix humanity's role of bearing the good, for example. Humanity faces an adventure that is very much open-ended.

This imperfection, this orientation toward a history, means that humanity is created free (signified by God's speaking to humanity from the very outset). Addressing a word to someone presupposes a freedom on his or her part. We do not address the word to objects. To talk to someone and to engage in a dialogue implies that the other can respond. What therefore characterizes humanity from the very outset is its ability to respond.

Elohim blesses humanity and tells them to be fruitful, multiply, dominate, and so on. Humanity receives a commandment. Once again, we encounter a misunderstanding because this has nothing to do with an order of creation or a law. To be sure, there is an order of creation, but humanity is not included within it. In the same sense, humanity is not subordinated to a law. A major error has been made in relation to the Old Testament by translating the Hebrew word *torah* with 'law' in the meaning this word has today, because modern law has become something objective, theoretical, and abstract. In the Old Testament, a commandment is always a personal word addressed to someone within a human relationship. The text therefore informs us that this word that God addresses to humanity does not create within him or her a nature, but a word that is the beginning or starting point of a dialogue in which humanity can obey or (to a certain extent) disobey.

Humanity is placed at the summit of creation as a consequence of this word, and humanity will dominate the fish, birds, animals, and so on. What this means exactly is very important in the theological perspective of the authors of the text because from here on in, there are no gods in nature: neither the forces of nature, nor the stars, nor the animals are anything more than what they are. They are not powers. When the text tells us that humanity will dominate the creation, it tells us that humanity is not subject to the play of a set of higher forces. On the contrary, humanity is to rule over all of creation; hence, verse 26 opposes all polytheisms and mythologies. It is a radical polemic against the world of that time and the cultures of its peoples, dominated as they were by all kinds of gods and evil powers, and everything that came with them.

The twenty-eighth verse is another text that has led to many difficulties: 'Be fruitful and multiply, fill the earth and subdue it, have dominion over the fish of the sea,' and so on. The 'be fruitful and multiply' has been much discussed recently because of the birth control and abortion questions. It certainly does not mean that we must have many children. It means carry out your work, which of course includes having children. 'To multiply' is commonly reduced to having children, from which has come an orientation in life that holds that to have many children is to be blessed by God. The text does say 'bear fruit,' but children are not the only fruit: there are many others, such as spiritual, intellectual, and moral fruit. It is all these different kinds of fruit that humanity is called to bear. As a result, this text cannot be used to condemn a couple that refuses to have children, for example.

As noted, humanity is called to dominate over the fish and the birds, etc., except that this role of domination is like the one God exercises over the creation. Humanity is there to direct the world. You could say that ultimately the image here is that humanity on the earth is what God is in the entire creation. What this means is that humanity is called to rule within the image of God, and consequently can only use the means employed by God. In other words: as God rules over the world, not by his power but in and through love, so humanity is given to rule in and through love. We will soon see how important this is for the events that follow.

A great deal of effort has gone into drawing from these texts the moral, ethical, and metaphysical consequences. However, these texts have no such purpose; they are not moral, ethical, or metaphysical but existential, as it were. They seek to reveal who humanity is, including its relationship with God. Nothing is said about a human nature, its permanence or variability; and to draw anything from these texts regarding such matters is a terrible mistake. It is also impossible to derive from them any moral implications for our own behaviour. Not only were these texts not intended for this; but we always forget that they were deliberately placed before the ones that describe the break in the relationship between God and humanity. No implications whatsoever can be drawn for the present from the condition of humanity before this break with God. For example, these texts do not advocate vegetarianism; nor can they be used to justify the kind of exploitation of the riches of the world seen today, or the *techniques* used to dominate the earth. These errors of interpretation have mostly been made in the grip of Greek philosophy.[9]

All this ends in verse 31 with the proclamation: 'This is the great good,' or, alternatively, 'God saw that it was very good.' We have already noted that this concerns the whole, all that God has created in its unity and totality. This means that the whole of creation is a kind of unbroken unity, and that a communality exists within and with the Creator. In this whole ensemble there is accord and harmony. Humanity is bearing the image of God within this whole; and this means that the creation in its entirety is not a mere object for God, not even an object of his love. God loves what is before him, but not as you love a thing. In this whole there is now the image of God, which means that there is the possibility within the creation of a response to the love of God. There is a mediator within this creation. God loves, but the creation needs to respond to this love, and mere things cannot do that. We now see the full meaning of humanity ruling over the creation: so that humanity

---

9 In his five-volume work *Histoire des institutions* (Paris: Presses Universitaires de France, 1–2: 1961, 3–4: 1962, 5: 1956), Jacques Ellul explains that Western civilization was founded on three 'pillars': Greek philosophy, Roman law, and Christian revelation. These three 'perfections' turned out to be completely incompatible, which gave Western civilization much of its internal dynamism. For example, the Greek invention of universal knowledge and what it implies for what it is to be human is in complete opposition to the Jewish view of being God's creatures, which gives all human activities a relative character. From this, it must not be concluded that our current universal science and technology derive directly from the Greeks. The transition from these activities being unique cultural creations that have no separate and independent existence to their present forms, in which they are separated from experience and culture, is complex and turbulent. I have described it in my book *Living in the Labyrinth of Technology* (Toronto: University of Toronto Press, 2005), which is dedicated to the memory of Jacques Ellul.

can bring to God the love of the whole of that creation. It is the primary vocation that the text attributes to humanity.

This opens up a second possibility, namely, that the one called to respond to this love could just as well not respond. Since there cannot be any restricting or restraining in a relationship of love, humanity could decide not to respond. It follows the theme of perfection and non-perfection, of freedom and non-freedom, which finds expression in the attitude of Adam, from whom Elohim awaits a response.

I believe that in the Bible a relationship of love can be characterized by two elements. First, it is a relationship that is total; it is a unity and thus involves and commits the entire being, without any reservations. When, for example, the prophets speak of the love of God for his people, they always use a vocabulary of physical love that can be very graphic in order to make it very clear that this is not about spirituality, nor some vague love 'in the clouds,' but a relationship that involves and commits the totality of God's being. The other element is that love, in the Bible, is a relationship freely engaged in, and the one who loves submits himself (or herself) constantly to the one who is loved. I believe this is fundamental in the whole orientation of the Bible. To say that God loves is to say that God submits himself to human initiatives. For example, when Jesus Christ is revealed to us in the New Testament as the witness of God's love and the incarnation of that love, it is because he submitted totally to whatever humanity wanted to do with him. In the Sermon on the Mount also, love implies this kind of acceptance of the superiority of others over yourself. I believe these are the two primary elements of a relationship of love in the Bible.

What ruling over the world without love implies becomes evident after the break between God and humanity. Skipping ahead to chapter 9, we find that a portion of the text we have examined is repeated, but with a difference: 'Be fruitful and multiply and fill the earth. The fear and dread of you will be on every beast of the earth, on every bird in the air, on everything that creeps on the ground, and on all the fish in the sea. They are delivered into your hands.' The difference between these two texts is considerable. In the first situation there is no question of fear since everything is in harmony and in communion. In the second text, the domination is one of violence that brings fear. The two relationships with the animals are very different. The first domination, as we shall examine later, is by means of a word: Adam gives the animals a name, thereby attributing to every creature and the whole creation a certain level of autonomy in relation to himself. In the second case, every creature fears this new kind of human domination.

I am not sure that we understand very well the far-reaching implications of God's love. For example, we cannot base marriage on the texts we have examined. Humanity invented marriage, which is not to say that marriage is bad but to say that humanity (and not God) invented it. In other words, God does not set up an ensemble of institutions nor a destiny from which humanity cannot escape, or which people cannot disobey to do something else. This is what I mean when I say that humanity has no destiny, but instead is placed before a very large number of possibilities.

The Seventh Day

The conclusion of this first creation account deals with the seventh day of creation.[10] The number is significant because it is the number of perfection. Six days are announced with the words: 'It is the evening, it is the morning,' followed by the number of the day. For the seventh day there is no evening and no morning. Nothing is said. Hence the seventh day is an open-ended period; it is an episode that is not closed, which means that today we are in the seventh day. Or, to put it in another way, this means that all of human history takes place on the seventh day. The structure of the first creation account is extremely significant. In the first six days the cosmos appears, and this is followed by the appearance of human history. The text reveals the next act in the creation, which begins with the history of humanity.

Now on this seventh day, it is a question of God's 'resting'; and this resting is the crowning of creation. God steps back from his creation and no longer acts. It is not that God stops being the Creator, but that he no longer makes new things. This development implies a certain freedom on God's part, because if God was the 'first cause' or 'prime mover' and thus impersonal, this cause would continue to function and there could be no decision to rest. For this and other reasons, such a view represents a serious theological error. No decision to rest would be possible on the part of an impersonal 'first cause' because it would

---

10 For additional thoughts on the topic of God's rest, human history, and reconciliation, see chapter 12 in Jacques Ellul's book *What I Believe*, trans. Geoffrey W. Bromiley (Grand Rapids, MI: Eerdmans, 1989).

have to go on acting indefinitely. What this first creation account tells us is that God manifests his freedom in his decision to rest.

God's decision to rest takes place within history. The implication is clear: it leaves humanity its freedom in history. God stops acting in order not to interfere in the activities of humanity. Once again, this revelation is fundamental and decisive with respect to all other religions because of this difference. As soon as God has created humanity as the element that brings love and implies freedom within this world of harmony, he will not constrain what he has created to be free. God withdraws in order to leave the field free for humanity. It is for this reason that it is so important that God is a person and not some philosophical abstraction. When I say that God is a person I do not mean to define him. I am simply saying that God acts toward us as a person who is able to leave the field free for us, as it were.

Must we conclude from this text that God is indifferent (or absent)? Such an interpretation is out of the question because it would fly in the face of this being the seventh day and the crown of creation. It is therefore not possible that God simply withdrew, especially since the relationship of love between God and humanity continues to exist. What happens instead is that in history, humanity (with its projects and independent actions) succeeds in disturbing God's rest. We are told this very clearly in the Psalms, for example. In other words, we reach the astounding understanding that God does not direct everything, even to the point of resting and not directing anything. This God intervenes in history only through a dialectical relationship with humanity. He literally inter-venes by coming into the middle of things, but always in the rest he chose, which implies doing so with a certain distance.

It is important to understand this clearly. There is no providence in the Bible. God does not step by step, minute by minute, dictate what is to happen in the world, thereby establishing the reality of that world, as it were. This idea of providence is another terrible theological error. The world was given to a humanity that was created free and able to act as it saw fit. If this humanity broke with God it would become independent, but God does not break his relationship of love with humanity, and therefore engages himself in the course of action that humanity establishes. This is the message which we encounter throughout the entire Old Testament and which culminates in the person of Jesus Christ, where we see a God who completely submits himself to human decisions, to the point of accepting what humanity wants to do with God himself.

This is the reason why the Bible is so complicated. All along we see a humanity going its own way, and God coming into the middle of human activities only in order to give meaning or direction to people or to warn them about the consequences of their actions.[11] The clearest example of the latter is probably the story of Israel wanting to establish a monarchy. Remember that this was during the time of the Judges, when God was the King of Israel. However, Israel decides they want to have a government like all the other peoples. They want to have kings like everyone else. The prophet Samuel responds that this is out of the question, because you cannot reject God. But the people insist, and Samuel consults God about the demand of the people to replace the system of judges with a king. God answers, 'It is not you who they are rejecting but myself, and you must tell them what will happen.' Then comes Samuel's warning about the monarchy: 'You want a king, but be warned: he will take your young men for soldiers and your daughters for the harem, your properties to raise taxes,' and so on. To this Israel replies that this is all right with them, and that they want a king in spite of everything. The important thing is to be like all other peoples and have a king that can lead them in war. So God allows them to have their king, but here we encounter a rather extraordinary development. Saul, the first king, goes mad; but David, the second king, is transformed by God into the prophetic image of the Messiah. The whole business is very complex: God warns Israel, allows them to act; they see the consequences as the first king becomes mad; God salvages what Israel has done and transposes it to a spiritual level, and obtains from it the greatest good possible. There is no question of a restraining or constricting action that transforms humanity into an object with no choice but to do what God imposes. Human beings have to make their own decisions and their own history.

God's rest is the purpose given to the whole of human history. Near the end of the Bible, we are told that the final objective is to enter into the rest of God. This does not mean sleep or boredom but the perfection of love. That is what God's rest is. God blessing the seventh day re-

---

11 As noted, every culture (including the Jewish one) has to create a set of meanings and values to make life possible in an ultimately unknowable reality. Integral to these meanings and values is a set of myths which serve as the absolute points of reference for their orientation in that reality. As a result, human life is alienated. When God intervenes, He reveals the true meanings and values, which are other than those of an alienated culture.

minds us that all of human history is under his blessing. After all, the whole of history unfolds during this seventh day. In other words, the seventh day proclaims the whole orientation of creation, which is hardly static since it is to attain God's rest, which is the perfection of love. However, when the break comes between humanity and God there no longer is that unity in love, since humanity is no longer the free element in creation that responds to God's love. Hence, the seventh day of each week will be consecrated to remind people of the rest of God.

The Sabbath for Jews, and the Sunday for Christians, has commonly been turned into a day of all kinds of constraints. To enter into the rest of God on the Sabbath does not mean being bored. Sunday, for most Protestants, has been a day in which you were forbidden to do almost anything. For the Jewish people, this problem came from interpreting the Commandments as constraints, and these constraints were the greatest on the Sabbath. However, the Sabbath is meant to be the day when people are not constrained, when you do not need to work and instead enter into God's rest. Not to have to work means not being under the condemnation of work, of the obligations of the world, and even of death. On that day, people can rediscover a perfect relationship with God. We need to recover the meaning of this rest of God in order to discover the significance of the seventh day, which gives meaning to all the others.

3   The Second Creation Account

Introduction

We now arrive at the second creation account, which begins with the second chapter, verse 4. As I have said, many commentators have noted that the two creation accounts contradict one another in many respects. For example, we have seen that the first account begins with water; we shall soon see that the second one begins with a desert, without water or any growth. In the first account, the animals are created first, followed by humanity; while in the second account Adam is created first, followed by the animals to see if there may be a helper among them. In the first narrative, the universe is created first and humanity last; while in the second account, humanity is created first, followed by a garden as habitat. God is characterized by the Word in the first account, and by his forming and building in the second account. The name used for God in both narratives is different as well. The second account is thought to be two to three hundred years older than the first and has a more anthropocentric character, since humanity comes first followed by the garden, and the animals are all created in relation to and for humanity. The first account is of a higher 'intellectual' character, but the second one has more detail.

The real question is not the contradictions, but why the authors who put the entire text together kept both accounts, as opposed to sticking with the first. We have seen that the usual explanation by commentators in the grip of science and progress was that the authors who put the text together simply did not have the benefit of our scientific and intellectual development, and therefore integrated the two accounts as best they could without apparently noticing the many contradictions. I find these kinds of explanations entirely unacceptable because they do not even bother to explore the possibility that the second account is there for a very good reason. It is only if no such reasons can be discovered that the hypothesis that the authors of this text were not up to par should be entertained. Failing this, these commentators have not done their homework. In other words, the question is: Does the second account bring us something new and important over and above the first account? And, possibly even more important: Does the question addressed by the second account correspond to the one addressed by the first account? If the question that drove the elaboration of the first account is not the same as the one that drove the second, it is impossible to speak of the second account as a duplicate of the first.

To reply to this central question, I will begin with the names of God in the first and second accounts. In the second account, the name used for God is referred to as the sacred tetragram, made up from four consonants that are not vocalized, namely YHWH. As such this name is unpronounceable, although it may be vocalized in different ways, such as Jehovah or Yahweh. However, in order not to make a mistake, the Jews would never pronounce the tetragram; and everywhere they encountered it they replaced it with Adonai, which means Lord. Doing so ensured that none of the letters of the tetragram were pronounced, with the result that no mistake could be made.

What is the significance of God's name being unpronounceable, and what meaning could the word itself have? In the traditional commonly used translations, without attempting to translate it, the tetragram is sometimes replaced with 'the Eternal.' This translation is completely wrong if it is associated with the metaphysical idea of eternity. Apart from this, the translation itself is not entirely wrong because the tetragram derives from the Hebrew verb *hayah*, which means three things: to be, to arrive, and to begin. The tetragram is the verb *hayah* in the first person, thus meaning 'I am': God is the only One who is. The question of the existence of God never comes up in the Bible, because he is the One who is. (As an aside, I recognize that in contemporary philosophy there is an extensive discussion regarding the Being of being, but that is an entirely different matter also). The tetragram approximately means: I am, I come, and I begin.

The tetragram is used as the name of God when the Bible speaks about God revealing himself. The name Elohim is used when the Bible speaks of God in the objective sense: the God who creates the world, the God of the nations, the God who is distant, or the God who is discerned in his works. In the latter case, for example, when people contemplate the stars or the universe they may experience a sense of grandeur that brings them closer to God. The Bible tells us that what this person experiences is Elohim. He realizes that there is a Creator, there is a God, and he is impelled towards something he cannot discern in nature. On the other hand, when God enters into a personal relationship with a human being, he is not Elohim but the One who gives his Name, thus revealing himself as being the One who is at the very heart of all life and who hands over his Name. God reveals himself to Abraham as Yahweh, and he did the same with Moses and with all the prophets. Yahweh is the God who establishes contact with a person he chooses, and this God can only be known by a revelation. You cannot take hold of Yahweh who reveals himself as the Being of beings unless he gives himself to you. Elohim, on the other hand, can be known through his works.

In Jewish thought (this was typical for most cultures in the Middle East at that time) to give someone your name was to provide that person with a hold on you, because the name was the spiritual being of someone. Knowing someone's name was therefore much more than having the ability to call that person, get his or her attention, and begin something together. When you knew someone's name you acted on that person's interior being, and that person was given over to you. It is the same kind of thing when in other civilizations people have an aversion to being photographed, because possessing someone's image means that you can act on that person. In the Bible also, having someone's name is to act on that person. As a result, when Yahweh gives someone his name, it means that he accepts that this person acts on him. To a certain extent Yahweh gives himself over to people. However, there is a limit, as signified by the fact that the name is unpronounceable. God gives his name, but it is not one that any human being can say. This is what might be called the dialectical movement of a hidden God who reveals himself; and when this God reveals himself we know that he is the hidden God.

To put it more precisely, when God does not reveal himself to us we can have relatively clear ideas about him. We can imagine whatever we like and make it as precise as we like. Human beings think they know who God is, as long as God does not reveal himself. However, when God does reveal himself, the first thing you learn is that everything you thought about him is false. You then learn that he is the hidden God whom you cannot find. This is the double meaning of the given name being unpronounceable: God is both revealed and hidden.

The second creation account no longer speaks of Elohim but only of Yahweh. It is no longer a question of the One who creates, organizes, and directs, but of the relationship that exists between God and humanity. This is why this text begins with humanity. In the first account, it was a question of understanding who God is in relation to the universe as a whole. In this second text, it is a question of the relationship between God and humanity. This is an entirely different issue, which calls for a different response: a narrative that begins with humanity, and then proceeds to situate everything in relation to that humanity. This is not a matter of anthropocentrism; instead, a second theological question is asked that requires relating everything to humanity.

In any case, in the seventh verse we are told that with regard to his soul (in the Jewish sense) or being, Adam becomes a living being, which qualifies his person: 'He blows into his nostrils the breath of life and it is man, a living being (or, living as to his being) (or, living as to his soul).' The Hebrew word for soul, *nefesh*, is the equivalent of the person; and this person, according to the text, exists because of an act of God, who does not simply make Adam live but makes a person out of him, that is, a living being as to his soul.

The translation of many words in this account is very important. In the fourth verse, the Hebrew word *toledot*, usually translated as creations or origins (the origins of the heavens and the earth when they were created), means generations, and is frequently used in the Bible to speak of genealogies. Here the text does not deal with the creation act of the first chapter but with descendants, the way a baby is created as the fruit of the act of love; and this is what the Hebrew word designates: a series of generations. In other words, this account begins with the birth of the heavens and the earth, in the strongest sense of that word. Throughout this text we encounter a number of words strongly associated with sexual relations and birth – words that have a positive quality to indicate that everything done is good. We also find a number of words with a negative quality, indicating an ensemble of potentially bad elements.

Another word that stands out is Eden (in verses 8 and 10), which designates sexual communion encompassing sensual pleasure and joy. It goes without saying that it is pointless to look for a particular location where the garden might have been. Nevertheless, generations of exegetes did exactly that. They managed to find two of the rivers: the Tigris and the Euphrates. For example, Father Chaine devotes fifty pages to an attempt to locate Eden geographically. I believe that the name alone precludes any sense of a geographical location since it indicates a human reality.

The text says that the garden of Eden is in the east, which is a very important term in the Bible. The Hebrew word *qedem*, translated as east, means 'from where the Messiah comes,' and 'from where the Messiah will return.' When vocalized differently, it means 'the glory of God.' However, the Hebrew word literally means 'what precedes'; and this is not difficult to understand since the sun rises in the east. It can also mean 'what was in the beginning.' It is worth noting that there are two equivalent biblical meanings: the east as eternity and the east from which comes grace. Of course, this is a very different view of eternity from the one we are used to. We think of eternity as an infinity of time, but in the Bible there is no relation between time and eternity. In the biblical perspective, eternity is not a very long time, and time is not a bit of eternity. There is no relationship at all. Eternity is from where grace comes, which is something altogether different. We need to put aside our time-related notions of eternity. Eden in the east does not mean that the Messiah came from, or that Jesus Christ will return from, China, so to speak, but that he will come from where grace is. Hence, Eden in the east was where grace was to be found, in the sense of a free gift, thus forging this remarkable connection between Eden as sexual pleasure and joy, and as grace.

The names of the four branches of the river flowing from Eden present us with a play of words that is very ambiguous. The first, *pishon*, means 'that which spreads out far in the distance,' but in a negative sense, pejorative if you like, because it is in excess. It is the equivalent of hubris in the Greek sense, and of immoderation; and it also has the meaning of transgression. In other words, it is the image of a river that overflows, which designates excess and transgression. The second river, *gihon*, is the counterpart of the first, but it grows in a positive sense, that of being large and growing larger in a harmonious way. The verb used is *gacha*, which is the moment the head of a baby appears during the birth process. It is a very characteristic term. In other words: with the first river there is the meaning of immoderation, frenzy, and transgression, and with the second river that of the appearance of life. The name of the third river, *hideqel*, also has a negative meaning, of something sharp, violent, hard, and that pierces. The name of the fourth river, *pherat*, has the positive meaning of being fruitful and productive.

Hence the names of the four rivers form two pairs of positive and negative elements, which signify that Eden, as the universe given by God to humanity, includes all possibilities. There is the possibility of the harmonious growth following birth, of death and destruction, of frenzy and madness, and so on.

I do not believe that this play on words is merely coincidental. The first river surrounds the land of *chawilah* 'where there is gold, the gold of that land is good, the bdellium and the onyx are found there.' The ambiguity continues because, while it is the land of gold, there is also the bdellium, meaning 'in poverty.' So you see, there is gold along with poverty. There is here a series of clever plays on words, of puns, to show us the contradictions of the universe, which appear to be commensurate with humanity.

In this garden of Eden we find two trees, the meaning of which is also symbolic. The tree of life is in the centre, and there is also the tree of the knowledge of good and evil. The translation of the Hebrew as 'knowledge' is weak, and 'affirmation' may be better. Adam may eat the fruit from the tree of life, but not the fruit from the other tree. To understand this, we must recognize that there is no question here of knowing an objective good or evil. From a biblical perspective, there cannot be a reality called 'the good' and another called 'the evil' – 'the good' is what God says and does. There is no 'good' in itself, for the obvious reason that if there was a good in itself it would be prior to God and able to pass judgment on him. It is the all too common attitude (for example, of the liberals in the nineteenth century) who argued that the God of the Old Testament was terrible and barbaric in his ordering of wars and massacres. From the point of view of 'the good,' God should not do this. In other words, human beings discern a good apart from God, on the basis of which God can be judged. The Bible is much more radical: 'the good' is simply what God says and does.

Hence, the tree cannot be for knowing good and evil, but for having the ability to decide what is good and evil, and to do so without God. That is the problem: It is God who decides, but there is a tree that would allow human beings to decide what is good in his place. There is, of course, the traditional Christological interpretation going back to Tertullian, an early church father, who made the astute remark that the two trees were in the same place. Two trees cannot both be in the centre of the garden; hence, the two must be one. You can immediately see the Christian typology: it signifies the cross, already present in the middle of the garden of Eden. The fruit of this tree, which is both the fruit of life and the fruit of the discernment of good and evil, is of course, Jesus Christ. He is the only One who *is* life, and who at the same time discerns good and evil in the sense of separating the two. This early Christian interpretation has reverberated throughout Christianity. Such a symbolic interpretation is absolutely not imposed by the text itself. The situation is analogous to the one we spoke of earlier, of seeing Elohim as a Trinity. It is a Christian reinterpretation of the text, which is not wrong from the perspective of Jesus Christ but which cannot be affirmed on the basis of this text alone.

I will conclude these introductory remarks by responding to some of the questions regarding the many translation problems that we encounter in our Bibles. A little background information may be helpful. St Jerome did a rather poor job of translating the Hebrew text into Greek, which often resulted in different meanings from the original. This text was subsequently translated into Latin, with another host of mistranslations. Worse, all this was done under the strong influence of Greek philosophy; and this became the basis for much Christian thinking. It should come as no surprise, therefore, that very little remained of the original Hebrew thinking.

For example, the distinction between good and evil is not the fundamental one in the Bible. It is the distinction between life and death, clearly put in Deuteronomy 30, verse 15: 'See, I have set before you life and good, death and evil.' Good and life are the same, and so are evil and death. The reason is simple. God is the living One; hence, if you are in communion with him you are at the same time living and in the good. The two are the same. If you break the relationship with God, you are separated from life and hence in death and evil. God is the only One who can say that this or that is good. There is no good outside of him, separate from him. In Hebrew thinking, there is no pre-existing evil but only what humanity says is evil. The absolute evil is a human morality, because by means of it humanity or a society claims to be able to discern what is good and evil, which amounts to human beings putting themselves into God's place. It is why we are constantly warned not to judge anyone or anything. Only God can do so. The difference is that God declares the good and never the evil. The latter is impossible, because his word is inseparable from the act that brings forth. God created humanity free, which is inseparable from the possibility of disobedience and thus of separation from the good and from life.

It is for this reason that in the second creation account it is never said that this or that is good. As soon as humanity appears the situation becomes ambiguous, because there are the two possibilities of the good and life on the one hand, and of evil and death on the other. For example, we have seen how the text emphasizes the ambiguity of the situation of having gold and living in poverty at the same time.

In Hebrew thought there are no such things as a fallen humanity or fallen angels. For example: when in the opening verses of the book of Job we encounter Satan, it never says that Satan is a fallen angel. What we are told is that God summons all his creatures, and among them is Satan, who has a particular role to play. Nothing is said about Satan aspiring to dominate God. This also is Greek mythology. Satan is the Accuser, and that is his role before God: to point out the occurrence of evil. God does not accuse. We have a hard time getting away from our Lucifer-related images, but these are entirely foreign to Hebrew thinking. Satan simply seeks God's justice. He is the agent of that justice by demanding that justice be done to those who do evil.

It is for this reason that Satan is exactly the opposite of Jesus. When Jesus says he sees Satan fall from heaven as a bolt of lightning, he means that the Accuser no longer exists before God. The Bible speaks of Satan only in the book of Job, and therefore in relation to a humanity that has separated itself from God. Humanity is doing something other than what God expects from it, and this doing something else will be called evil. Satan claims that Job will become like everyone else the moment he encounters difficulties. God permits Satan to put Job to the test to see if Job is a good man, and what this means must be understood in the context of the entire revelation. Death and everything that comes with it must not be seen as a punishment for evil, but as a consequence of breaking from the living One. In the same vein, whenever we accuse someone we become Satan. Whenever we cause divisions between people we become devils, since Diabolos is the one who causes divisions. It is important to understand that the Bible often personifies a certain reality in these phenomena of accusation and division.

After the break with God, is it possible to live in the world without judging? It is certainly necessary, since the world is no longer innocent. Nevertheless, human beings do not have the right to judge, even though they are obliged to make distinctions between good and evil.[1] This is the terrible situation in which humanity finds itself. Following the

---

1 See Jacques Ellul, *To Will and to Do*, trans. C. Edward Hopkin (Philadelphia: Pilgrim Press, 1969), for a discussion of how morality is necessary for societal order but that it can never express God's will.

break with God, we all have this need to classify everything, whether people or things, as good or evil; but when Jesus enters into the midst of all of this, he completely upsets all morality, in keeping with the Old Testament. He constantly shows that what we declare to be morally good is often not so. However, Jesus never made distinctions between good and evil. For example, he does not judge the Pharisees. What he says is: 'Woe to you.' This is not a curse; what he says is that they are unhappy. He does not blame them, but tells them they are wretched because they are fundamentally mistaken. Jesus tells them that to be happy is not to follow the ways of the world, but the way of God, which is love.

Human Life in the Garden

I will now turn to what the second chapter reveals regarding humanity, which includes some things already encountered in the first. The following four elements appear as the most important: the name of Adam, the question of freedom, the question of service, and the question of the Word. The first man is called Adam, which means, literally, red earth or clay. Adam is a common noun, and in Hebrew is preceded by an article: *the* Adam, signifying that he belongs to the materiality of creation and has what you might consider to be an animal nature. At the same time, the name Adam is unique (or specific to him) and different from the Hebrew *isch*, which means humanity, analogous to the German *mann* or *l'homme* in French. Being a unique name as well as a common noun, this means that Adam cannot be a single man. Similarly, when Eve is created it is not one woman. The Bible is not speaking of one couple. All of humanity was created in Adam, which is precisely what this common and generic name means. Hence, for Hebrew thinking, there are no scientific problems as to whether there was one first couple or whether there were more people, who appeared in central China, southern Africa, or somewhere else, and when this all happened. The Hebrew authors of this text were not concerned with these questions. Jewish commentaries provide us with clues as to the kinds of questions that may have preoccupied them.

For example, the Hagadah (a commentary from the first century B.C.) explains why the Hebrew word translated as Adam is in the singular as opposed to the plural. The reason for there being only one person is to teach us that whoever destroys one human being destroys the whole of humanity. It also teaches us that no human being, no group, and no race can regard itself as superior to another. This is why Adam in the Hebrew is a generic name in the singular, as well as a common noun in the plural that designates all of humanity as opposed to a particular individual; but being in the singular it represents all humanity in one being.

Concerning the question of freedom, the text affirms two things. The seventh verse reveals that Adam lived by the spirit. There are two Hebrew words that mean the same thing: *nefesh* refers to the person, a being, a soul (in the Hebrew sense); and *ruach* refers to the breath of respiration as well as the spirit. This reminds us of Jesus' saying that the wind blows (or: the spirit breathes) where it wills, and when you hear the sound of it you do not know where it comes from or where it is going. This saying maintains the ambiguity of breath and spirit. The same Hebrew commentary explains that just as we cannot keep our breath within ourselves for very long, so also we cannot keep the spirit. This identity between breath and spirit teaches us that no one can possess the spirit. No one should believe that they can possess the spirit, be a mystic in communion with God, or become a spiritual being. The spirit and breath are like a movement or exchange with the outside world. The breath referred to here is a sign of and condition for being alive, and so is the spirit. All this represents a very important first aspect of human freedom. Human beings are free if they are not stuck on possession; they must move as with respiration and so with access to the spirit, which is always moving. Hence, human beings are free to the extent that the spirit is free.

The second aspect of freedom comes from verses 16 and 17, which deal with the commandment: 'You may eat from every tree in the garden, but not from the tree that permits the discernment of good and evil; for on the day you eat from it, you have died.' For many, this text is proof that God is not good because he imposed this interdiction. I would like to go back to what we discussed earlier, namely, the matter of declaring good and evil by saying: This is good and that is bad. What this really means is to put oneself in the place of God. Only God speaks the good. Either you say what God says or you say something else, and that is a problem. Putting yourself in God's place inevitably involves breaking the relationship with him; and since he is the living one (the totality of all being), any claim of replacing him involves cutting oneself off from life, which results in death. The text is commonly translated as: On (or from) the day you eat of it, you will die. However, the Hebrew text is in the imperfect tense; consequently, the future tense should not be used. It is not at all a punishment or penalty that is imposed. What the text is literally saying is that from the very day you ate of it you would be dead. It is not that you will die sometime in the future. What this means is that from the very moment you would wish to decree what is good and what is evil, it would mean that you are already dead. It is not a matter of a punishment, but of a process of breaking off with God by no longer listening to him, putting yourself in his place, from then on saying by yourself what is good and evil in his place; and you have begun to be dead. At this point, living in freedom is impossible.

The situation is analogous to one in which a parent warns a child not to touch a hot stove because she will burn her hand. Burning her hand is not a punishment. There is only a punishment if the parent says: If you try to touch the stove, you must go to your room. The parent warns the child of the reality: to touch something hot is to burn your hand. We have hopelessly confused God's warnings with commandments. In the entire Old Testament, God only warns his people of what will happen if they do this or that.

What our text reveals, therefore, is that the freedom of humanity exists only if they remain in communion with God, this communion being a relationship of love. All along we have seen the importance of love and sexual communion and so on, and all this is directed at the relationship of love between God and humanity, even in the most physical sense. Hence, what is commonly understood as a command-ment is not at all a law imposed on humanity; it is not an imperative, a constraint, or something negative, but a condition for being alive. Humanity is told that in order to continue to live, it is not enough to eat from the tree of life, but you must remain in your relationship with God and receive the spirit, the spirit that comes and goes as an element of freedom; and because of this, you cannot claim the right of deciding what is good and evil in God's place, instead of listening to the Word of God. It is the very condition of freedom, because God reserves for hu-manity the possibility to do otherwise.

Next comes the question of service. In the fifteenth verse we read that Yahweh takes humanity and puts them in the garden of Eden to work it and to keep it. It is rather amusing that many commentaries say something to the effect that this is ridiculous. Why work in a garden when it has already been explained that the soil produced all kinds of fruit by itself? Why did the garden have to be guarded? Father Chaine, in his commentary, concludes that the writer had a bad day and even a lapse of memory. I think, on the contrary, that this text is full of meaning.

Humanity is called to render a service, but one that is useless.[2] Of course, the garden did not need to be cultivated since it was fruitful, and it did not need to be guarded since there were no external enemies. This is exactly the point: there is no necessity to work and there is no necessity to be productive. All there is, is the Word of God. God tells humanity that they are there to cultivate and keep the garden. What humanity is therefore faced with is: 'God says that I should do this, it serves no purpose, but I will do it.' What God says is the good. If, on the other hand, humanity begins to say, 'Of what use is it?' that is like the tree of knowledge of good and evil. 'Since the garden doesn't require cultivation, I do not need to work, and since there are no enemies, I do not need to guard it, so I won't do it.' That is the evil. This response may be morally legitimate: 'Since it serves no purpose, I will not do it.' But God said: 'Do it'; and that is the trouble, to have confidence or not in the Word of God. This is the situation humanity had to face. In any case, it is clear that it is impossible to derive from these well-known texts the law of work. Work as such does not exist for humanity as a law of creation.

That this text isn't about real work is confirmed by the use of the Hebrew word used for working the garden, namely, *avoda*, which means worship. In other words: 'You will worship God through working and guarding it, knowing very well that these actions are unnecessary; but it is simply a form of worship, and you honour and adore him by it. It is not in order to produce, but to honour in reciprocity.' All the early Jewish commentaries have strongly suggested that what this means is that God did not create humanity for nothing. He did not launch humanity into an emptiness. Humanity has a role to play. Leisure is not a life, and empty leisure is not good. This role, according to the Hebrew word *avoda*, is to bring the whole of the garden of Eden before God so that all of creation will adore God through this human service. When humanity serves God for nothing and without an objective, they bring the creation to worship God.

The above, I believe, is the meaning of verses 15 to 17. We begin to see where the story of good and evil comes from. Humanity could refuse to work, but this has consequences that we will soon examine. The refusal to work for nothing led to the necessity of having to work for something. There no longer was any choice.

---

2 See Jacques Ellul, 'Meditation on Inutility,' in *The Politics of God, the Politics of Man*, trans. Geoffrey W. Bromiley (Grand Rapids, MI: Eerdmans, 1972).

I now turn to the question of the Word. The text describes the impressive scene where God has all the animals pass before humanity, each animal is given a name, and God accepts these names. As we have seen, giving a name means to dominate spiritually over the creation. In other words, in the first chapter, humanity is called to rule materially or concretely, while in the second chapter they are called to do so spiritually. Humanity is to rule as God does by means of the word. By giving a name, humanity participates in the spiritual sovereignty of God over creation. They have received the gift of the word, that God and God alone can give. The verses in question were at the core of a theological argument during the fourteenth and fifteenth centuries. The text tells us that when humanity gives a name they define a reality; that is, when Adam calls an animal by a certain name, it really is the name of that animal. There is no distinction, as the one made during the fourteenth century, between the name and the real thing. In the text, the name and the thing are one and the same, and the name is absolutely identified with it. In our century we face the complete dissociation between the thing and the verbal form, which no longer corresponds to any reality.[3] In this text, on the contrary, the word of humanity is true, it defines what is real, and at the same time a meaning is given to the whole of creation.

Finally, I would like to respond more fully to some of your questions. To return to my earlier example of a child being warned not to touch a hot stove, this story is an analogy of the kind of misinterpretation that has been made of the Old Testament. All throughout, God limits himself to warning: This is what will happen if you do this or that. There are no eternal rules. God, the living One, warns that to separate yourself from him is to be dead. From the very beginning of the first chapter of Genesis, God reveals that there is only one domain, as it were, foreign to him and that is the non-being, the *tohu wabohu*. It is important to understand that when freedom is introduced, it is not already constrained, because then you cannot speak of freedom. I believe that the problem with this kind of reasoning is that it is logical but not biblical. In the Bible there are no constraints, no choices, if you like, but instead there are orientations or conditions. What freedom means, and particularly what Christian freedom means in the New Testament, is that it is

---

3 These issues have been developed in Jacques Ellul, *The Humiliation of the Word*, trans. Joyce Main Hanks (Grand Rapids, MI: Eerdmans, 1985); and *Propaganda*, trans. K. Kellen and J. Lerner (New York: Vintage, 1973).

not an indeterminate, indefinite, or undefined freedom. It is not the freedom of a donkey placed midway between two bales of hay identical in all respects, including size, taste, and smell, and there is therefore no reason for the donkey to go to the one rather than to the other. Freedom is not a matter of doing anything whatsoever.

Christian freedom is defined by the relationship of love and only by this relationship. Theologically speaking, freedom and love are indissociably linked.[4] You cannot love under duress, you must be free, and you are free in a relationship of love and only through that relationship. This is what the second chapter of Genesis is about. If Adam loves God, he will as a matter of course and spontaneously do what God says, since it pleases both. If Adam does not love God, he will do something else, and at that point he stops living. Just think of your relationship with your spouse. Do you love your spouse because of obligation, constraint, necessity, a cross to bear, and so on, or is it out of freedom? Do you believe that your freedom would be all the greater if you did not love him or her? If you get right down to it, it is that simple. You cannot love someone if you are not free; and the ultimate form of freedom is expressed in loving and not in hating. It is not by destroying the other that you find freedom. We hear enough about that in psychoanalysis. We can have a good laugh about the notion that in assassinating your father, you liberate yourself. Each time the Jews attempted to address their God as Master (the Hebrew word is *Bel*), they were rejected because God cannot accept being called Master, for obvious reasons. He is the liberator and not the master. All this is extremely coherent.

Man and Woman

We will next examine the portion of the text where woman appears, and deal with five questions. The first regards her name. It is Adam who gives her that name; and, as he does with the animals, he says (according to verse 23): 'This one shall be called woman (*ischah*), for from man (*isch*) this one is taken.' The fact that he names her, just as he did the animals, could mean that he dominates.

There are two points I would like to make that are surprising. The first is that in most of the known languages, the word woman derives from a different root than the word man. In Hebrew they have the same

---

4 See Jacques Ellul, 'Lifelong Love,' in *What I Believe*, trans. Geoffrey W. Bromiley (Grand Rapids, MI: Eerdmans, 1989), 66–86.

root. *Isch* means master, but since it is Adam who gives her this name he transfers this mastery to her. *Ischah* means the one who will now be the master.

Father Chaine,[5] as a commentator in the grip of positivism, argues that undoubtedly this hints at matriarchy. This is confirmed by verse 24, which tells us that the man abandons his father and mother and follows the woman. I believe there is much more to all this. *Ischah* is the result of adding a suffix to the end of *isch*, which has a precise meaning: in the direction of. Hence *ischah* literally means: in the direction of the man. In other words, the woman establishes the direction towards being human. The man is not human, so to speak, as a given. It is the woman who establishes the direction toward what it is to be humanity. She drives man to become fully human. That, I believe, is the meaning of *ischah*, which has enormous implications.

The second point I would like to make is that when Adam meets the woman, he becomes aware of himself: 'This time, bone of my bones and flesh of my flesh.' Each of the two needs the other in order to know him- or herself. The text tells us that man knows woman, that he knows himself thanks to woman. The Hebrew verb *yada* has a triple meaning: sexual knowledge, experiencing the value of someone or something else, and participation. Thus, man achieves self-knowledge thanks to woman, through woman, and by means of woman. It also corresponds exactly to God's recognition that 'it is not good for man to be alone.'

This brings me to the second question. When God says that 'it is not good,' it is the exact opposite of 'it is good,' which we find throughout the first creation account where everything is approved by the declaration that it is good. In other words, this is the first 'not good' in creation, 'it' being the solitude of man. Consequently, the evil is the break between man and woman; and this throughout the Bible remains absolutely fundamental. It is based on what could be considered as a kind of ontology or an overall conception of humanity. Because man does not know himself except by knowing the woman and vice versa, we can now understand why the Bible is so harsh with adultery and homosexuality – as flawed conceptions of what it is to be human. We have failed to understand this because we have made it into a simple question of morality; and once this is done we are lost, because neither morality nor nature can give us any firm guidance. In the Bible it is not a question of morality but a question of what humanity is, and this can

---

5 J. Chaine, *Le livre de la Genèse* (Paris: Cerf, 1949).

only be discovered through the relationship *isch–ischah*. Making a moral issue out of adultery or homosexuality continues to permit Christians to judge and condemn others, which is a double error.[6] The text affirms

---

6 Unless they are carefully interpreted in the context of his work, Jacques Ellul's comments on homosexuality appear to be contradictory with what he is saying elsewhere in this book. It remains a difficult and painful subject both within and outside the Christian community.

A major portion of the work of Jacques Ellul is a sociological and historical analysis of the times in which we live. It is his contribution to our understanding of who we are and where we are going. By carefully examining many spheres of human life, he shows that people created *technique*, but it now has a greater influence on us than we can exercise over it. In other words, *technique* is the greatest threat to human freedom and hence to our ability to love during this period in the history of humanity.

Technique makes human life exceedingly stressful and difficult. Efficiency takes precedence over everything else. In addition, there is our anxiety regarding the future: growing unemployment, the threats of terrorism and war, the possible collapse of ecosystems, the many poisons moving into our food webs and threatening our health, and much more. We must leave much of ourselves behind in our participation in *technique*. To top it all off, *technique* desymbolizes human experience and culture, and along with it our meanings, values, moral directions, religious support, and hope for the future, which are all essential for making human life bearable. The epidemic use of anti-depressant drugs is but one symptom of the difficulties of living our lives under *technique*. In the face of all of this, we seek a way out. The explosion of all manner of sexual behaviour during the last half century is one of the most important symptoms of this struggle. Very simply put: it is as though deep down we realize that our socio-cultural being is enslaved by *technique*, with the result that our desire for freedom must be channelled through our biological being, and what better way to do this than through sex acts? In *The New Demons* (New York: Seabury, 1975), Ellul explains that sex has become the transgression of the sacred of *technique*. Ellul follows cultural anthropology and the history of religion in that the creation of a sacred also involves the creation of a profane. To reintegrate this profane, there is a sacred transgression which performs that role. In his book *The New Demons*, Ellul explains that the secular sacred of *technique* in our civilization is accompanied by its sacred transgression constituted by all manner of sex acts. Hence the explosion of pornography, sexual symbolism in advertising (especially in the 1960s, '70s, and '80s), etc.

For those among us who are heterosexuals, let us begin by examining the incredible influence this continues to have on everything related to sex. It predisposes us to all kinds of things that otherwise might not come into our minds. For example, it explains the ever-present 'soft' porn that appears to correspond to real needs of real people. It has become a secular religious cult of sex. Who among us is not affected by this cult? Apart from these 'cultural' influences, *technique* also exerts profound biological pressures. What is coming up our food web is affecting our bodies in the most fundamental ways, from weakening our immune systems to affecting the hormones that regulate so many functions, including sexual ones. It should come as no surprise that some of us confront a further brokenness in our lives because who we experience ourselves to be does not correspond to who we are physically.

monogamous relationships, which during the tenth century B.C. was highly unusual since there was not a single monogamous society in existence. Certainly the Jews were surrounded by completely polyga-

---

During the 1960s, when the influence of *technique* was beginning to make itself felt, many people celebrated various new liberties: we could wear our hair and dress any way we wished, sleep with anyone we desired, and have the religion of the day to boot. Falling all over ourselves in self-congratulation, we failed to realize that we were fundamentally mistaken. If we lived in a traditional society, these would have been incredible liberties indeed, but we lived in a society increasingly dominated by *technique*. All these details regarding our behaviour were completely irrelevant to the new emerging technical order. They did not matter in the least as long as we diligently submitted ourselves to a new technical conformity, that of using the latest *techniques* in our work and play. Ellul's comments must be understood in this light. Those who boast that the explosion of all manner of sexual behaviour is a manifestation of a newfound freedom are so possessed by *technique* that they confuse freedom with slavery. It is the worst kind of error a human being can make as we try to live meaningful and responsible lives on this earth.

When Christians make this error in interpreting our times, the consequences are even graver. In Genesis, God reveals his image of love in our being male and female, as a man and a woman complement one another in love to enrich each other's humanity. When humanity broke with God, we turned to other gods and their secular equivalents to defend ourselves against relativism, nihilism, and *anomie*. It distorted our lives and our communities; and the entire Jewish and Christian Bible shows how much sex was a part of this struggle. It is this aspect of the biblical message that is extremely difficult for us to accept as we struggle under the pressure of *technique* as our sacred, which we transgress through sex. In this context, I cannot identify with or condone any of the positions in relation to homosexuality outside or within the church today. Without exception, I find them superficial and even hypocritical because they do not discern the real meaning of our sexual despair. What Jacques Ellul sharply criticizes is our attitudes to homosexuality, especially when this part of our brokenness is interpreted as something else. It is important to remember that the Bible includes many accounts of our struggles with sexuality, including polygamy, adultery, incest, and homosexuality (practised by heterosexual men on each other or on boys). Jesus' dealing with the woman caught in adultery should remind us that, as a Christian community, we have a long way to go when it comes to practising our freedom in the domain of sexuality made possible by God's forgiveness and love. It would be wise to follow Jesus' advice to take the beam out of our own eyes before we attempt to remove the splinter out of someone else's. My own limited experience has shown me that the more conservative the Christian community, the greater and more frequent are its sexual aberrations. Whatever we do and say should be compared with our task of being present in the world as Jesus teaches it, which Jacques Ellul interprets in part 3. Rather than being caught up in every politically correct fashion of our times, let us move on to working this out, also in the domain of sexuality.

The most extensive treatment of this topic can be found in Jacques Ellul's *Les combats de la liberté* (Paris: Le Centurion/Labor et Fides, 1984); and in *The New Demons* (New York: Seabury, 1975).

mous societies. There is no question that this affirmation of monogamy on their part, as well as their establishment of cities of refuge, made them stand out. In the case of monogamy, the Jews were clear: it is a question of becoming human, and this complements what we have learned about humanity being in the image of God.

The third question picks up where we left off in the first chapter regarding humanity being in the image of God. Here we find one being who is two, or two within one being. To this we can add another remarkable explanation by the Haggadah of the seventh verse, where we are told that God fashions humanity. It may appear to you as a small detail, but it is rather interesting. There is a grammatical problem here. The Hebrew word is written here as *wayyiser* but grammatically there should have been only one *yod*, written as a letter y. In a language made up of consonants, this presents a major problem because an extra letter cannot simply be ignored. So why have two? The word *yod* means creature. Hence the Haggadah commentary explains that had the word been written with a single letter, there would have been only one creature. When the two letters are used, it means that there are two creatures within one word and within one act. Hence the seventh verse could be read as 'God fashions humanity in two creatures.' It corresponds to the first chapter stating that he makes humanity, he makes them male and female. It is exactly the same phenomenon. We encounter a kind of unity along with a division, a kind of tearing or splitting apart within the being of humanity; and this helps us understand the relationship between man and woman as described here. There are some simple details. The woman is the man's helper after none was found for him; and she becomes a part of his spiritual thrust, as it were. All this will be expressed later as woman being the glory of man. But the glory of humanity is the revelation; hence, it is woman who reveals the reality of man. Moreover, she is man's only counterpart, and he has a stronger link with her than with his father and mother. Here we encounter a unique idea: in antiquity, a man would not leave his family to follow a woman. Normally, it was the reverse.

Then there is the question of reciprocity, and for this I will refer to an excellent study of this text made by Emmanuel Levinas,[7] one of the great contemporary Talmudists. What these texts teach us, according to him, is that, for the woman, the man must be the sign that there is a

---

7 Emmanuel Levinas, *Du sacré au saint: Cinq nouvelles lectures talmudiques* (Paris: Éditions de Minuit, 1977).

humanity to be assumed: she not only provides the man access to love, but also helps him assume his humanity. And vice versa: the woman, as the keeper of love (using a Talmudic expression), must be for the man the sign that in love he will find the lost unity. Here is the reciprocal role we have lost. If we had kept this in Christianity, we would not have all the problems we do now. The man must be, for the woman, a sign of the humanity to be gained. She is not the woman who must stay at home, the housewife, the one who has babies, or who is the keeper of love alone. She is the woman who assumes one of the faces of all of humanity. Reciprocally, the woman must constantly teach the man that in his engagement in work or public life he will never find back the lost unity, but only in love. All this is much more than a simple question of complementarity. There are not only two complementary beings; *ischah* is not merely the feminine of *isch*, so to speak. On the basis of the totality of what it is to be human, there is a sharing of the masculine and the feminine.

Finally, there is the famous question of Adam's rib. God builds the woman from the rib he has taken from the man. There are numerous explanations. What I believe to be one of the weakest ones began with Thomas Aquinas, who said that it was all for the best because had God drawn the woman from the head of man, she would have been filled with pride; had he drawn her from his feet she would have been a slave; hence, it was best to take something obscure, such as a rib, to do the least harm. There have been many variations of this argument, such as, What would have happened if the woman had been built from the heart of man? and so on. All this is meaningless. A slightly better explanation derives from an Arabic saying that someone being my rib means an inseparable friendship. However, since this is taken from an Arabic text dating ten to twelve centuries later, I believe the direction of influence likely to be the reverse: the Arabic text was inspired by the Hebrew one, since we know that the Arabs knew the biblical text. Hence, I don't believe this is an explanation either.

This leaves us with three other possible explanations. The one I appreciate very much, because it keeps the ambiguity of which we have often spoken, is based on the Hebrew word *tsela* translated as rib, but it can also mean a fall. It comes from the verb *tsala*, which means to limp, hesitate, and then fall. Hence the word means rib but also a fall, disaster, or misfortune. I therefore find this word full of meaning as it is used here, in view of everything that follows. You could say either that the woman, ever since her creation, was a prime factor in the break with

God since she was taken from the rib, or that she is drawn from that break as embodied in the man. The fact that man would fall was already inscribed in him, and God took it out. This is no more than a hypothesis based on a play of words like so many others; and in any case, it is not the most important thing, and certainly not the most profound.

Two other explanations of the rib remain. What I have just described with the interpretation of falling down is expressly rejected by the Talmud. The commentators have rejected it with horror, in the conviction that it is absolutely impossible. Instead, these commentators, who are extraordinarily skilful in plays of letters, have come to a different interpretation. However, there are two schools of interpretation because the rabbis are divided over this. One school argues that the rib should be seen as a face; while the other school, also basing itself on a play of letters, holds that the rib is not really a rib but the last vertebra in the spinal column of the man. Both interpretations are possible; hence, there is the school of the face and the school of the last vertebra!

What is ironic is that these two paths of interpretation arrive at the same thing. If the woman was drawn from the face of the man, she is the other face; that is to say, she is absolutely the equal of the man at the summit of his dignity. If, on the contrary, she was drawn from the last vertebra we are talking about absolutely the most useless appendage in the man. Remove it and it has absolutely no effect. What this means is that for the woman, God undertook a creative act as fundamental as for the creation of the world. He created the world out of chaos, out of nothing; and so he created the woman from nothing. She is the summit of dignity, above that of Adam, because Adam was made from red earth but the woman was drawn from next to nothing. Hence, this was the summit of creative acts. We see the importance the Talmud attributes to the creation of the woman. This reaches its height with Levinas, who says that the creation of the woman from the rib is the most beautiful idea conceived by God, in that in this way he created the other who is the same. For love to exist, it is necessary that the other be another, yet that they are truly similar and truly the same. To draw something out of Adam to fashion the woman was to say that in this other, who was really an other, there were two 'sames'; there were two that were taken in Adam. But in that case the taking of the rib results in a wound (according to Levinas), and the woman exists to heal together the tear in the being of humanity. At the same time, the man can only encounter the woman at the cost of this tearing; after this amputation, so to speak, he depends totally on the woman for the accomplishment of his humanity. With this text regarding the rib, we come back to what we have already seen twice before, once with the *ah* ending in *ischah*, the woman who points the way to what it is to be human, and also in the double *yod* in *wayyiser*. All along, the text insists on the woman being not only the equal of man but the one who gives him the meaning of life. Here, I believe, is the substance of this text dealing with the creation of the woman.

This conception of man and woman is altogether different from anything that appears in the literature of that time and beyond. Nowhere else has the relationship between a man and woman the greatest possible importance: as the image of the relationship between God and humanity. Throughout the Bible this relationship is less schematic and simple than the way it is usually thought of. It is a highly diplomatic relationship that is flexible and complex. Finally, I must confess that I have never understood how the negative attitudes and beliefs concerning women emerged in the Christian community, and even less how they can possibly be defended.[8]

---

8 See Jacques Ellul, *The Subversion of Christianity*, trans. Geoffrey W. Bromiley (Grand Rapids, MI: Eerdmans, 1986), 69–94, for a discussion of the man–woman relationship and morality.

4 The Break between God and Humanity

The Serpent

The first six verses of the third chapter of Genesis are often thought of as dealing with the origin of evil. I believe, however, that we should not draw from this text more than it says. I will examine three elements of the text: first the serpent, then the temptation itself, and finally what is traditionally called the fall. Only then will I consider the question of the mythical or historical character of this narrative.

The serpent cannot be regarded as a supernatural being. It is not the Devil, which is an interpretation that came much later. Nor is it the dragon that appears in the book of Revelation. The text is very clear on the serpent being a part of the creation: 'The serpent was more subtle than any other creature that God had made.' The snake is clearly a part of the creation and not at all a metaphysical evil. This can also be affirmed theologically, in the following manner.

Why does the Bible not pose the problem of a metaphysical evil or of the origin of evil? The Bible, as the book of God's revelation of his plan for our salvation, contains what is important for that salvation and for re-establishing the relationship between God and humanity. It is important to always remember this. It does not contain a doctrine, nor does it seek to provide us with intellectual satisfaction. In other words, it is intended to help us take what might be called an existential position, as opposed to revealing mysterious or transcendent things that happen in heaven, such as the appearance of the Devil and the subsequent struggle between God and the Devil. The Bible never speaks about these things, since they are not our business. It is important to note that nowhere does the Bible talk about a revolt of angels, Lucifer (an invention that came about much later in Christianity), or the existence of an evil in itself. We are always tempted to import these kinds of ideas into the text under consideration, but it is only in the book of Revelation that the Bible talks about the existence of a demon, the beasts of the abyss, or the dragon who wages war in heaven against Israel or against Jesus Christ.[1] The significance of this is that we are told about these things, not at the beginning of human history, but after the crucifixion and resurrection of Jesus Christ. In other words, we are told only when the Bible can assure us that this has indeed happened, but Jesus Christ has made love and life victorious.

We are not told about these things within a kind of tragic perspective of uncertainty, as a drama unfolds itself in heaven in which we do not play a role and over which we have no influence. We are not provided with some kind of abstract knowledge, but we are told only at the end, to commit us to Hope.[2] If from the beginning we had been told that there is a Satanic power which is the near equal of God and which caused humanity to fall, we would have been confronted with a problem that existentially we cannot do anything about and that, philosophically or theologically, we have never been able to resolve. Hebrew thinking radically cuts short this kind of speculation. There simply is no talk of any of this, no Lucifer, no evil, and so on. We encounter it when evil or the dragon can only be thought of in relation to Jesus Christ and within salvation in Jesus Christ.

If the serpent is nothing more than a creature, it is obvious that the important thing is not what it is exactly, nor that it speaks. When Karl Barth was asked whether he believed that at one point the serpent really spoke, he rightly answered that the important thing was not whether the snake spoke but what it said. This surely is the real question. For there to have been dialogue and temptation via the intermediary of the serpent, there must have been a certain relationship between humanity and the serpent. In fact, the text shows two such relationships. The first is that this animal is related to the dust, just as humanity is. The fourteenth verse puts it, 'On your belly you will go, and dust you will eat,' and we have already learned that humanity was created from dust and will return to that dust. Second, in Hebrew there is something much more indicative in telling us that the serpent was the cunning one or the

---

1 Jacques Ellul, *Apocalypse*, trans. George W. Schreiner (New York: Seabury, 1977).
2 Jacques Ellul, *Hope in Time of Abandonment*, trans. C. Edward Hopkin (New York: Seabury, 1973).

subtle one. The Hebrew word *arum* immediately establishes a relationship to the man and the woman, of whom in the previous chapter the twenty-fifth verse tells us that both were naked, the man and his wife, and they were not ashamed.

The Hebrew word used here for naked is *arumim*, which is the plural of *arum*; hence, the words naked and cunning can be interposed. There is a connection: both the man and his wife are naked (*arumim*), and the serpent is the cunning one (*arum*), which can just as well be translated: both the man and his wife were cunning, and the serpent was naked. The use of the same word to designate the man and the woman as well as the snake shows that there is another bond between them.

The nakedness of man and woman is rather important, but it has led to a series of misinterpretations. Nakedness is commonly translated as innocence, resulting in attitudes such as that of the nudists, for example, who claim if you can live naked you are innocent. In the Bible this is not at all what is meant. To be naked is to be vulnerable and to be weak; it is always associated with a lack of strength and a lack of protection. What the text means with man and woman being naked is that their only protection is their relationship with God. It is God himself who protects them, and they need no other protection. This comes up again with Cain when he is put under the mark of God. God says to him that he will protect him. When Cain replies no, the Hebrew says that he no longer wants to be naked, meaning being weak and under the protection of God. He thinks he no longer needs any protection and begins to create his own through various *techniques* and the building of a city.[3]

The cunning of the serpent is to make use of the weakness of humanity to separate it from God, thereby making it weaker and far from its protector. The whole purpose of the serpent is to distance the woman and the man from God.

We are told that the serpent is cunning and intelligent. This is not to be interpreted as a fault or an evil. We are not told that the serpent is bad because of it. In fact, Jesus tells us to be as cunning as serpents. Moreover, according to Proverbs, out of cunning comes wisdom; and one of the patriarchs, namely Jacob, is called 'the cunning one.' We must be careful not to read anything into the text when it tells us that the serpent is intellectually the most developed of all of God's creatures. 'Of all creatures'

---

3 Jacques Ellul, *The Meaning of the City*, trans. Dennis Pardee (Grand Rapids, MI: Eerdmans, 1970). This book has some remarkable exegeses of later Genesis texts.

means that in some sense it knows more than Adam. But what is this knowledge?

The Hebrew word translated as 'serpent' is vocalized as *nachash*, which comes from a verb which has two meanings that cannot be translated with a single word because there is a whole context of meaning. *Nachash* means, first, 'to lead astray, to mislead with a view to the future.' It comes up a number of times in the Bible in the context of a crossroads where the wrong choice is made, so you go off in a direction that is completely different from the one intended. Probably around the time this text was written, the word also began to mean, 'to practice magic.' In other words, the *nachash*, by virtue of its name, signifies knowledge obtained by magic. This would mean (we will soon see how this develops, since it is only one aspect) that the serpent attempts to lead humanity to exceed the limits of their knowledge by means of something like magic in order to know the future, and to know something about the powers that can be used. This is the kind of knowledge offered by the *nachash*, who is the knower of magic.

The last thing to keep in mind about the serpent is that in the Canaanite world in particular, religions were centred around it. We know that in the Bible the animal that, time and time again, brought trouble to Israel was the bull, which was one of the divinities of the world in which Israel developed. Nevertheless, the serpent was one of the most important gods, at the very centre of religion as the symbol of life and fertility. Once again the text is polemic. The choice of the serpent in the text is not accidental, not simply because it is *nachash* but because it was a god of the world around Israel. It is in this context that the Bible reveals that this creature is simply one among all the others and nothing more. The serpent is not some eternal being, it is not invulnerable, it must submit to the condemnation of Yahweh; and it is only a creature who, although intelligent, uses that intelligence badly. Hence, it is through the serpent that this text attacks all religions. This, I believe, is the second element of the temptation, the first being magic. Through the serpent, both magic and religion are attacked; and these are the two important themes below the surface of this narrative.[4] What

---

4 This topic demands careful attention. Religion, magic, and morality are human institutions. At best they allow us to live in an orderly way so that humans do not engage in endless and random acts of exploitation and violence against one another. At worst they become authoritarian or even totalitarian. Christians and non-Christians can work together to make society and its institutions more just and open, but never do

in the Canaanite religions was the element of life becomes the element of death in this story. When the Jews took the serpent as the point of departure of Adam's error, they wanted to express the fact that the religious phenomenon symbolized by the serpent is the evil. This text from its very beginning has a strong anti-religious character, and thus desacralizes the world.[5]

The Temptation

We should not read into the text any preconceived ideas as to why the temptation came via the woman. It is not because she was weaker or more evil than the man. She undoubtedly had a substantial influence on him. After all, the text tells us that she is the perfect helper for him, and thus shares with him everything she lives through. I also think we should get rid of our usual interpretation of the temptation itself. A first interpretation is that it was a kind of testing of humanity by God, as if God placed humanity before a choice between obedience and disobedience. I believe that such an interpretation goes against the whole narrative of the creation. Critics of the Jewish or Christian faith have frequently made the argument that it is a terrible God who amuses himself by trapping humanity in temptation, but this is based on a completely erroneous interpretation of the text. How can there be a temptation when the relationship between God and his creation is one of love? There can be no question of God separating himself from his creation in order to test it after he has said all along that it was all very good. I believe, therefore, that this interpretation of the temptation does not come from the text and is entirely wrong.

Another widespread interpretation, which I believe to be equally foreign to the text, asks how it is possible that God imposed a prohibition. If God said, 'You shall not do this,' he was obviously taking the chance of inciting humanity to do it. If you read the text as it is, God does not say anything of the kind. It is the serpent who first says, 'So God said that you shall not eat from the trees of the garden?' To this the woman

---

these institutions embody God's will. Judaism and Christianity are to be lived out in faith in concert with others, rather than as institutionalized religions. See Jacques Ellul, *The New Demons*, trans. C. Edward Hopkin (New York: Seabury, 1975); and Jacques Ellul, 'Faith or Religion,' in *Perspectives on Our Age*, ed. Willem Vanderburg (Toronto: House of Anansi, 2004), 69–90.

5 See chapter 4, 'Faith or Religion?' in W.H. Vanderburg, ed., *Perspectives on Our Age: Jacques Ellul Speaks on His Life and Work* (Toronto: House of Anansi, 1997).

replies that God said not to eat from the tree that is in the middle of the garden. Nowhere does God say this. What this means is that insofar as the relationship between God and humanity is one of communion, humanity knows the good through that communion, and no barrier is imposed by God. There is, so to speak, no objective knowledge of what must be done and what must not be done. In our world of the separation of God and humanity, this relationship with God might be called a mystical relationship, if you like; and in such a relationship there are no things that you must or must not do. Such a relationship cannot be translated into objective formulas. For Adam and Eve no problems arise, and they do not come up against any prohibitions.

What the text now describes may be interpreted as the first step toward the break between God and humanity. The serpent, although intelligent, does not know such a relationship, and verbalizes what God said by asking, 'Did God say that you shall not eat of any tree of the garden?'. We then encounter the first induction toward the temptation, when the woman replies that they can eat the fruit from all the trees in the garden but (and now it is she who verbalizes a law), that God had said that you shall not eat the fruit from the tree in the middle of the garden. This constitutes a switch from a lived communion to what I would call a legal analysis. The discussion then changes, because the relationship with God is no longer the same. She translates it by saying that there is a law. Until now she did not know it since she simply lived it. The woman now faces the temptation of morality. We have now uncovered the three aspects of the temptation, and this is at the very heart of the problem. The first aspect is that of magic, the second that of religion, and the third that of morality. This is the key to understanding our text. God has made a creation for love, for glory, and for praise; and out of this creation humanity is going to make a magical, moral, and religious universe that is the opposite of the creation God had intended.

The switch in direction takes place with the promise of the serpent, to the effect that 'your eyes will be opened, you will know good and evil,' and so on. The serpent thus causes doubt to arise in the heart of the woman, and also plants a question. One could say that being cunning, the serpent has a kind of Socratic approach. It knows very well that God did not say that they cannot eat from any tree in the garden, and you can see the kind of provocation it uses. It leads her to reply, 'No, God did not forbid us; but it is true that there is one tree we must not touch or eat its fruit.' This is how the serpent induces the woman to question things. She is led to desire, to take the fruit as a wish to no longer depend on anyone but herself. When the serpent speaks, the evil does not yet exist in itself. What the serpent says is true: if they eat of this fruit they will know both good and evil, and it happens exactly as it says.

There is a play of words when the serpent tells her that she will not die. In Hebrew, the phrase 'you will die' is vocalized as *temutun*, but the serpent pronounces the negative 'you will not die' with a repetition *mot temutun*. This is a verbal form particular to the Hebrew, which implies the immediacy of the action. A literal translation would render this as: 'you will not die immediately.' Many Hebrew scholars agree with this. This is what the serpent promises, and again it is true; but the whole thing hinges on the repetition of a single letter that stands between a truth and a lie.

Going back to the first verse of chapter 3, it is easy to see how this temptation develops in our own lives as we try to make sense of God's revelation in our Bibles. Did God really say this or that? Doubt appears, and along with it the temptation to know better. This is also the temptation faced by all exegetes seeking to know God better, but (and this is the change in direction), to do so from an independent point of view, namely their own, which they advance in any discussion. Are we certain that God said, 'You shall not eat from the tree in the centre?' I am not introducing doubt but a question which, from an intellectual perspective, is a reasonable one, even though the Bible teaches me that I can only know his will and answer the question as to whether or not it is really true by submitting to his word. In other words, will I be the judge of God's word by asking, 'Did God really say this?' or will I first submit to his word in order to understand it? Then, in the fifth verse, we are told that 'God knows very well that (not only will you not die, but) when you eat of it, your eyes will be opened and you will become like gods, knowing both good and evil.' This statement verges on an accusation against God, to the effect that God wants to safeguard his privileges by preventing others from becoming gods; and, more fundamentally, there is the accusation that God hides certain things, and that therefore we had better get to know what he has in mind in terms of his intentions. This is what the phrase 'God knows very well that ...' means. In other words, we are faced by what has been called *gnosis*, which is purely intellectual knowledge about divine mysteries. It means that God is placed in the context of intellectual knowledge, and not in the context of love.

The two steps just described, namely, 'Did God really say that ...' and 'God knows very well that ...' amount to my saying that I know better

what lives within God, or what he has in mind, than what God has revealed of himself. Hence, in these two steps we encounter religion once
more, because all religions have said exactly that. They all claim to be
able to judge the truth of this or that revelation, and all religions have
claimed to establish a knowledge of secret and mysterious things. In
this way, the religious process estranges human beings from God.

The serpent claims that 'your eyes will be opened and you will be
like gods, knowing good and evil.' Since this claim is in the future, it
distances humanity from the present by telling them what will happen.
Humanity will be focused on a future and will abandon what they now
experience and live in favour of what they could be experiencing and
living, with the central element being the knowledge of good and evil.

There are two converging interpretations, both sound in my opinion.
The first points out that knowledge in Hebrew is not limited to an intellectual operation, is not merely something conceptual, since it implies a
profound and deep relationship as well as a power. To know, to speak,
and to have power are interchangeable terms. In other words, to know
good and evil means to decide good and evil and to have the power to
define them. Until now the will of God had been the good, and there
was no evil because there was nothing else. Now, humanity has the
power to say, 'This is good and that is bad,' and to do so independently
from the will of God. This is the first interpretation of what knowing
good and evil means.

Gerhard von Rad[6] has another interpretation based on a long and
very beautiful study in which he shows that in the Jewish texts from the
same period as this one, the phrase 'good and evil' has no moral content at all. Since in the Jewish world of that period, everything was
subject to a judgment of good and evil, it was a kind of shorthand
designating everything. Hence, the meaning von Rad gives to the expression 'knowing good and evil' is that 'you can do everything.' This
interpretation fits remarkably well with the assurance that they would
be like the gods, able to do everything. He concludes that what the text
says is not an issue of morality but an issue that he calls 'titanesque,'
which is hubris or the unleashing of human madness, frenzy, and the
exceeding of all limits.

It seems to me that these two interpretations are not at all contradictory. In one case it is humanity that decides good and evil, and in the

---

6 Gerhard von Rad, *Genesis: A Commentary*, trans. John Marks (Philadelphia: Westmin-
   ster Press, 1972).

other case it is the unleashing of hubris, the Promethean endeavour. This phenomenon is closely related to the one I dealt with earlier, namely, that of magic and religion.

The last element of the temptation that I will consider is found in the sixth verse, where we read that 'The woman sees that ...' but the Hebrew literally says, 'She sees that evidently the tree was good for food.' In other words, the serpent appeals to the evidence. In the Bible this is fundamental because it always mistrusts evidence.[7] Contrary to Descartes, the evidence here is surely the path of evil. She sees that 'evidently the tree is good for food, a delight to the eyes, and useful for understanding,' in the intellectual sense. This text is equivalent to that found in the first letter of John 2:16, which speaks of the lust of the flesh, the lust of the eyes, and the lust of the spirit, which are the same three temptations, so to speak. The fruit is good to eat, beautiful to the eye, and useful for intelligence. She sees this as evident, and from that moment on her eyes are opened and in a sense evil begins, because she on her own and for herself decides what will be her food, what will be her aesthetic, and what will be her intelligence. She appropriates for herself what, until now, has been a gift, a blessing, and something which until then had merely existed, but which now has to be useful for understanding.

We now begin to grasp the orientation of the text, which is far removed from our conventional understanding of the temptation, and in any case has nothing to do with sexuality. It is also important to note that the authors of this text did not make a philosophical lesson out of it and not even a theological lesson, as I am now doing. Instead they put it in a poetical and mythical form, which was understandable for their listeners.

In response to your questions, I would like to add that the living word of God is not a law. It is only when it becomes fixed that it turns into a law. We see this process happening in churches all the time. We are once again beginning to appreciate the difference between the written and the spoken word, and the difference between ritual language and speech that brings something new. In church communities we have always experienced that when this word is spoken *hic et nunc* as a living word, a spoken word, and when it is received as such, then we are not under a law. If, on the other hand, it is intellectualized and formalized, as it were, then you find the development of morality all over again.

---

7 Jacques Ellul, *The Humiliation of the Word*, trans. Joyce Main Hanks (Grand Rapids, MI: Eerdmans, 1985).

The Reformation attempted to give back to preaching its primary importance. After all, preaching is the act of the Word here and now. God speaks, and after the sermon is finished there is no point in conserving it. However, the Reformation failed. The Word can again be made a living word by someone who believes and applies it. But when, for example, we take the Decalogue as an objective law, then we have the moral problem all over again, because we make a law that we can then impose on others, and use this law to judge others. In this way the law is made false. It becomes a morality, even though Christianity is fundamentally non-moralistic. In the same vein, we are again facing a situation where the Word is shut up in a religion with a magical use of the Bible, as when, for example, people open up the Bible to any page in the conviction that they will find the answer to their question or problem. Today we are surrounded by such magical and moralistic uses of the Word. We always have to remember that there is nothing that is closer to an error than the truth itself.

The Fall

The fall is a widely accepted notion, yet in the Bible there is no such thing, nor for that matter, an original sin. There is no question of obedience to an evil, nor can we say that humanity chose evil. Instead, what is happening in this text has to do with humankind wishing to choose on their own and to be on their own. In short, humanity wants its independence. This causes a break, and in its autonomy humanity becomes creator and judge of the will of God. It is in this situation of brokenness that humanity will develop, bit by bit, what is foretold in the text. Humanity progressively develops a religion, magic, and a morality.

In its autonomy and brokenness, humanity sets up another relationship with God. We have seen that in the creation God gave Adam freedom, and now Adam conquers his freedom, which turns into an independence. We have a series of terms that qualify the two different relationships. Freedom was lived in trust, it was founded on love. There was such a relationship with the Other, and this was the central element: God was absolutely the Other, yet there was a total and complete relationship with him. There was freedom, trust, and love in the relationship with the Other. Now, with independence, we have an entirely different picture: a will to power, autonomy, and the absence of a relationship, there not being any Other. This is the new creation, as it were, established by humanity.

Thus, humanity gains its autonomy, and in addition wants to have everything immediately. This is an essential aspect of the break. As I said before, humanity was weak, they were naked. Since the relationship between God and humanity was one of love, as was the relationship between man and woman, this meant an ongoing development: love can never be something static, complete, or accomplished all at once. Humanity is the image of God, and the couple is also the image of God in love, naked love. It is what I would call an expanding love. It is an image of God that is constantly reinvented through love. Love invites a history of patience. In the Bible, the love of God is the story (or the history) of the patience of God. What this text about the temptation reveals regarding the upcoming break is that humanity wants everything right away. The tree is good for food, desirable to the eyes, and good for understanding; and they take it immediately.

To deal with the issues you have raised, we need to confront the frequently asked question: Why does God permit this or that to happen if he is really God? I believe that we need to understand that the only relationship for God is one of love, which means running the risk of not being loved in return. This brings us to the central problem, namely, that when you love someone you cannot compel or constrain him or her, and you must accept the possibility that he or she does not love you. For example, if God sought to obtain the love of humanity through seduction, God would be the Crafty One instead of God. The Crafty One obtains by seduction what should have been the gift of oneself. In the words of Karl Barth, 'When God says yes to humanity, he gives humanity the possibility of saying no.' I believe that if we do not understand this, we do not understand the very heart of the revelation. When God says yes to humanity, he says yes to what that humanity is in its journey and development, which means that in advance God opens up the possibility of humanity replying no. Hence, there is no hidden pre-existing evil, but simply a God who, because he loves, is vulnerable. Because he loves humanity, he gives it the possibility of breaking off that relationship and living without him. To love is to allow the possibility of breaking up and not to compel the other to continue that relationship without love. I believe this is the deepest mystery of God's revelation in Jesus Christ.

Myth and History

The last question I would like to deal with is that of whether this narrative has the character of a myth or whether it is historical in nature. We simply do not know the facts of what happened, any more than for the first days of creation. Nobody was present at the beginning, and when people were present they did not pass it on from generation to generation. We do not know what Adam told his children and what they told theirs, and so on. Hence, this narrative has a mythical character: it was put together to reveal a fundamental truth that reaches to the very heart of our lives, instead of telling us the factual details.

However, there is another dimension of a mythical narrative, about which I disagree with Paul Ricoeur.[8] Following an old theological interpretation, he regards this mythical narrative not as referring to an origin, but to the history of each one of us. In other words, this is not a story about God, Eve, and Adam but instead a universal and permanent history that begins and begins again with each and every person. According to this interpretation, each one of us in our lives begins this story anew, so that this narrative describes the individual history of each person in every generation. There is no before and after, because this situation of brokenness is all there has ever been. I cannot accept this interpretation because it amounts to accepting that what we know and live at present in terms of the creation, the human situation, and the relationship between God and humanity, is what God created and wanted. If there has not been a *before*, in which the relationship of God and humanity was one of love and communion, and an *after* in which this was broken, Ricoeur's interpretation would be correct; and the situation we all live would begin with each and every one of us. However, if God is the One revealed in the Bible, it is radically impossible that this world, our lives, and our relationship with him is what God created and wanted. Hence, I believe there must have been a break at some given moment; but we simply do not know whether this moment was situated in time. Probably no date or historical period can be assigned to it. Nevertheless, I believe that this narrative is undeniably historical in the sense that it teaches us true knowledge (which is not the same as exact knowledge) about the transformation of the relationship between God and humanity. I believe this is supported by the name Adam, designating not one person but the potentiality of humanity from its very beginning. We thus have a narrative, not only of what recurs in all our lives but also of the transformation of what was once the creation. In this sense, the narrative is a historical one, but not one

8 Charles E. Reagan, ed., *Studies in the Philosophy of Paul Ricoeur* (Athens, OH: Ohio University Press, 1979).

that flows from a scientific historical investigation. This, in my opinion, is the crux of the present hermeneutical debate.

What the Bible reveals is the incredible adventure of how God wins back the creation through his love without either seducing or compelling it. This helps us understand why Jesus warns us so severely not to judge. It is not merely a question of evil. When we say to ourselves that something is good, we can be sure that at that very moment we do wrong. We are put on guard against any discrimination of an objective good and evil, which implies that the greatest aspirations of humanity are representations of evil. Yet we cannot live without making judgments, without having values, and without plans for the future. We are still on this earth and not in the kingdom of God. We need to live in and help evolve societies. We cannot do otherwise, but we must make sure a society never becomes an ideal or a sacred. These societies will never embody justice, freedom, or love. The best we can hope for is that they are liveable, and to achieve this is no small accomplishment. The Bible radically condemns all utopias.

All we can strive for is to create a society with a certain equilibrium so that everyone more or less has a certain well-being, in the knowledge that it is not likely to last very long. As Christians we must engage in this process and live in what is relative, without adopting the absolutes of our society. According to Barth, in faith we accept that we are useless servants, but servants nevertheless.[9] What I do serves nothing before God because he could do it without me, but I will do it anyway. As Christians we are not martyrs, angels, heroes, or extraordinary people. Recall that Jesus, somewhat mischievously, asks the question: What is so extraordinary when you love the people close to you who also love you, since non-Jews and non-Christians do the same? (Matthew 5:46–8). This is the situation we must live. In so doing, we must never tempt the creation or question the word of him who loves us. Again, Jesus shows us the way. During the triple temptation, he does not argue with the *Diabolos* or give his own answers. Instead, he cites biblical texts, that is, he refers to a word of God. By not taking it upon himself to answer, he reveals his full obedience and love for his Father, finding no need to add to what God has said.

This is in sharp contrast with what Eve does. It is not that she wants to do what God has forbidden, but that she wants to take on her own what God gives every day, because knowing the good is communion

---

9 I have been unable to locate the exact quotation.

with God. Eve appropriates this for herself and makes of it a kind of intrinsic quality, to ensure that it is renewed from day to day instead of waiting for the grace, communion, and love of God. The other aspect is that she transforms her relationship with God into one that is religious, magical, and moralistic. It is this double element of the appropriation and transformation of her relationship with God that is the central element in the narrative we have just examined.

We have also begun to discover why the proclamations of Judaism and, later, Christianity, were so upsetting and shocking: they called into question everything humanity regards as having superior values and having ultimate importance. However, the trap into which Christianity fell was to reconstruct these same values, in the form of a new aesthetics or building the cathedrals, for example. Without question these cathedrals were very beautiful, but they were also a catastrophe in the sense that they petrified God's word, as it were. In saying these things I acknowledge that, since we are not yet in the kingdom of God, we are incapable of doing things differently.

I must confess that I find it irresponsible to plunge a congregation into the hermeneutical crisis we face from time to time, because there may be people who have only a very simple understanding of the gospel. I may run the risk of disturbing them in a way they may not be able to handle. For example, the philosophies of Husserl and Heidegger have plunged us into a hermeneutical situation of such complexity and difficulty that I can honestly say that when I was a member of a committee struck to sort out this hermeneutical business, I really thought I was in danger of going mad. It was the only time in my life that such a thing happened to me. I do not have a bad head for these things and succeeded in mastering the issues, yet I really thought I was losing it. Hence, when this obscure material is thrown at clergy who may not be very strong intellectually, they will not be able to master it and it will drive them crazy. These kinds of issues are best left to a dozen or so intellectuals who know this stuff well; and when they have come to the end of this kind of exercise they will have to see what may be retrieved, if anything, that may be useful for the edification of a community. We certainly do not have the right to terrorize people with this kind of thing.

When you are an intellectual you are called to use your head and cannot do otherwise. It is impossible to close the door and say, 'From here on in I will ask no more questions.' If I can manage to live by an explanation until I can find, or God provides, a better one, that is not too bad; and if, moreover, this small path I have made leads to elements that might help others to find their own path, this is about all we can expect to accomplish. In our present situation, that is, after Eden and before the kingdom of God, we cannot do anything else, and it is not useless. I cannot agree with Ricoeur that there is an inevitability in human life, because that appears to go back to a notion of original sin without any possibility of doing otherwise. God's way was not to use his authority in order to re-establish community with his creatures, and as intellectuals we cannot do the same thing with others. God instead chose the path of the reincarnation through the birth, life, death, and resurrection of Jesus Christ, and that has become our path.

It is possible to speak of an original weakness in the sense that human beings are finite, and in this Ricoeur is, I believe, correct.[10] Human beings as creatures are finite, and to the extent that they are naked they have this weakness, because the fullness of their lives depends on grace and not on something within them. Their being is in God and none other.

It is not for nothing that the Bible is a book of the Word. The Word mediates, and the work of Jesus Christ is a mediation. In contrast, what is immediate and evident in terms of knowledge always resides in the domain of error. However, the knowledge that comes via the intermediary of the Word is in the domain of truth. As I have explained in my book *The Humiliation of the Word*,[11] what is evident is related to seeing. The Bible distinguishes strongly between reality as the domain of seeing, and truth, which is the domain of the Word. There are very few explicit visions of God in the Bible. When God appears to Moses it is only to him, and the people see only thunder and lightning. When Moses comes back from the mountain, he wears a veil because his face looks so unbearable to the people. When Elijah asks to see God, there is that remarkable account in which the thunder passes and Elijah knows it is not God, the storm passes and Elijah knows it is not God; and finally, there is the murmur of silence. Then he realizes that this is God. In other words, God is not seen but when he has passed, people realize that he has been there. It is only in the last part of the book of Revelation that reality and truth are rejoined in the new creation. In the meantime, science works on reality, but it will never attain truth. The error of going by the evidence from reality is to attempt to penetrate the domain of truth by what is nothing but the domain of reality. The Apocalypse is a book of visions because there is fusion between reality and truth. It

---

10 Charles E. Reagan, ed., *Studies in the Philosophy of Paul Ricoeur*, op. cit.

11 Jacques Ellul, *The Humiliation of the Word*, op. cit.

shows how God assumes the totality of human history, along with everything humanity has made, to bring all this reality into truth.

Just a note: All we know about the earliest human reality is from skeletal remains, that is, when death was part of that reality. Beyond this we cannot go, hence we cannot know anything about human life before the break with God.

5   The Consequences of the Break between God and Humanity

The World Humanity Creates, and God's Decisions

We have seen that the text does not support the concept of a fall, but rather a break that humanity brings about in its relationship with God. Via this break, humanity engenders a number of consequences; and there are others as well that flow from the decisions God makes. The latter must not be confused with a curse. God never pronounces a curse on humanity. I will study these consequences as an ensemble, after which I will deal with a contemporary theological current that interprets sin as being entirely positive.

A first consequence that follows from the break is the man's and woman's discovery that they are naked. This is not a question of sexuality, morality, or modesty, but one of weakness. They seek to overcome this weakness by making clothing for themselves. Throughout the Bible, all the way to Revelation, clothing means protection. The symbolism is very coherent: the awareness of weakness leads to a search for protection, which from then on becomes a part of human history. This protection was not required prior to the break with God because He was their protection. It is a pattern that recurs time and time again: humanity refuses God's protection, preferring to make their own history and to rely on their own abilities to make clothing, *techniques*, and other means of protection.

There is a second aspect to this discovery of weakness. Recall what I said earlier about the meaning of being naked resulting from a play of words in the text, since the word used can also mean cunning. The man and the woman become *arum* like the serpent, that is, they share something of the same nature. The Hebrew text is very clear: the man and the woman discover each other in a new way, which means that there is not only a break with God but also with each other. The text that follows confirms this with great precision. As they discover that they are cunning they discover one another's vulnerability, which ends a relationship of love and communion to make way for one involving an intellect used for critique and questioning, as seen with the serpent. So also, the man and the woman pose questions before God. Their awareness of weakness and cunning leads to fear: they are afraid of God and they hide from him. From now on, the relationship with God is broken and is no longer based on love and communion. In other words, they are now able to have an objective knowledge of God, without love. It reminds us of the letter of James, where we read that the demons also know God and they tremble. There are two ways of knowing God. There is the knowing in love, through which communion is maintained and evolved; and there is a knowing in a broken relationship that is exterior, questioning, and critical. Through this knowing, God appears to be terrible and all-powerful. If you believe that God is all-powerful, then all you can expect is to be terrorized by him; and this is exactly what we find in Christian circles that regard God in this way. For example, the preaching of the Puritans had a constant element of terror.

The second consequence, which also follows spontaneously from the break, is humanity becoming responsible, in the etymological sense of that word: being called to respond. You cannot be responsible by yourself in an abstract way because it is a matter of responding to a question. The man and the woman encounter two questions, 'Where are you?' (verse 9), and, 'What have you done?' (verse 13). These are, in fact, the two questions that God continues to address to humanity. This is because, throughout our lives, we do not know where we are (not simply in a geographical sense, of course), nor what it is exactly that we are doing. The Word of God reaches humanity even when they flee, but it is not destructive; it neither negates nor leads to their death. God does not ask these questions because he does not know. On the contrary: the questions are there to help them to understand, by guiding them toward an awareness of the situation. Humanity now has to answer for itself, which before the break (when there was communion) was not necessary because, in a sense, God answered for them. In the Bible we see this same relationship with Job and with Jesus Christ, where God replies. Following the break, it is humanity who needs to respond for itself.

These questions put humanity in an extremely difficult situation because they really cannot respond. In order to truly answer, they would be obliged to recognize that they are now outside the communion with God; and this would imply a self-condemnation. Failing this, humanity has no choice but to give a false response, which amounts to not being fully responsible. At this very moment, humanity discovers their true situation and now knows evil. As we have seen, until now there was no evil anywhere. Humanity knows evil, not when they disobey, but at the point where God's questions make them realize that they cannot answer him. It is this situation that leads to all the systems of justification. It reminds us of Paul's texts on the law, where he says that if there had been no law there would have been no sin. This does not mean that had there been no law, it could not have been transgressed, and hence there would be no sin. What it really means is that if there was no law you would not have to respond, and you would not have been led to the discovery that you could not respond. It is this inability to respond to God's questions that results in the discovery of evil in the world.

From this situation flows the third immediate consequence of the break with God, which is the accusation of the other. Humanity refuses to respond in truth and to accept the punishment for their mistake. They throw the blame on others, which follows immediately from the discovery of the knowledge of evil. The man accuses the woman of having given him the fruit from the tree, and also accuses God for having given him the woman. In other words, Adam says he had nothing to do with it; it is the fault of God and the woman. When God asks the woman what she has done, she accuses the serpent for having tempted her. What is fundamental here is that the man and the woman become participants in the power of accusation. Accusing one another is a consequence of the break in communion, the objective knowledge of the other outside of love; and from this flows the process of accusation. God is never the Accuser. In the Bible the Accuser is well known and goes by the name of Satan, which means exactly that. There is thus no need to postulate a pre-existing evil or a pre-existing Satan, because it is at the point where the man and the woman begin to accuse one another that Satan, personifying the universal power of accusation, comes into existence.

In addition to the above three consequences that flow directly from the break between humanity and God, there are others that flow from God's decisions. First, we need to understand what God says to the man and the woman. God does not announce a curse but a covenant; and in the biblical perspective this is absolutely central. Normally, the consequence of humanity breaking with God should have been death because God is the living One, the totality of life, he who gives life and embodies all of it. When you no longer have a relationship with life you are dead. Nothing is more simple than that. Yet despite the break, humanity is maintained because God does not wish to annihilate his creation and permit the power of the void to triumph over it. Humanity is maintained, but in an entirely new situation. What is rather extraordinary is that in this situation created by humanity seizing its independence and autonomy, God does not punish them for what they have done, nor does he re-establish the situation before the break. Instead, God decides to participate in the situation in order to transform it, which is the entire history of the Old Testament. Every time humanity takes the initiative and does something that turns out badly, God does not cancel out what humanity has done, but he plays his part in order to remedy it and create a new relationship that is liveable for both parties. This relationship can no longer be one of communion because that has been rejected by humanity. God and humanity have been separated. It is as if God establishes a new state of affairs, which in this narrative will be referred to as the covenant.

The covenant recognizes a particular situation in the world, a humanity now making its own history, and limits the damage that has been done. Humanity should have died immediately, but they continue to live as a result of God's limiting the consequences. They must live in this situation caused by the break with God, for which he establishes a new statute or covenant. This is the first of God's decisions.

The second decision made by God is to curse the serpent. As a consequence, the situation takes on a new dimension. Until now, as we have seen, the serpent was just an animal, be it the most intelligent and clever one. The curse brings about a radical change. On the one hand, the serpent is marked by a sign of shame and defeat. The Semitic symbolism of the time is very clear. It is not a question of the snake having had legs and feet before the break. It has to do with the custom of that time of dragging the vanquished over the ground on their bellies, as shown, for example, on the Chaldean stelas. On the other hand, the serpent becomes a symbol of the power of hostility between the woman and her descendant. This is very significant from two points of view. The serpent will eat the dust. To make sense of this, we need to remind ourselves that even the more urban people of the time had a thorough knowledge of nature; hence, they knew very well that serpents did not live on dust. The serpent eating dust is therefore not based on an observation but on what God later says to Adam, namely, that you are dust and to dust you will return. In other words, the serpent will eat what Adam is made of. It implies a relationship between the two in which the serpent has mastery over the material substance of Adam by absorbing the dust of humanity. This brings out the mythical and symbolic dimension; and for the Jews this explained the religions involving the serpent. As we have seen, the Jewish writers took the serpent as a model because they were surrounded by people whose religions involved serpents. What this text says, therefore, is that these religions consumed the dust of humanity, or in a sense absorbed humanity. Here we again encounter the anti-religious character of this narrative.

The second aspect of what the serpent becomes is related to the hostility between the serpent and the woman's descendant. Once again, this is not an observation of nature. The Hebrew word is very clear. It does not say descendants (in the plural) but a descendant (in the male singular). You could almost say that it is an absolute term, which implies majesty. Consequently, Christians have traditionally regarded this as a reference to Jesus Christ as *the* son of man. In any case, this gives the serpent its full significance and importance. The serpent can hurt his heel, which in the Hebrew writings of that time meant to entrap someone or to lure someone into a trap. However, the son of the woman, or the son of humanity in the absolute sense, will kill the serpent.

In sum: what at first was nothing but an animal with no metaphysical significance has become much more than that: the instrument of the break, the instrument of accusation, the bearer of God's curse, the devourer of the material substance of humanity, and a participant in the final combat between the absolute Serpent and the absolute Man, as it were. At this moment the serpent becomes what in later texts is referred to as the ancient serpent, the dragon who lives in the depths of the waters, and so on.

A third decision made by God regards the woman and the man. I must confess that I am always surprised at the superficiality of the common interpretations of the text; and I will therefore stress that there is no question of a curse on the woman or the man. For the woman, there are two new elements. First, there is her suffering in giving birth, which is therefore no longer entirely natural. Her vocation now is the maintenance of life, which will become evident from the name she is given according to the verses that follow. She ate from the tree to reach a higher situation, but instead she finds herself in a lower one, not being 'as God.' It is a common misunderstanding that this text simply deals with the physical suffering associated with giving birth. From a historical perspective, it is worth noting that this suffering has increased considerably in our civilization, to the point that it is almost inconceivable that a young woman of our time would be capable of having fifteen children in about the same number of years. In earlier civilizations, things were different enough that no special clinics and medical care were required; and in some cases, the woman even took care of it herself and recovered relatively quickly. We have again made some progress with the newer methods, but that does not take away the stupidity of the traditional interpretations of this text. Instead, what the text symbolizes is the complications in the relationships with children being a source of much suffering for many women, from many points of view. The break with God affects the entire process of bringing babies to adulthood.

The second new element for the woman relates to the desire for her man, who will now rule over her. The break with God also causes trouble here. The woman will be directed by her desire, and the man by his need to dominate. Again, I do not believe that this is simply a natural sexual matter. Of course, this is not excluded; but clearly, the sexual desire of the man for the woman is more or less as great as hers for him. The real issue is related to what the woman did. She desired the tree of knowledge and became desiring in her orientation. This became her situation: a creature dominated by her desire. The man becomes the one who dominates, thereby reversing the former situation, where he followed her. It was the woman who gave direction to the created couple. This is now reversed as she becomes directed and dominated, and as the man becomes oriented toward power and domination.

This brings me to the man's situation. While God does not reproach the woman for what she did, he does reproach the man: 'You listened to the woman and ate from the tree,' and so on. Hence, it is the man who disobeyed. Within the couple, he had a certain responsibility for their orientation and wisdom, and therefore should have responded to the woman. He stands accused, but once more this is not a curse. This accusation translates into a triple development.

The first new element concerns work, and the suffering that accompanies his vocation. He was called on to cultivate and guard the garden, which, as we have already seen, was in a sense a play and a joyful pastime. It turns into a burden, evolving into work in the etymological sense. He has to submit to this burden in order to survive. The soil that bore fruit as a gift of abundance from God now becomes infertile. Both man and woman have to participate in the maintenance of life through children and food, which was already their vocation, but it is now accomplished in suffering.

The second new element is the responsibility the man and the woman have for what happens to nature: 'Cursed is the ground because of you.' There are thus two curses, one on the serpent and the other on creation. This follows from what we have already seen. Since humanity was the head of creation, their betrayal and mistake falls on creation, and they bear the guilt for that. In passing, I note that this flies in the face of the thesis that accepts the notion of sin but rejects any association with guilt. There may be something to this within the context of psychoanalysis, but here the text clearly states that humanity bears the guilt of creation's being cursed because of what they did. Humanity has dragged creation into the break. As a result, the burden of work becomes the sign of creation's curse, and the suffering of creation is a reflection of humanity's mistake.

The third new element in the situation of the man and the woman is death. As the text says, 'You will return to the dust from which you were taken.' However, for most contemporary theologians, death is not something new in the sense that in their view Adam had been created mortal, or in any case, created finite. I believe Ricoeur is correct when he talks about the finitude of human creatures.[1] Humanity is not eternal. It is this that differentiates them from God. This is why, under normal circumstances, they would have had to partake of the Tree of Life. In communion with God, this would have been an end that might be called normal. It would have been a completion of life without suffering and without sadness.

God's decision changes several things. First, there is the awareness of dying; and humanity will be haunted by this vision of death. Here we encounter a difference between man and woman: the woman is the one who gives birth, and the man has the awareness of death. For those who argue that the differences are purely cultural (which I accept in a great many instances), I would point out that nevertheless there are some differences. I am, of course, not saying that the woman does not have an awareness of death, but that in the traits of the female person it is less dominant than in the male person. I believe this is one of the fundamental differences between men and women, but I certainly don't want to make a big deal of it.

---

1   Charles E. Reagan, ed., *Studies in the Philosophy of Paul Ricoeur* (Athens, OH: Ohio University Press, 1979).

Another new thing with regard to death is that in all this we see no promise of eternal life. There is no reconciliation and no resurrection, but only a complete death. 'From dust you have come and to dust you will return,' and that is all. What this means, I believe, is that from the moment the break came between God and humanity, God withdrew his Spirit. Humanity remains alive but without this Spirit of God. Here we uncover the root of what we have been living with for centuries, namely, the distinction between material life and spiritual life. This is one of our greatest weaknesses, so destructive of the unity of human life. This unity, which was an ensemble of communication within communion, ends with the break between humanity and God, between the man and the woman, and the inner break between the material and spiritual life, now radically separated. The inner unity is entirely lost. At this point, death becomes what the Bible calls the king of terrors. If there is no promise, no resurrection, and no eternal life, but only the serpent in the dust, then death truly becomes the king of terrors.

Finally, we encounter a warning from God to humanity. If you wish to live without me you will discover what you are without me, namely, a creature destined for death. Humanity is nothing else and nothing more. Everything is finished; and yet, from the biblical perspective, this is the point of departure of a history. Hence, something else had to intervene because the Bible has no notion whatsoever of an immortal soul. From an ontological perspective, there is nothing immortal about humanity; and humanity has been reduced to this by the break with God. Job says that he knows that he is going to his death; but that he also knows that his Redeemer lives and that he will rise on the last day, and when he does, his eyes will see God. In other words: I will disappear because I am nothing, but my Redeemer (and this is something rather complex in Job) is alive because he belongs to God and is from God. The resurrection appears just as the creation did, that is, from nothing: God re-creates.

However (and this always evokes within me the greatest admiration when I am faced with this revelation), God does not re-create entirely from nothing but from what humanity wanted to be. In other words: God gives to every person the fullness of what they hoped for, and this is the resurrection. It is not a process that automatically continues life by a kind of purgatory in which there is a hidden life, much like seed hidden in the soil. We fully die and God raises us from nothing, but it is ourselves he raises because God never wanted to annihilate the history of humanity. What happens to the finitude of human life is explained in the book of Revelation,[2] where we are told that this finitude is maintained, in the heavenly Jerusalem, by the presence of trees from which people will eat in order to live indefinitely. Hence, there is that limitation of people having to do something in order to continue to live. This resurrection is clearly the new creation, which has nothing whatsoever to do with an immortal soul. The immortal soul is a Greek invention, which Christian theologians began to absorb through Greek philosophy in the second and third centuries.

Now, in response to your questions: What the Bible refers to as the Word is not the same as what we call language and communication. The text describes a universe of communion. It is not necessarily the case that the serpent verbalized by means of words and phrases. The serpent was the point of questioning. In not having to respond to his own questions, the serpent was not responsible. The serpent questions, as opposed to God doing so, and in that sense he substitutes for God. We are so steeped in the celestial mythology acquired from our civilization, of devils, fallen angels, and so on, that it is very difficult not to project this into the text. I cannot find anything like this mythology in the Bible.

Jewish theologians have developed other interpretations of the resurrection and eternal life, with the same intellectual rigour and care exhibited by the authors of the creation narrative. For some, to belong to the people of God is to have his Spirit. When a Jew dies, this Spirit in him or her returns to God, and the rest disappears. There is no concept of a personal resurrection. The texts that refer to a resurrection are interpreted as a resurrection of the Jewish people as a people, and not as individuals. Other theological schools developed as well; and in the time of Jesus there were those who believed in the immortality of the soul, and still others in the resurrection.

A Modern Reinterpretation of the Text

There is a strong tendency in contemporary theology to regard the break between God and humanity as being essentially positive in nature. There are a number of themes I would like to highlight. First, a certain emphasis is given to humanity's not being created fixed, or once for all times. It is a creation that will evolve. However, this development would have been impossible within the narrow confines of the relationship with God because of divine paternalism. Humanity could

---

2 Jacques Ellul, *Apocalypse*, trans. George W. Schreiner (New York: Seabury, 1977).

never have become itself. It could only do so by breaking with God, along the lines of the psychoanalytical necessity of 'killing' one's father. According to this view, the death of the father is necessary to permit the child to develop. In the same vein, humanity must develop by itself after the beginning that was provided by God. Humanity then progresses in order to become adult. This kind of argument is used by contemporary theologians to convince us that we are now of age. It is emphasized that only in this way can there be a human history, which would have been impossible within a communion with God. After all, history is full of conflicts, tensions, and breaks. Humanity, therefore, had no choice but to claim its independence and to break with God even if that meant disobeying him. It is only then that humanity began to invent, to develop *techniques* of all kinds and all the rest, in order to overcome material challenges. Everything of the greatest value, such as the creation of a history, of science, *technique*, and so on, could not have occurred without the break with God.

In this context, Paul Ricoeur and others have argued for a reinterpretation of sin as the source of human freedom. It is at the origin of all social life, as seen, for example, in the putting on of clothes as a social act. According to this theology, which assigns a positive value to sin, it is sin that represents the true grandeur of humanity, to the point that humanity becomes aware that they are truly like God, thanks to having distanced themselves from him. According to Ricoeur,[3] this is a fact that has remained dormant during the 'innocence' of humanity. Sin thus becomes the promotion of one's self-awareness and launches the adventure of becoming human.

However, things are not left there. Attempts have been made to show that, by separating from God, humanity did exactly what God expected all along. The argument goes as follows. God had a plan for humanity which, of course, he did not wish to impose but which nevertheless began with the human decision to break with God and become independent. All along, according to this interpretation, God wanted humanity to evolve in order to come of age. All this could not happen as long as God remained the Father and humanity was confined within a close communion. God wished humanity to have a history and to exploit creation, which had been made for this very purpose. It was therefore necessary for humanity to quit 'playing around,' since everything came so readily, and to engage in some serious work. Humanity had to take hold of

---

3   Charles E. Reagan, ed., *Studies in the Philosophy of Paul Ricoeur*, op. cit.

knowledge in order to realize what God had in mind for them. Hence, the fall, to use the traditional term, was essentially positive, and could not have been avoided in any case because of God's plan for humanity. Consequently, there is no original sin as an evil since it paved the way for a completely positive interpretation of human history, science, *technique*, and so on, all originating in the break with God. This was the position of Ricoeur until 1968, when he changed his mind.[4]

The only objection I will make to this modern reinterpretation is that it raises the following difficulty. Humanity now does on its own what God freely gave, but which has been taken over. In other words, humanity has become possessed by a spirit of conquest. Humanity now accomplishes in domination what God wanted to be done in love. Hence, humanity is driven by a will to power. After this, whatever people want to say about the history of science and *technique* leaves me indifferent; because what really matters is whether or not, at the very heart of all of this, there is the spirit of conquest and the will to power. All this talk about killing the Father, and having become independent and so on, is the expression and point of departure of the spirit of conquest and the will to power. I believe the results speak for themselves. With the evidence from human history we can perhaps at least agree that it has been profoundly shaped by this spirit of conquest and this will to power. This, I believe, is the real issue and the tragedy of this theological reinterpretation: it has not really succeeded in eliminating the negative aspect of sin. What it has accomplished is to overlook, or refuse to face, the real problem of the spirit of conquest and the will to power. For myself, this is the crux of this theological development. I could add all kinds of details and elaborations, but it would not change anything fundamental. As a footnote, in response to your question, I will add that since 1968 Ricoeur has practically abandoned his theological studies. Generally speaking, this whole reinterpretation is already rapidly losing ground, especially in the face of the environmental crisis, which has at least shaken the confidence of a few of these thinkers. The historical ascendancy of humanity has become a dubious assertion. We were warned all along that God's kingdom will not come in this manner. However, we ought to remind one another that everything humanity does is taken seriously by God, more seriously than we often do. We may say that all this serves no purpose whatsoever, but that is one thing God never says.

---

4 Ibid.

Other Consequences

I will now turn to the concluding verses in the third chapter, and discuss three themes. First, there is the name of the woman and the clothing. Second, there is the ejection from the garden, and, finally, the new situation of humanity outside the garden.

In the new covenant with God, Adam does not revolt but accepts God's decisions and his own altered situation. His behaviour is thus very different from that of Cain, for example, who refused to accept God's decision and new covenant, thereby worsening the situation. The first thing Adam does is give a name to his wife. Life will continue, and it is the woman who must assure the work of life. In this context, Adam names her Eve, as the living one who transmits life. It is a name which is close to, and derives from, the tetragram as the name of God. The Hebrew name for Eve shares the last three letters (hwh) with the tetragram. The elimination of the first letter (Y) is significant since it designates 'I.' In other words, she is the living one by continuing God's work of life on the level of nature, but since the 'I' is missing Eve is not life itself, and life is not within herself. The Bible frequently distinguishes the two. She is alive but not life-giving. She does not bring forth life. She is not life in an absolute sense, and she cannot say, therefore, I am. Only God can say this.

It is Adam who gives her her name, and Jewish commentators have recognized many significant elements in this. Perhaps most importantly, Adam and Eve have taken hold of the promise of God. We have seen that life will continue even though humanity has separated itself from the living One; and Adam puts the new covenant into practice. The fact that the man gives her the name marks the distance between the man and the woman. The woman is no longer *ischah*, which derives from *isch*, to signify that they are one being, the woman being the feminine part and the man the male part. The new names, Adam and Eve, are entirely different, signifying a certain distance and an entirely different being. The communion and total unity between the man and the woman will never be re-established. There is more. Adam's giving a name to all the animals that God brought before him was a sign of his domination. Here also, attributing a name to Eve means establishing his domination. She is no longer exactly 'flesh of his flesh and bone of his bones,' because she is now other; and it is as such that he dominates over her, and their relationship will be marked by this domination. Just as the perfect relationship between the man and the woman is broken, so also the relationships with all members of humanity are opened up to domination and the establishment of hierarchies. Outside the lost communion, relationships can only be maintained by constraint and domination, thus ushering in what will become a legally ordered universe. In other words, the relationship of domination becomes transcribed in terms of obligations, duties, and constraints. As a number of rabbis point out, from then on those who are at or near the bottom of these hierarchies will call this domination into question by becoming swollen by pride, conquest, and so on; and those above them will seek to dominate but not in the image of God, as was the case before the break, but in order to exploit, thereby also becoming swollen. We frequently encounter this in the Bible in relation to hearts swollen with pride, for example, along with the warning not to live this way. In sum, the relationship of communion is replaced with relationships of hierarchy and domination.

God makes clothing from skins and gives them to the man and the woman. We have seen that clothing signifies protection; hence, he gives them a sign of his protection. God thus rejects the protection that humanity wishes to create for itself, because earlier in this narrative we saw that the man and the woman had already clothed themselves with leaves fastened together in order to have their own protection. The significance of this can be more fully understood from the later account of Cain, to whom God extends the sign of his protection. Cain refuses because he does not trust it. He decides to make his own by, on the one hand, developing various *techniques,* and on the other, building the first city (whose name means 'beginning'). This is profoundly significant in that God had made a beginning, but after the break Cain wants nothing to do with God's beginning and protection. Cain wants his own beginning.[5] This is in sharp contrast with Adam, who accepts to live under God's protection rather than his own.

The Hebrew word used for God's *making* (of the clothing) can also mean the making of a sacrifice. In other words: the clothes came from a sacrifice, and for the authors of this text it may have been a sacrifice of animals, comparable to those made in the temple. However, here it is God who makes the sacrifice; the clothing is a sign of grace because the meaning and purpose of a sacrifice was to pardon and redeem (in this case, Adam and Eve). It is therefore more than a matter of protection. In

---

5 See Jacques Ellul, *The Meaning of the City*, trans. Dennis Pardee (Grand Rapids, MI: Eerdmans, 1970).

a few texts in the Old Testament, but primarily in the New Testament, to clothe means the act of God by which he covers someone's sins. When God clothes a person he no longer sees their sins. A clear example is found in Isaiah 61, verse 10 ('… for he has clothed me with the garments of salvation, he has covered me with the robe of righteousness …'). The book of Revelation speaks of people clothed in white who were washed in the blood of the Lamb. However, in a sense we can say that the clothing made of skins speaks of a grace that has not come to perfection, and points to the perfect sacrifice that leads to being clothed in white during the last days, spoken of in Revelation.[6] The clothes given to Adam and Eve are a prophetic announcement of the final destiny of humanity; and that is exactly how the rabbis came to understand it as early as the second century B.C. Despite the break, humanity is headed for salvation, eternal life, and glory. God has anticipated everything, whatever decisions humanity may make. From the very beginning, there were the two trees of the cross to mark God's intention and his love; and if humanity decided to break with God and gain their independence, this cross would become the historical cross of the salvation of humanity. The cross would have remained in Eden had the break not occurred. Whatever humanity decides, God has already prepared a response to their intentions.

Many simplistic explanations have been given for humanity being sent out of the garden. Most of these can be eliminated by a careful reading of the text. I will begin with the Tree of Life, which humanity must no longer put their hands on. It may be thought that this tree maintained humanity's life in Eden. This happens to correspond to a number of Assyrian and Babylonian myths that speak of a wonderful garden which has a tree that produces a certain fruit that when eaten regularly renews one's life. This presents no particular problem, because our text clearly means that from now on human beings have a limited time to live, from which there is no escape. This follows directly from God's decision regarding death, that humanity is dust and to dust they will return. Humanity is thus prevented from escaping death.

There is another important element that I wish to highlight before we get into the deeper meaning of this text. The text says that humanity has become as one of Us. The God who speaks here is the one we encounter in the first chapter, namely Elohim, who is a plural, and who reigns objectively as it were, without any personal relations, because he is not

---

6 Jacques Ellul, *Apocalypse*, op. cit.

revealed. This is not Yahweh, but the God of astronomers and philosophers. This God recognizes that humanity now has the power to decide good and evil, which makes humanity equivalent to this God (but not to Yahweh).

We must go much further to reach the deeper meaning of this text, which gets at the significance of the separation and exclusion from the garden. We need to ask what humanity's situation would have been like if they had remained in the garden of Eden and if they had eternal life. Humanity would have been in the presence of God without communion with him. In other words, humanity would have been in the presence of a God whom they no longer loved. The break had occurred, love no longer existed, and there was (according to the earlier texts), the issue of fear. Adam was afraid. Humanity would therefore have an objective knowledge, as it were, of this God in their separation from him. They would have been in the presence of the holiness of God while being excluded from it, and in his power while having broken with him. It would have created the situation that the Old Testament speaks of on several occasions, namely, that no one can see God and live. Hence the encounter with God's full power and holiness after the break would be mortal, and yet, according to God's decision, they would not die. The situation would have led to a state of living death. As I mentioned before, in the epistle of James we are told that the demons also know God, and they tremble. It characterizes their situation. Adam would not only be afraid, but he would be in the situation of a person who is dead and who continues to live. Moreover, he would be in this situation for all eternity without any way out. In other words, it would have been a non-historical situation in which humanity was stuck, much like a pinned butterfly; and all this in the presence of God but without communion and love and without any possibility of moving forward. There would be no history, and hence no possibility of redemption through which God once more reveals his love. The gift of this love is eternal life, but this would be impossible because humanity would already have it.

When we bring together the three elements we have just indicated, namely, the absence of the possibility of redemption, the presence of a God regarded as One who judges, and an eternal life in this situation, we would have a description of the equivalent of Hell and eternal damnation. We need to understand that Hell has nothing in common with what Dante describes. In the Bible eternal damnation would be the presence of God, who is entirely holy, but whom humanity is unable to love. In other words, the expulsion from the garden, which is commonly interpreted as still more punishment, is instead, along with the provision of clothing, a preparation by God for the possibility of redemption, reconciliation, salvation, and eternal life. Were it not for the expulsion from the garden, none of this would be possible.

Finally, we need to ask why no return was possible. Outside the garden, Adam must cultivate the soil from which he was taken. Jewish commentators have noted that a relationship is nevertheless maintained between this soil and the garden of Eden. We have been told that four rivers with living water flowed out of this garden; hence, a relationship of life remains. However, the flow of this water is in one direction only, and there is no way back because the cherubim guard the entrance to the garden. The Hebrew word for cherubim means 'terrible ones,' and I have never been able to understand why in some paintings they are depicted as nice little angels. With the 'terrible ones' at the entrance, humanity cannot go back, which means that from here on in God is the hidden One. This is further substantiated by the text, which declares that humanity, now separated from God, must stay out of his presence because no one can see God and live. There is no way back to God; and this text condemns all human attempts to do so, whether it be through mysticism, magic, or religion. This text is in radical opposition to any human pretence to knowing God, to using God for human purposes, to recreating a religious world, or any other attempt to ascend to God. The biblical relationship is always in the other direction, that of God descending towards humanity and revealing himself to them. There are no other possibilities. Christians have, of course, interpreted the flow of living water from the garden as an image and prophecy of baptism.

I recognize that there have been endless misunderstandings regarding these and similar texts. How can the Bible condemn so vehemently any attempt to get closer to God by the building of the tower of Babel, the ziggurats, the towers of the Assyrians, and so on? Did the people doing so not have the very best of religious intentions? Nevertheless, our text explains very clearly why the road back to God's presence is barred by the 'terrible ones.'

I will conclude with a reflection on the situation of humanity after their exclusion from the garden. First, humanity is no longer the image of God. The relationship between the man and the woman is broken, and since this was the image of God, there simply is nothing left of it. For some theologians, such as Thomas Aquinas, something nevertheless remains; for him, it was reason and intelligence. Calvin agreed with this. Other theologians, such as Karl Barth, argue that this is a serious mistake because it implies an image of God that is other than that of love. I believe the text is very clear in its explanation that the image of God is love. However, I do not wish to rule out the possibility of once again becoming the image of God if he grants it through grace and if humanity fully embraces that grace. In any case, we cannot seize it for ourselves because the road back is blocked. There is dissociation of love in two directions, namely, *agape* on the one hand and *eros* on the other. *Eros* is taking hold of the other in order to dominate him or her, while *agape* is the love that gives (including him or herself). As long as we live by *eros*, which is the love through conquest by any means, we cannot be an image of God. It is only possible in *agape*.

Second, humanity now has a knowledge of good and evil that is separated from God. This means that humanity decides what is good and what is evil, even though they do not know what it is; and it certainly has nothing to do with God's decision or will. It simply becomes a question of conscience, morality, and the like. In addition, humanity can now experiment with good and evil. Special attention must be paid to the word 'and' in this experimentation with good and evil, which is in direct conflict with the orientation of the Bible. God wants to conduct humanity towards a choice or a decision. In Deuteronomy, God says that he places before his people the good and life, and the evil and death, in order that they may choose the good and life. It is one or the other. In contrast, what the text refers to as knowing good and evil is not an either/or but a combination of the two, possibly leading toward a synthesis. In other words, humanity does not want to choose, but to have it all. Humanity wants the good *and* the evil, and not having to decide between them. This is fundamental because God excludes this possibility. We can observe this attitude all around us: many wish for God, but also like to hang on to everything else. We seek God's grace, and continue to build a world in which everything costs money. This is the moral situation of humanity: we wish to decide what is good and evil, and have both.

Third, humanity remains in some harmony with nature, but after the break nature was diminished because of humanity. Chouraqui[7] puts it well: nature has become desert-like and is dumbfounded at having been created to become the place of humanity's suffering, sin, and death. In other words, from here on in nature is no longer the place of

---

7 André Chouraqui, *Le livre de l'Alliance* (Paris: Éditions du Bibliophane, 2003).

humanity's honour, having been diminished to *tohu wabohu*. This is not all. To be sure, nature has not become bad. What appears bad to us is not bad in itself. Verse 18 is clear on this point: the soil will yield thorns and thistles. These plants are not bad in themselves. They are bad insofar as they are now incorporated into the work of humanity. The promise in the book of Revelation that the lion will not harm the lamb, nor the serpent the child, symbolizes a reconciliation. Just as there has been a break between humanity and God, so also there is now a break with the natural milieu. The latter is not bad in itself, but it is bad for humanity because of the break with God.

As a fourth point, I would like to make two remarks regarding the notion of original sin. The situation our text describes is, as Paul says, the same for every person: all die in Adam. This is not because of some kind of hereditary process, but a collective personality. We readily accept a kind of horizontal solidarity between all living human beings, but there is also a kind of vertical solidarity with all the human beings who went before and those who will come after us. Before God humanity is an ensemble. In the text we have examined, Adam is neither a myth nor a symbol, but the person we all are. We are all included in Adam as part of this ensemble. This is what Paul means when he says that all died in Adam. Hence, there is no original sin but there is a perspective of humanity as a whole, in a sense synthesized before God in Adam. It is in this sense that it is possible to speak of a sin that is repeated indefinitely, which I will sum up with what I believe is the excellent way in which Karl Barth put it.[8] Barth said that when humanity chooses it never turns out to be right. In contrast with God, humanity constantly chooses evil, ruin, and death, because humanity is not God. To will the good, salvation, and life is the work of God alone. No one can take care of this in his place. In other words, if humanity could truly choose the good, salvation, and life, they would be God. It is God, and God alone, who is the Living One and who loves; and therefore, everything he says and does expresses the good, salvation, and life. There is a complete identity, and no one else could accomplish this. Hence, following the break with God, humanity in its rebellion constantly chooses what is not God, namely evil, ruin, and death. That is what sin is all about; and following the break, it cannot be anything else. This is the situation of humanity as a result of its choice. At the same time, it is a

---

8 Karl Barth, *Church Dogmatics*, vol. 4: *The Doctrine of Reconciliation*, trans. G.W. Bromiley (Edinburgh: T. & T. Clark, 1956).

point of departure of God's efforts to regain the ground that was lost as a result of humanity's decision. All of history is a result of the joint efforts of God and humanity.

Some Additional Reflections in Response to Questions

In order to examine the role human freedom plays in all of this, I would like to briefly return to the text in Deuteronomy where God says to his people that he places before them the good and life, and the evil and death, in order that they may choose the good so as to live. The situation has nothing in common with a teacher who lays out a great many things and tells his students to sort them out for themselves. The people are in the presence of their living God, who intervenes in their lives to say that this is the good and that is the evil, and I am with you. In other words, God commits himself and involves himself in this decision. His people are not left to themselves in their chosen independence in order to make the choice. When God places them before a decision, he is with them; and because of this they are in the presence of everything that is indispensable for choosing the good. This is no longer impossible even though, following the break, humanity apart from God can only choose the evil.

We observe exactly the same thing when God speaks to Cain. God tells him that evil is crouching at his door, but that he must overcome it. God offers him the power to do so but will not do it on his behalf. In any case, he respects Cain's decision. All along, God is preparing to go all the way to accomplish salvation through Jesus Christ. Jesus loved as God intended humanity to love (*agape*). From that point on, the situation of humanity changed fundamentally, and his followers were placed in a situation of freedom in Jesus Christ.

I have noted that as people of our time, place, and culture we are steeped in Dantean images of Heaven and Hell: the former full of angels, and the latter full of devils torturing the damned. It is difficult not to read these images back into the text; but, as I have said before, nothing of the kind can be found anywhere in the Bible. All this is exacerbated by our curiosity and desire to know. However, the Bible has not been given to provide us with knowledge but to reveal what God deems necessary for our lives, which is an entirely different matter. In order to live, do we need to know about the battles of angels, Lucifer, and all the rest? It so happens that the Bible is very discreet about these matters. It may not be enough to satisfy our curiosity, but it is all that is revealed to us. I will attempt to summarize what I believe can be said about these things.

In the Bible, angels are not specific beings. Angels are the carrying out of the will of God *hic et nunc*. They are an image intended to inform us that the will of God is being executed. In the same vein, demons are not specific beings but abstract realities such as the break, fatalities, necessities, and everything else that is opposed to freedom. In using the term 'abstract realities,' I am not implying that these realities are not lived. For example, love is a word but it is also an ensemble of things that people live. I believe that from a biblical perspective, none of these realities can be thought of as being supernatural.[9]

I will elaborate this in greater detail for the biblical notion of the demonic. First, the biblical authors lived in a cultural context fully convinced of the presence of devils and their powers. As a result, a diversity of natural phenomena were considered demonic. However, this far from explains everything.

A second aspect of the demonic resulted from the transposition of human actions to a religious level. This happened when human beings attributed ultimate values to ordinary things or actions. It is the kind of thing the prophet Isaiah ridicules with his story of the person who cuts down a tree, uses the branches for firewood to cook his food, a part of the trunk to make the table and chairs at which to eat it, and the base of the trunk to carve an idol, before which he prostrates himself in worship. Here is a human action that ends up becoming an idolatry, which may be regarded as demonic. However, this second aspect also remains completely dependent on human actions.

There is a third aspect which escapes humanity, in the sense that certain ordinary realities appear to take on supernatural powers. Of this, I believe the Bible also gives us a number of examples, as in the case of money as a spiritual power, the state as a political power, and the city as an alienating power. Money is nothing but a convenient means of exchange; yet it is much more than that in the sway it can hold over people's lives and over entire communities. Even after we eliminate all the human aspects, there remains an irreducible core, which may be regarded as a kind of locus of power that is independent of individuals and societies. In the same vein: Where does the power of the state come from? If one person kills another, he or she is a murderer. The same is true if two people kill someone. The same is still true if three people kill someone. We can go on, but at some point there is a change, namely,

---

9 See Jacques Ellul, 'Politics: The Realm of the Demonic,' in *Living Faith*, trans. Peter Heinegg (San Francisco: Harper & Row, 1983), 234–48, for a discussion of the demonic.

when the state condemns someone to death. Where does the legitimacy of this action come from? In our contemporary societies, where there are no longer any certain reference points and therefore no legitimacy, it may be argued that the state has also become a murderer. However, in earlier societies this was not the case, and the state's power over life and death was considered normal. It was certainly more than a simple convention between the members of a community, or a cultural norm. I believe that all this constitutes what, in the New Testament, is referred to as the principalities and powers (*exousiai*), the powers that intervene in the world. Of course, this has nothing in common with the representations of devils as seen in the Middle Ages, for example. What the Bible refers to are certain powers that are independent of human actions.

There is a fourth aspect, similar to the previous one, in which such powers are given names. An obvious example is Satan. Satan is the accuser and the separator, but this must not be thought of as a person or supernatural being. I believe that what is being referred to are all the forces that act as powers of accusation and separation in the world and in human history. These clearly act independently from God, in the sense that he is the God of reconciliation and never of accusation; but it does not follow that they are therefore supernatural. There is another way the Bible talks about this, namely, in cases where the Bible speaks of someone possessed of a demon. Some of these can probably be interpreted as psychological, but there are others in which people appear to be possessed by a destructive spirit. The latter case is, I believe, the equivalent of what I said about the accuser, the separator, and other powers of evil and destruction.

This brings us back to an earlier question of why God permits such powers to exist. As I have sought to explain, this entire reality came into being with the break between humanity and God. From the moment the communion was broken, the accusations flew and relationships were damaged. This shows the enormous responsibility humanity bears for all this, since the break included the launching of these powers. It started with humanity, yet these powers represent something more. As we have seen, the entire creation was, in a sense, displaced by humanity's decision, thereby triggering an entirely different spiritual universe. Through their decision, humanity abandoned a creation consisting of love and freedom in order to enter one of necessity.

Many theologians have attempted to go much further than the biblical texts in order to bring everything together in a rational, coherent system of thinking that could answer the above kinds of questions related to the origin and role of evil. Again, the revelation was not given to us to satisfy our curiosity in these matters. It should come as no surprise, then, that any attempts along these lines have created difficulties that have never been resolved. As far as the origin of the above powers is concerned, it is impossible that they were created by God. If they were created good but later rebelled, then where did this rebellion come from? It simply pushes the problem to another level. If they were not created by God and came to exist independently, God cannot be good by allowing this. No one has ever found a way out of this dilemma.

In conclusion, I will briefly comment on nature's ability to address God. We are accustomed to thinking that humanity has language and is able to communicate, but nature cannot. I do not see it that way, as long as we do not limit communication to talking. For example, many of us have experienced some form of communication with animals. They express themselves and can make themselves understood. The Psalms speak of the creation singing God's praise; and Jesus said that if you were silent the stones would cry out. I have no problem with nature addressing God, even less so before the break.

PART TWO

The Love That Seeks Us Out
(Job 32–42)

The book of Job may be divided into four parts. There is a prologue in verse which sets out the story, including the conversation between God and Satan. This is followed by the exchanges between Job and his friends.[1] A third part includes the discourse by Elihu. In the fourth part (again in verse), God's blessing returns to Job. We will begin with the third part, which in turn divides into three elements: Job's discourse, followed by that of Elihu, and ending with God's appearance. I will begin with Elihu.

The discourse of Elihu has drawn an enormous amount of criticism claiming that it was added later and that it really does not contribute anything to the book as a whole. The reasons for this conclusion are numerous and diverse, but we should nevertheless take them seriously.

First, there is the argument that the style of the seven chapters in question is different from the remaining text. Some specialists observe that the vocabulary is not the same, in the sense that the third part uses words that are different from the ones used elsewhere, even though they refer to the same things. It is influenced by the Aramaic language, which would date this part of the text much later than the rest. Another argument is that Elihu's discourse is completely ignored by Job and God, in the sense that no reference is made to it. There is an argument to the effect that the way in which Elihu revisits Job's discourse shows that he has available to him the written text, and it is this text that he discusses. I must say that this is a rather clever observation, since he

---

1 Unfortunately, audio recordings of Jacques Ellul's study of the first two parts were either not made or were lost.

repeats some verses from Job's speech word for word. Hence the conclusion that Elihu is working from a written text.

Still another argument holds that Elihu appears out of nowhere only to disappear just as mysteriously. We simply know nothing about him. Elihu is also absent in the concluding part. I must confess that I find this far from convincing, since there are other instances like this in the Bible. Melchizedek is an obvious example. He is the king of Salem, which means the king of justice and peace, who suddenly appears in order to bless Abraham and then disappears. We know nothing about him, and yet the New Testament presents Melchizedek as a model of a bearer of God's blessing. I therefore find this argument entirely unconvincing.

I have already mentioned the fundamental criticism that if the seven chapters of Elihu were taken out, it would change nothing. The discourse of Job, which precedes it, fits very well with God's reply. It is therefore concluded that the text of Elihu adds nothing to either the thought or the actions of this book. He supposedly does little more than repeat what Job and his friends have said. Furthermore, the critics disagree over who Elihu represents. Some say it is Satan and others say it is God. All this shows that this text is indeed very difficult.

There have also been debates over the identity of the author of these seven chapters. For some, it is the same author as the rest of the book, but these chapters were written much later. Others argue that it was so much later that it must be a different author. What is more fundamental is the conclusion of many critics that these seven chapters must have been written by a very religious but narrow-minded rabbi who was deeply offended by the perceived excesses of the book of Job. It was his way of toning it down and refuting certain elements. This reveals the usual bias of historians who assume that anyone who is deeply religious must also be narrow-minded. Also, I find the implied assumption that there can be no offensive or extreme elements in the Bible more than a little curious. It rests on the idea that truly religious authors impose a moral judgment on the text and thus tend to tone it down. According to these pre-judgments, Elihu attempts to moralize the rest of the book.

Faced with all this, I would like to ask the following question. Is it conceivable that in Israel people could play around with a text that was regarded as a part of the canon, that is, part of the revelation of God? From a historical perspective, we must remember that the canon of what we call the Old Testament became fixed approximately 180 years before Jesus Christ, and the book of Job was widely regarded as one of the oldest books. According to the rabbinical tradition, it goes back to the days of the patriarchs around 1200 B.C. Hence, the canonical status of this book has been established for a very long time. In such a case, is it really possible to believe that some rabbi takes it on himself to add a piece here or there and to reorganize things a bit? Is this what Christians do with the Bible today? Would we add a little discourse or reorganize things whenever we are upset at something? In both the Jewish and Christian communities this is unthinkable and absurd. The discourse of Elihu was already in the book of Job before it became accepted as part of God's revelation.

One of the most recent hypotheses holds that Elihu's purpose is to ridicule Job's friends. Here is this young man who is so full of himself that he essentially says that no one has understood anything and that he will set them straight. However, what he says is banal. I have no difficulty with the idea that possibly Elihu has a touch of this arrogance, but to dismiss his entire text without examining it more closely is completely unacceptable.

That brings me to the last group of exegetes, who indeed ask what this text really says. Some hold that it says absolutely nothing after all. In one instance that is all the commentator says about it. Others feel that Elihu's intervention upsets the flow of the book of Job. A person might be impressed by this virtual anonymity, but I take it as another one of these exegetical fashions that will pass. I believe we ought to begin by recognizing that this text is a part of the canon accepted as the revelation of God. It is hard to believe that the rabbis would have admitted a text into this canon which they regarded as stupid and adding nothing.

I believe we should examine two things. The first is the place of this text within the whole. Is it possible that a text that supposedly says nothing is inserted between two others that are completely fundamental? After all, the text of Job which precedes it shows him to be an image of the Messiah, and is followed by God's revelation. I find it impossible to believe that between these two texts of such great importance someone stuck in a long piece that says nothing, and that no one noticed this.

The second point has to do with the names of Elihu, who is described as the son of Barakel the Buzite of the family of Ram. These four words are full of meaning. Elihu means 'He is my God.' Virtually all Hebrew scholars agree that when the Hebrew for 'he' is used in the composition of a name, it always designates the God of Israel. Hence, Elihu means 'YHWH is my God.' It is also important to note that God is never called YHWH in the book of Job until he reveals himself as such. He is called Elohim, El, Eloha, El-Shaddai, and so on, but not YHWH. (I will return to this later). I think this fact alone hints at this text having some importance. Elihu is called the son of Barakel, which means 'Elohim has blessed him.' Hence, Elihu is the son of the benediction of God. Again, I would say that this is full of significance. Elihu comes from the land of Buz, which in Hebrew refers to 'he who is despised.' It is the word which the prophet Isaiah uses to designate God's servant, the son of man. Again this is a qualification not without some significance. Finally, Elihu is of the family of Ram, which means 'from above,' in the sense of the heavens. Putting all this together we have Elihu, YHWH is my God, son of Elohim's blessing, bearing the title of the despised servant, and coming from the heavens. I find it impossible to believe that someone could put these words together to head up a text that has no meaning or value whatsoever. In other words, I am turning the pre-judgments of the above exegetes around. They begin with a presupposition based on a rapid reading of this text, which admittedly is somewhat redundant and, from a literary point of view, not very beautiful. I would rather begin with the above two points.

I would like to add, as a footnote, that the rabbinical tradition never discusses these kinds of questions because they take the text as revealed and reliable to the letter. However, I am always a little disappointed that the commentators in this tradition rarely examine the symbolism in names, preferring instead to make calculations using values assigned to individual letters. I also find that the Talmudic explanations of this or any other text tend to be on the level of each verse as opposed to the whole. Hence, I did not find this explanation of the passage of Elihu very helpful because it sticks to explaining the text verse by verse.

7   Elihu (Chapters 32–37)

Chapter 32

I think this chapter confronts us with two fundamental questions. The first regards wisdom: many days and years do not teach wisdom. It refers back directly to the text about wisdom in chapter 28. Elihu contrasts wisdom with the intelligence that comes from God's Spirit. He challenges tradition and experience to the benefit of the true revelation. It is an important teaching. Within people there is the spirit that is the breath of the almighty One, which gives intelligence. Recall that in Hebrew the word *ruach* should be translated as spirit; and there is also the word *hevel*, usually translated as breath. The latter word, when used in Ecclesiastes, is commonly translated as vanity. We tend to oppose the ephemeral character of this breath (respiration) to the enduring character of the spirit. It is very significant, therefore, that the Hebrews, when they thought about God's work in people, his wisdom, and his revelation, chose the word breath (what is most fragile and ephemeral) to express this idea. At the same time, it is this very breath that, for a living being, is all-important. In God's revelation, what is the most important is most fragile and transient; and reciprocally, what is most fragile is the most important, and this leads to true wisdom. I believe there are very good reasons why God chooses what is the most fragile to reveal himself to people, namely, the Word. If God revealed himself in all his power, we would be annihilated. God has to reveal himself through what is the most fragile and humble, namely, breath.[1]

---

1 Jacques Ellul, *The Humiliation of the Word*, trans. J.M. Hanks (Grand Rapids, MI: Eerdmans, 1985).

Job's friends relied on their human intelligence and even claimed to have wisdom, but they failed to convince Job. Elihu stops talking to see if they will say anything more, but they remain silent. He then begins to speak in God's name. He is created by God and it is his Spirit that inspires him. In other words, by speaking in the name of God, Elihu is his witness before God reveals himself, and this is the key to understanding his entire discourse. He is the prophet, so to speak, who goes before God's revelation. God reveals himself later. In the meantime, there is a human being who speaks the wisdom of God and announces his judgment.

This brings me to the second issue. Elihu is not the defender of anyone and he takes no sides. The Hebrew text speaks of giving no title of superiority or supremacy to anyone, which means that before God we are reduced to nothing, as dry grass and so on. Status has no importance whatsoever. Elihu says he cannot bestow any titles or flatter anyone, because his Creator would quickly remove him. If he found someone to be very good and important he could not call him lord, because God is the One who preceded the entire creation, with the result that he cannot acknowledge any form of superiority or title on the earth. Elihu has received one single mission, namely, to articulate the Word of God with a human voice. For now we can acknowledge that he is a messenger from God in the form of a prophet or an angel (the subject of angels comes up shortly); and for us he may appear as the image of Jesus Christ.

I believe these are the two important aspects of this chapter. On the one hand, there is the opposition between human wisdom and God's Spirit; and on the other hand, there is the messenger of the Word of God who takes no sides and does not bestow status on anyone. One final remark: We will continue to encounter, in a number of verses, the problem that many translations deviate considerably from the Hebrew.

In response to your questions: I would say that the reason God chooses the most fragile means for his revelation is to avoid the possibility that people are able to say that this or that is the truth. We know very well that we are constantly tempted to do this. The histories of the Jewish and Christian communities are full of examples of the difficulties this can create. It also means that we can only discern false prophets following the events in question, and why the only possible relationship with God is one of faith.

Chapter 33

Having dismissed Job's friends, Elihu now turns to Job. He begins by pointing out that he himself is also human. Before God I am like you, I too was formed from clay, fear of me will not trouble you, and I will not crush you. He is responding to Job's repeated demands for God to appear, and his fear that if God does so he will be crushed. Elihu in effect tells Job not to be afraid because he speaks in God's name but is himself a fellow creature. Again, we recognize the image of Jesus Christ who is a man and yet is fully God. It is as if Elihu were a screen between an all-powerful God who speaks and Job who is afraid. It is an expression of God's love to first send a messenger in order not to crush people.

Next, Elihu revisits what Job has said, including his accusations. For example, in the tenth verse, he cites Job word for word. This is how God treats me, and, in addition, he does not speak to me. In verses 12 and 13, Elihu explains to Job that God does not have to account for his actions. He does not have to speak to Job, and yet he does. An explanation of three ways in which God expresses himself follows. The explanation of the first can be translated from the Hebrew as: God speaks once, and he does not repeat it a second time when people do not take it seriously. The first time God speaks plainly, clearly, and to the point, but he will not do so a second time. We have the Bible and we will not have more.

There are other forms of God's speaking as well, including dreams and visions, but in a sense these are less clear and certain. At all times, God chooses means that are open to discussion because he respects people's freedom. Our liberty rests on the need to interpret what God says. This answers a long theological debate around the question of whether God's Word constrains us. If God is God, how is it possible that when he speaks to us we may not be convinced? The answer is that God's Word is given over to our interpretation so that we remain free before the God who reveals himself as the One who liberates. The text explains that dreams and visions are open to interpretation in order to keep people from pride. If a human being could possess the complete truth of God, Adam would have succeeded in some sense.

Elihu sheds new light on suffering as a Word, another way of God expressing himself. It is not a means of punishment, a way of redemption, a hidden good, nor a path to perfection, but a call to repentance in order to bring people back to God. It reflects the account in the gospel of Luke, when Jesus was asked about the crimes committed by the Galileans who were massacred or by the people on whom the tower of Siloam fell. Jesus answers the people that this is not their concern, but if they do not repent the same thing will happen to them. It also reminds me of the novel by Thornton Wilder entitled *The Bridge of San Luis Rey*. Following a terrible accident, someone investigates the life of each person who was killed to find out what they did to deserve such a death. It turns out that they had simply finished everything they had to do in their lives. What Elihu says is that suffering must be interpreted as a call to repentance. It is not an occasion for us to judge whether those who suffer deserve it. The text makes clear that Job's claim that his suffering would lead to his death is not true. Elihu explains that suffering leads to encountering God in repentance. When that repentance takes place, we meet the angel of intercession who protects people, prays to God for forgiveness, and announces that a ransom has been paid. It is this angel who has found the ransom, hence it cannot be something that a person could possibly offer, even by a human sacrifice.

At this point, youth and strength are restored, and something much more important happens. In verse 27, people recognize themselves as sinners. We should pay careful attention to the order in which things happen when there is suffering. People take note and repent. The angel intervenes and says that the ransom has been paid. God forgives and grants grace. It is then that people become aware of having sinned, because they have been saved from the grave. As the text says: I have sinned and violated justice but I have not been punished as I deserved. In other words, people know this only when they have experienced forgiveness.

It is exactly in this way that Job's situation is completely turned around. He had endlessly complained that he was being punished without having deserved it. What this means is that he had not yet encountered God's grace and pardon and had not realized that God's grace had presided over things all along. He now recognizes that he had sinned but was not punished for it. God is now recognized as the One who, by extremely indirect and fragile means, constantly calls people to repent in order to re-establish a relationship with them. Contrary to what Job has argued up till now, God pursues our salvation and not our death.

The text declares that two times, three times, God does all these things for people. Of course, these numbers are purely symbolic. It is the Hebrew way of saying that it is permanent, continuous, and constant. I believe that Elihu, following up on what has been said thus far, contributes something rather new and important regarding the way God works. There is a kind of flexibility within a permanence that takes into account and makes use of many diverse elements of what is happening without ever deviating from a movement toward salvation and without the slightest waver toward death. Despite tremendous turbulence, by the use of the Word, dreams, visions, and suffering, God constantly changes his pedagogy according to the culture, the historical time, the particular person, and so on. I believe that this is what the text means – it is fundamental to the entire revelation. In other words, there is not a kind of progress occurring in the revelation of the Old Testament. For example, God does not reveal himself more clearly in the prophets than in the law. Instead, what we see is an extraordinarily diverse pedagogy adapted to the time, place, and culture in order to enter into our ways of thinking. It is the presence of God who constantly seeks us in love, without ever imposing himself. We see this in the reading of the Bible. People with little background and education receive something · from it, as do people with a great deal of learning. I have been studying these texts for at least fifty years; but when I reread the texts we discussed I again heard new things, and I am totally convinced this will never stop as long as I live.

Chapters 34–37

In order not to make this study session too long, I will focus on chapter 34:10–33, chapter 35:5–16, chapter 36:5–15, and chapter 37:13–24. As is evident from our preliminary discussion of these texts, it is not uncommon that the usual translations do not correspond very well to the original Hebrew texts. I do not wish to trivialize the difficulties involved. First, each word must be formed by inserting the required vowels – usually by doing so according to tradition. Whatever word is thus formed has, of course, several meanings. Then comes the interpretation of the text. You know I am fond of reminding you that one of the great Talmudic rabbis has written that each text has seventy-seven meanings plus the true meaning, which only God knows. We must struggle with these texts knowing full well that we will never exhaust their meaning. I also feel very strongly that the study of the Old Testament requires a knowledge of the Hebrew language. If someone does not possess this knowledge, it is better to work in groups in which at least one or two members know the original language. For the New Testament it is different – I do not think knowing Greek is as important. One of the great mistakes of Christianity in the Middle Ages was to rely too heavily on St Jerome's rather bad translation of the Hebrew text into Latin for its knowledge of the Old Testament. This caused many misunderstandings between the Jews, who read the Hebrew text, and the Christians, who relied on this Latin translation. We can never claim to have an exact translation, and even less to have fully understood the text. We can neither possess nor hold on to the Word; and this brings us back to our discussions regarding breath and spirit.

We have also seen how a quick reading of a text can mislead us. At a glance, this text in the book of Job appears to affirm little more than the idea that God is righteous and powerful. Only a very careful reading begins to bring out new understandings. It is important to ask questions such as: Does Elihu present more or less the same arguments as Job's friends, who constantly argue that he was guilty? A careful reading of the text shows that this is not the case; and we will continue to see that Elihu never judges Job.

Next, I will turn to what I believe to be the principal themes in these texts. These are the justice of God, sin, and the power of God. Beginning with the first theme, we are constantly told that God is just and that he cannot be anything else but just. According to the text, God does not know inequity, nor does he violate justice. He is not accountable to anyone and his authority is vested in himself. As chapter 34:13 puts it: Who gave him charge over the earth, and who entrusted the universe to his care? He does not have to answer to anyone, and no person can make demands with regard to his justice. This said, four observations can be made regarding God's justice.

First, it is a justice for others and not one driven by self-interest or egotism. Verse 14 tells us that if God only thought of himself and withheld his spirit and breath, all would perish. Also, his immense power does not push people away. In chapter 36:5 we read that God is mighty but he does not make fun of others and he does not reject anyone – God is for everyone.

However, we must not ask him to judge before his time. In other words, we must not ask God to pronounce good or evil in the course of human history. This reminds us of Jesus' parable of the wheat and the tares: gathering the tares before the harvest will also uproot the wheat. God acts in his own time and there is no automatism of any kind in his actions. It is therefore impossible even to speak of the injustice of God until after the final judgment, and certainly not during human history. We are told that just because we do not always experience his anger does not mean that he is not concerned about crimes that are committed.

Moreover, this justice for others does not differentiate between people but treats everyone alike. As Elihu says, God does not keep track of who is powerful and who is not, who is rich and who is not, and so on. It means the same thing as Jesus' saying that God makes it rain on good and bad people alike, and makes the sun shine on the just and the unjust. This God will not judge people differently because all are the work of his hands, as declared in chapter 34.

It is not for people to criticize God. What is happening here is that Elihu turns things around, just as Jesus does in the parable of the prodigal son. In it the father asks his oldest son why he takes offence to his being good to his brother. Elihu says the same thing. Hence we cannot accuse God of not exercising our kind of justice, which is based on punishment.

The text associates God's justice with his power and sovereignty; and what is becoming apparent is that there is no difference between this power and this justice. We cannot say that God is powerful and that he is just but, instead, that God is powerful because he is just and he is just because he is powerful. This clears up a problem for which I could never get an answer from any pastor when I was young: In the book of Judges, why are the judges military leaders? It is because in them there was no difference between being just and being powerful. They derived power from God's power and because of that they were just; and because they were clothed with God's justice they were powerful. It completely goes against our idea that there is a conflict between power and justice. However, in God they are the same.

Another characteristic of God's justice is the complex relationship that exists between the actions of humanity and those of God. We are told that God lets people be but that there will be consequences. We are also told that injustices and evil come from people, from our fellow beings. People cry out against excesses of oppression and complain about the violence of many. The consequences of the works of people come back on them as a kind of 'logic' of human behaviour. It is not God's will to sustain evildoers. Chapter 36:6 says this explicitly. Of course, this challenges our conceptions because, ever since the Middle Ages, we have made God the cause of everything, the cause of causes, and the final cause. This has nothing to do with what the revelation tells us: God allows people to develop their lives and their history, and yet he intervenes.

This mix of the actions of God and those of people is a big problem in the Old Testament, with which I have struggled in my book *The Politics of God and the Politics of Man*.[2] God is present and he intervenes. For example, he makes the great to appear and disappear (34:20). We see the same thing in chapter 36:7 where we are told that he puts kings on their

---

2 Jacques Ellul, *The Politics of God and the Politics of Man*, trans. G.W. Bromiley (Grand Rapids, MI: Eerdmans, 1972).

thrones, he maintains them for a while, but they are full of pride and this causes their downfall. In other words, God intervenes but then he allows things to develop. If he names a king and then that king turns out badly, God lets it be, including all the consequences of this evil-doing. For example, one of the prophets tells us that God 'whistled up' the Chaldeans and they came from the north. However, they were so extreme in their persecution, torture, and killing that God annihilated them. There is a kind of logic here. If God calls a king, he expects him to do his will, but if he does not there will be consequences that fall on people and that may cause them to rebel. God is present in each moment of our lives and in our history, but this does not mean that he directs it – he is always by our side. When we read in Matthew that no bird will fall without the *will* of your heavenly Father, the Greek does not say this at all. It says: without your Father, that is, without your Father being there. God is there when a little bird dies. God permits the 'causes' of history to operate but he is never absent from this history. He is always with us.

I believe these are the principal characteristics of God's justice, which are difficult to accept. We have a hard time understanding that the will of God is the good. We ourselves have already established a justice and a good, and God had better conform to what we have declared to be just and good. According to the Bible we need to learn to turn this around and to accept that justice is the will of God, and the good is his will. There is not a justice or a good above God. Instead, God declares what is just, and what he says is justice – not what we have declared it to be. God does not obey our conceptions, theories, and ideas of justice. This is why Elihu reproaches Job's friends: for having told him that his suffering was willed by God.

In response to your questions: I will attempt to illustrate this further with the example of the flood. God let people be, but this turned out so badly that it could no longer continue, both for the sake of the people and before God. God intervened and brought things to an end, and despite this people began again. The flood was no doubt the most massive intervention, but it was limited to a particular moment. It always happens this way in the Bible. Similarly, a prophet warns that God will intervene on this or that specific matter, and that is all. Hence, we cannot regard God as absent, nor as a kind of all-determining cause. God lets things develop, but there are moments when he intervenes. For example, Paul was converted by an intervention of God, but afterwards he had to find his own way. Many times, in his letters, he says that it is

I who say this and not God. In other words, a momentary intervention of God in your life could suffice. From then on you always remember that moment when the Word of God became true for you. God is not going to repeat this over and over again. We have to find our own way. In the Old Testament, the Jewish people are constantly reminded to re-member the day of God's intervention. Another example is when God intervenes in Cain's life. He warns him that evil is at his door but that he can overcome it.

I will now turn to the second important theme in these chapters, namely, that of sin. Job's friends constantly associate sin with what Job has done. Job argues on the same level. Elihu speaks about sin on an entirely different level, going much deeper as it were. He focuses on two aspects that are rather clear in the text. Chapter 36:9 tells us that God denounces their works and transgressions, that is, their pride. The other aspect is self-justification. For example, chapter 35:1–2 asks if we think we can justify ourselves before God. It is no longer a matter of specific deeds but of a certain attitude in life, namely, that of pride and the will to dominate as well as that of self-justification. Job exhibits both when he is proud of the good he has done and when he claims to be able to justify himself. This explains why in chapter 35:1–2 Elihu asks Job whether he thinks he can justify himself before God.

Moreover, there is a remarkable response to Job's assertion that avoiding sin does him no good. Elihu tells him that sin does not affect God but it affects others, and the remainder of chapter 35 develops this. Your justice, in terms of what you do, good or evil, does not serve God but your neighbour. When things turn ugly, people cry out against the excesses of oppression and the violence of many. People complain about their social and political situation, they seek to affirm their justice against others, and they demand punishment. Instead, Elihu explains that they should first ask where God is. No one says: Where is God my creator, who inspires songs of joy during the night, God who teaches us by means of the beasts of the earth and gives us intelligence through the birds of the sky? It amounts to a critique of our self-justification when we complain about others and strive to make social and political chan-ges instead of first concerning ourselves with our relationship with God. If, during periods of disaster in our history we do not turn to God because we think we can take care of ourselves, he lets us be. If you have no interest in the will of God and his love, says Elihu, then do not be surprised when God does not intervene. God does not respond to those who turn away from him. I believe this may well have caused the failure of some revolutions even though, as we will see, there is a place for revolution in our text.

To sum up: self-justification amounts to living as if I am self-sufficient and guided by my own justice. Pride is at the very heart of the will to dominate. Together they deny my need for God's justice and love. For example, if a Christian becomes a politician, thereby choosing the path of domination while attempting to remain faithful, he or she will certainly fail. We have seen many examples of truly authentic well-meaning Christians who as politicians were a disaster. Christians must follow their master in the way of non-domination, that is, the way of non-violence and non-power. However, we must never forget that we live by necessity and not in a world of freedom, hence there are times when this becomes impossible. For example, I think that pacifism cannot be politics but it can be a witness, and the two are totally different. As an individual I am entirely opposed to all uses of atomic power, but I recognize that if I had the responsibility of conducting the politics of our present government I would have no choice but to defend the use of nuclear power. To think and act realistically is entirely other than living by faith. Christians must always live with the recognition that, socially and historically, things work in certain ways but we must, at the same time, live with the possibility that God may intervene. However, as a Christian I may not expect others to behave this way. I can choose not to defend myself in the hope that God will intervene. All I can do is bear witness to the fact that if we take the risk of not defending ourselves, perhaps we will have God's approval. However, it is a risk that I may not impose on others and not on a mixed community of Christians and non-Christians.

The third theme I will discuss is that of God's power. The last part of chapter 36 and the first part of chapter 37 describe natural phenomena brought about by God. The text tells us that it is useless to argue with God because he is free with regard to his creation. With respect to humanity, God places his seal on the hands of all people so that they will recognize themselves as his creatures (chapter 37:7).

The Hebrew text also implies that people's hands are sealed, meaning that God imposes limits as well as placing a mark as a sign of belonging to God. People are obliged to recognize these limitations to the extent that they cannot understand or resolve a great many things (chapter 37:5). People have difficulty understanding even simple material things, symbolized in the text by not even knowing why their clothing is warm. If we have trouble understanding many material phenomena, how can we claim to understand the justice of God, which is infinitely more complex and abstract? Nevertheless, what differentiates God from humanity is that his justice is not corrupted by his power. I come back to what the text revealed earlier, namely, that God is powerful because he is just and he is just because he is powerful, even though this makes no sense to us. We can only trust, through faith, that this is the case.

God also reveals the two forms of his justice, namely, punishment and mercy (chapter 37:13). God accomplishes his will by one or the other, and in faith we need to accept both. This image that the text gives us regarding the justice of God is both awe-inspiring and comforting because we are assured that his power and justice are the same.

Following this reflection on what I believe are the essential elements in the text regarding the above three themes, I would now like to deal with the question of what this discourse of Elihu means. As we have already seen, Elihu is almost certainly a messenger from God. In the biblical context this means he is an angel (the Greek word for angel means messenger). In the Old Testament, such a messenger had no identity. What this means is that an angel is not a person, being not only identified with but identical to the message. The angel was the Word that was brought, and that was all. It is the complete opposite of how we think of angels.

It is now clear why Elihu came from nowhere and why he disappears after the message was brought. He is a messenger in three ways. The first is the message for Job. The only real criticism he addresses to Job is that he has created an impasse for himself. He reveals the contradictions that underlie Job's discourse. Job prays, but he also says it serves no purpose. Job calls on God to judge him, and at the same time he declares God to be unjust. Why bother praying, or hoping for God's justice? In revealing these contradictions, Job is not condemned. Three times the word 'revelation' is used by Elihu (not included in some translations). He reveals to Job his sin, namely, his pride and his self-justification; he reveals the contradictory nature of Job's protest; and finally, he explains what has taken place and reveals what will happen.

The second way in which Elihu is a messenger is in preparing the way of the Lord. The reproach addressed to Job, and the way he goes about it, corresponds exactly to what God says when he appears, later on. I think this is very important because it means that Job repents not only because God appears, but because he has been prepared for this by Elihu's message. Throughout the Bible (and we do not pay sufficient attention to this detail), God's actions are always announced first. He promises, and the fulfilment comes after. God always acts in two different moments in order to leave us time to reflect, to react, to meditate and pray. Think of the prophets. In this instance, God does not suddenly appear to Job. He first announces everything, even the animals he is going to show to Job. God's revelation is always structured in this way, in order to give people time to decide where they stand following the announcement and before the event takes place. Throughout the entire Old Testament this is exactly how things unfold. It also holds for our time, so that we may understand when God intervenes even though we do not know when that may be. We see the same thing here. Job is convinced by Elihu's message, of which the proof is that he says nothing more when God comes.

The fundamental reason why the Bible shows how things unfold in this way is that God does not wish to condemn humanity, in the hope that when he comes people will have heard and will be ready. He does everything possible to make this happen. If, instead, God suddenly appeared to humanity, it would be disastrous. If, on the other hand, people have listened to the Word and if they have repented, then God has no need to condemn anyone and has no need to manifest his crushing power. Nor will there be any need for God to justify himself to humanity.

Job has constantly brought a suit against God, and if he had continued with this it would have ended very badly for him. Instead, Elihu stops him by explaining the contradictory nature of his behaviour. God no longer has to appear as someone who has been accused by Job. He is no longer involved in a suit. This opens the possibility of God's love being re-established in his freedom. We also have this tendency to dictate what should happen and what God ought to do. We seek to entangle God in this process but God wishes to reserve the freedom of his love, and he does this by the preaching of his Word. As I have explained in one of my books, it is amazing that God chose the most fragile means to reveal himself.[3] If, on the other hand, God had chosen to use means of power, means that would mechanically act on us (such as a fully efficient information and control system), we would have lost all our independence with respect to him. In choosing the Word, the power of God is transmitted by the frailest and humblest means, which in a sense are inadequate. We see this clearly in attempting to make sense of this text. Apart from difficult translation problems, the text is open to misin-

---

3 Jacques Ellul, *The Humiliation of the Word*, op. cit.

terpretation, misunderstanding, manipulation, distortion, and trivialization; yet this leaves us a certain freedom.

Finally, Elihu prepares the way of the Lord by clearly announcing exactly how God will appear. The details are found at the end of chapter 36 and the beginning of chapter 37, and this will be revisited later. We have the announcement of the storm, the lightning that accompanies God when he comes (according to the customary images of that time), the wind that follows, the clouds that hide the light, and the light wind from the north that clears the sky, exactly as with the prophet Elijah. Once this happens God comes, and the prophet no longer has anything to say. This is why he ends with noting that we cannot go where God is and God does not respond to our wishes; and it is at this very moment that God intervenes. The prophets knew that they were not the ones who accomplished what they said. I believe this is what Elihu as angel, messenger, and prophet is all about.

In response to your questions: God's glory is the revelation of God himself as he is. In Jesus Christ God has revealed who he is in a double relationship. Jesus glorifies his Father in revealing who his Father is, and God glorifies the Son in revealing him as God. The theology of glory in the gospel of John is very important, but it rests entirely on the Old Testament. It reminds me of Pompey, one of the Roman conquerors entering Jerusalem, wanting to know what this glory of God, which the Jews spoke of, was all about. So he goes into the holiest place in the temple and finds absolutely nothing, because there is no possible representation of what is the glory of God. It is there when God is present, and there is nothing when he is absent.

8 God's Appearance (Chapters 38–39)

Practically all commentators regard this text as rather disappointing. Even though God appears, he does not reply to any of Job's 'existential' questions. After all, Job's entire effort has been focused on challenging the purely intellectual questions and theological constructions of his friends in order to situate his problem entirely on an existential level. All this appears to be ignored, and we are back to intellectual problems, including whether Job was present when various things were created. All this seems rather disappointing – apparently God is not answering anything. One commentator goes so far as to suggest that it is a waste of time to speak of God and his works or to ask God for a revelation regarding humanity and the meaning of life. Only God can speak of God, and yet he does not speak of this, with the result that humanity remains alone. This is a characteristic reaction to the fact that Job receives no reply.

God situates himself entirely on the level of his total power, but this power was never called into question. Yet it is this power that God reveals. It is not surprising, therefore, that most commentators have relatively little to say about this text. To at least get something out of it, historians and exegetes, by showing that fragments of this text are comparable to numerous others and that it has nothing original in it, have led some to the conclusion that it is a dreadful irony on the part of God. I must confess that when I read that text from this perspective, I find it downright devastating because Job is a very unhappy person. It makes God appear in the way non-believers often see him: a God who is only power, who crushes people, who reduces people to silence without replying. We have all heard these kinds of accusations, and this is exactly what a non-believer would get out of it.

However, I am convinced that this text has a hidden dimension, which is not to deny that if you read this text rapidly and remain on the surface, you will get nothing out of it. This is true for much of the book of Job as well as many other texts. You must really want to go deeper by taking a stand that this is a revelation, and you must respect it and meditate on it. In other words, you must be driven by a conviction that it is simply impossible that God has nothing to say. Hence, the first step in reading these kinds of texts is one of faith. If we truly believe that this God who speaks is deaf, mute, and blind to the cries of his creatures, then that is what we will find. If, on the other hand, we believe that the God of the Revelation is the exact opposite, then we had better read the text much more carefully.

From this perspective, I would like to make three preliminary observations. First, there is the question of the relationship between God and people. In this text, God reveals his name: YHWH. Everywhere else in Job God is referred to by other names: Elohah or El-Shaddai, which mean the all-powerful one or the divine one. YHWH is the God of the second chapter of the book of Genesis, that is, he who enters into relationships. Surely it is not accidental that in this part of Job we find the name of the God who enters into a relationship with people and who reveals himself to them. This is the God who becomes a personal God. I would not go so far as to say that this is a direct reply to Job, but it is God's attempt to approach him. It is perhaps not so much the content of what God says that is the most important but the fact that God comes closer to Job and speaks to him. To the existential questions of Job, God in effect replies: I am here. When he comes before us, he speaks as the One he is, namely, the all-powerful One who is not at our disposal. At the same time, God cannot simply be the distant all-powerful One, because he is also the incarnated God in Jesus. It is this ongoing movement: God uses his name, YHWH – I am the living One who is with you. He declares his power precisely because he is there close to us. It is the same thing as Jesus being always present but at one point there was the transfiguration, that is, his being all-powerful manifested itself. Hence, this change of name in our text is highly significant.

The fact that God speaks is equally important. When God speaks, his whole Word is present. Whatever the content of that Word, it is always first and foremost a Word that creates. When God speaks, he creates. Each time God reveals himself, he brings about a new situation. In coming to Job and speaking to him, God creates a new situation for Job, even when God says very little or nothing, and the new relationship constitutes a kind of new birth.

Finally, I would like to note that the situation is completely turned around. Job never ceased to question, and now it is he who is questioned. In chapter 38:4 he is asked where he was when God laid the foundations for the earth, and on and on. I do not believe that God is attempting to demonstrate Job's weakness and lack of power. Surely we can give the editors of this book more credit than that. As everywhere else in the Bible, God is busy turning around the relationship between the Creator and his creatures. People ask questions; and instead of answering, God asks them a question. From this we should learn that the Bible is not a book of answers but a book of questions. It begins with Adam being asked what he has done, and it culminates with Jesus asking his disciples who they think he is. God makes people responsible in the full sense of this term. He calls them to reply, and by doing so they become responsible. There is a much deeper sense to God asking us questions – it implies that we are free. For example, when Jesus asks his disciples the above question, he leaves them entirely free to reply and to make their choice. When God asks us a question, it means that he liberates us from everything that determines and enslaves us, so that we can freely reply to God's question. It makes us fully responsible. These, I believe, are the important introductory observations I wanted to share with you.

Next let us turn to the text itself, beginning with the vision of the creation. Parallel visions can be found in many places. Within the book of Job, in chapter 25 there is the discourse of Bildad, in chapter 26 that of Job, in chapter 37 that of Elihu; and they all more or less say the same thing about creation and the power of God. As a result, one commentator suggests that God takes up the arguments the others have given to show that they all spoke about these matters correctly. I do not believe this gets to the bottom of things, for three reasons.

First, I take this to be a demonstration of the mystery of the creation in all the things we do not understand about it. Today we see this in the development of science. The more we advance, the more we discover that we do not know. I must confess I am fascinated by this intellectual adventure of science: that time and time again things turn out to be more complicated than was previously believed. We may think that we more or less know the answers to the questions God asks of Job, but science keeps showing us how much there is that we still do not know. In addition, there are many things that appear to make no sense to us. Why do some animals pay little or no attention to their offspring (ostriches, for example)? The opposite is a mystery: why do other animals exhibit maternal love (such as lions)? The text speaks of an extraordinary diversity of animals. Wisdom is given to the hawk and discernment to the rooster, but both are denied to the ostrich; the extraordinary qualities of horses are celebrated, and much more.

There is also the question of the lack of utility. Job's friends seek to demonstrate that it is important to do useful things, also for one's salvation, and that the world is filled with useful things. Even serving God is useful. Job answers that this is not true, and that serving God is not useful. Later, God shows that the creation is not about utility but about a free gift. There is no point inquiring into the purpose of the creation, the purpose of the rain, or the purpose of the animals. Their value and significance derive from God's having made them. The creation was not made for humanity; and this is reflected by God asking Job to regard it apart from himself, as it were. As one commentator puts it, God places Job in the world of his creative freedom, a world that is 'motiveless' and gratis. We do well to remember that, although the garden of Eden was created for humanity, it was filled with many things that served no human purpose and which were not intended to serve people.

Job has to abandon the anthropocentrism evident in his discourse. He had put himself, his suffering, and his thoughts in the centre of everything. Although we can understand how he came to be this way, God desires him to go further and to recognize that despite his eminent place, he cannot conclude from this that only he counts. Everything else that exists counts for God as well.

Job has to learn that the world exists on its own. In chapter 38 we see a world that has its own playfulness, so to speak. Job also has to learn that God makes decisions for reasons he does not know, but this does not make what God does absurd (as Job has claimed all along). God now responds and tells him he has a design and a project, and that these have dimensions that Job cannot grasp. In the enormous abundance of what exists, there is nevertheless an order.

I will close by focusing on a few details. First, we are told that the sea has become like a newborn baby that God has wrapped in swaddling clothes. It signifies that the sea is but one newborn before God, as well as the extent to which he limits it. The importance of this must be understood in relation to the mythologies of Job's time, in which the sea represented the power of the void that constantly threatened to submerge the world, with the image of a flood in the background. The text turns this around completely by likening the sea to a newborn.

The dawn is likened to a person who plays a moral role. The wicked go by night, with the result that when the dawn appears they are deprived of their 'light.' In other words, the night is the light of the wicked; and when the dawn of God appears the light of the wicked disappears.

Later, in chapter 38:31–2 we encounter the constellations. This text reflects the very words Job used in chapter 9. In the Hebrew there is a play on words because of some double meanings. The Big Bear also means ringworm, Orion also means fire, and the Pleiades also means a pile of mud. Here we have the same words Job used, except that now there can no longer be a play on words because the text adds 'the constellations.' In other words, God says to Job that he has called his stars ringworm, fire, and a pile of mud, but he wants him to know that these are constellations. Job is asked whether he knows the laws of heaven and whether, from his place on the earth, he can tell what is written therein; or whether he can make the constellations appear in their time. I believe what God is getting at is whether Job knows how all these constellations are related since, like everything else in the creation, they are not dispersed in the heavens by chance. We will see later how important this is.

There is one last matter we must consider. Practically all theological commentators, including Calvin (as opposed to the historians and exegetes), have asked themselves if there was not another meaning to this text of a symbolic, mythical, or analogical character. Many attempts have been made to find such a meaning. For example, I tried to figure out whether there was a key to this text in the names of the animals, but I could not find anything. The rabbinical commentators have made a number of attempts as well, with a subtlety that often goes too far for my liking. However, I will give you an example of an allegorical interpretation of chapter 38:12–14 with respect to the dawn, given by the well-known Talmudist Rashi. The text tells us that the earth is transformed, as clay pressed with a seal, and dressed up in a shining garment. A little later it asks Job: 'Have you walked in the recesses of the deep, were the gates of death disclosed to you, and did you see the door of the shadow of death?' Rashi writes that this is an allegory of death and resurrection. The earth pressed by a seal is the earth that has taken on the greyish colour of a cadaver. This is founded on the meaning of Adam, namely, red earth. This earth has now been struck to the point that it is no longer alive and red. The dawn, which is the light of God, appears, and it clothes this earth with a shining garment so that it takes on the colour of life. In this resurrection the wicked are judged by being deprived of the light, and the arm that is raised is broken; and all this is further reinforced by God saying that he has opened the doors of death in verse 17. I have only given one small detail of this extensive allegorical interpretation, which covers a great many verses.

For Christians all this is further related to what we find in chapter 39:30, which contains the saying that where the body is, the eagles will gather together. Jesus cites this in the great apocalyptic text in the gospel of Matthew (chapter 24:28). No one appears to be able to make sense of this saying, including myself. I will point out that in Greek the saying refers to a cadaver, but the equivalent Hebrew word means the one who is pierced; so that the saying then reads: 'Where the pierced one will be, there will be the eagles.' For Christians the pierced one clearly refers to Jesus Christ. One possible interpretation would then be that where the crucified Christ will be, there the elect will gather. However, for me this raises more questions than it answers.

It is also possible to come up with analogical interpretations. I must say I am always somewhat wary of such an approach because in the past this has almost always gone much too far. Nevertheless, with this text I have an impression that God shows the world to Job in order to reveal himself. I base this impression on what we read in chapter 38:33: Are you able to understand the laws of heaven, or impose their authority on earth? It is not just a question of understanding the reason for this or that but of discerning God's creation. This is a perspective which is not at all that of Reformation theology. Does the creation bear an analogical marking of God, which would permit the discovery of certain truths about him? This was standard fare in the Middle Ages.

Before we dismiss this too easily, we should recall Paul's text in his letter to the Romans, which is more than a little embarrassing for a strictly Protestant Reformation theology. It is found in chapter 1:19–20 where we read that what we can know about God is evident to all people. God has made it known to them. Ever since the creation of the world, the invisible perfection of God, his eternal power and divinity can be seen with the eye when we regard his works. This is clearly very embarrassing for Protestant theology, which does not accept that the creation contains a natural theology. Hence it must be impossible to see the perfection of God in nature, and yet this is exactly what Paul says. I have had to consider the possibility that this astonishing description in Job says the same thing. To regard God's creation and to understand it paves the way for discerning a certain truth about God. One of the best commentators on the wisdom literature suggests that God refers to his creation so that it bears witness. The creation has something to say about God to humanity by speaking to people who reflect on it.

Going further down this road, I find something that Calvin wrote to be rather astonishing. In his courageous commentary on this text, he says that the wing of the ostrich is used with great joy, and that this wing is an allegory of God's joy. The world's situation is founded on this joy. It is amazing that the image of the wing of the ostrich could inspire Calvin in this way, considering that he generally was rather dry and humourless.

It is clear that people are unable to read the creation by their own means. Without God's discourse, Job would not have understood the creation by himself. God had to tell him, and this turns the situation around. The creation does not speak to people directly – it only speaks to us when God tells us that it does so. We learn to read the creation because God tells us there is something to read in it about him. God speaks to Job, and unveils the creation to him, Job understands what he did not see before, and now he can read this creation. In this way Job learns a number of analogies. I can see two of these in this text.

First, there is the analogy of the whole. Chapter 38 shows that all things are related to each other, and everything is created together. Many words are used that suggest a kind of communication: roads, paths, and gates. These help to create an ensemble of connections forming a whole. By analogy, God is not simply the God of everything, but the God of everything related into a whole. It makes me think of what physicists like D'Espagnat referred to as the principle of inseparability. What this means is that nothing in this universe can be separated from anything else. What happens anywhere has repercussions for everything else. This has enormous methodological implications. If a physical phenomenon is observed separated from everything else, the results will be wrong. I believe this gets at the same kind of thing as our text. As such, I think it is an analogy of the totality of God.

The second analogy that I see in this text is that of freedom. What all the animals that are described in this text have in common is their freedom. There is only one exception, namely, the horse. The horse is domesticated and obeys a master, and yet the horse reveals itself as free in combat. The horse rejoices in its strength, it sheds its fear, and hence the horse also has its freedom. All these animals are independent from people, who cannot prevail over these creatures of God. That being the case, how could people possibly prevail over God? In other words, the freedom of these animals is an allegory of the freedom of God. It is precisely this freedom of God that Job sought to curtail.

This brings me to my last observation. Many commentators have suggested that God is lacking in love in his dealing with Job. However, God listens to Job. He takes him seriously. He speaks to him, and in order to communicate he does not use a revelation that is so powerful that it overwhelms Job. Instead, God uses a mirror by referring to his creation. What he says in effect is: Look at this creation and you will see the God of this whole, the God of this freedom and so on. In other words, God veils himself in order to speak to Job, and he does exactly what Job asked of him. Job asked God to meet him on his level and to stop crushing him from afar. This is exactly what God does when he speaks to Job about his creation as an analogy of himself.

Once again, we see that when you persist reading a text in the conviction that it is a revelation, you never walk away empty-handed. However, you have to make that commitment to the text. In contrast, those who did not believe that this text contained a revelation, including the historians of the nineteenth and twentieth centuries, came away with absolutely nothing. We must remember that God's Word creates something new within us. Job is no longer the same person after God has spoken to him. We may not be happy with what God says, and we may not be convinced that he has answered our questions or dealt with our problems. Nevertheless, it brings us hope which allows us to move forward.

In response to your questions: I think it is helpful to remember what we learned in Genesis. The second creation account describes a universe with the garden of Eden, in which humanity lives. The name of this garden means the delights of love. Humanity was placed in this garden to bring God the delights of love. It would be terrible if the God of love failed by not encountering a response to his love. Of course, it would be within God's power to start all over again, but within his love it would have been a catastrophe. We must also remember that the role of humanity (created in the image of God) was to take care of the creation as God would, that is, not by means of power but by the Word. It is useful to keep this in mind as we work our way through Job.

9   The Two Beasts (Chapters 40–41)

Job now recognizes that his disputes with God are vain and useless, in the sense that what he has experienced in his life cannot be understood by means of theological, metaphysical, or philosophical arguments. All the normal ways of understanding God and the motivation behind his actions cannot get at the truth. Job recognizes that when he speaks about God, his words carry no weight, and because of this he can only be silent. What else can one be after God shows you his creation?

Perhaps Job's reaction is similar to that of our more thoughtful scientists, who recognize that, in our search for reality, our experience is that the more we discover, the more we also find that we still do not know. Knowing more is not necessarily knowing better. It may simply be knowing differently.

Even though Job acknowledges that he has understood what God is telling him, he cannot talk about it. He has been led to recognize that God is more mysterious than anything else, and he promises not to speak and discuss vainly again. Consequently, to use a phrase of Karl Barth, nature is not a second pathway of the revelation. When God shows nature and its mystery to people, they can only be silent because they do not learn anything more about God. Is this as far as we can go? Must we conclude that this work of the Creator negatively describes him? This would place us in the middle of the classical scholastic arguments that God cannot be positively discerned in his creation, but maybe he can be discerned negatively. I think this is complete nonsense because it corresponds to the situation in which Job found himself earlier. On his own, he had always concluded that God could not be discerned positively in his creation, hence there would have been no point to what God has just shown him. Job has to become silent in order to transcend his situation and go further.

After God speaks to him, Job announces his silence because he is defeated but not convinced. God has won but he has not won Job's heart, as is clear from his reply. The manifestation of God's power and the wonder of his creation fail to convert Job. However, this is not the entire story because there is another response from Job at the beginning of chapter 42. I do not agree with many exegetes who regard the two answers as virtually identical, to the point that they assemble them into one text. The two answers are in fact very different. In the first, Job limits himself to being silent but his heart is not in it. In the second, Job is converted and God wins his heart. More about this later.

The consequences of seeing Job's answers as being essentially the same can be far-reaching. When some exegetes rearrange the text by moving Job's first answer to combine it with the second, it implies that chapters 40 and 41 (the descriptions of Behemoth and Leviathan) are simply the continuation of the preceding chapters. Just as I believe Job's two answers are separated because they are different, so also the hippopotamus and the crocodile are not simply another two members of the animal kingdom. Job's first reply is not an interruption of a long description of many different animals and cannot be moved so as to be combined with the second reply. Doing so may create the appearance of a more coherent text, but I believe that these two animals involve an entirely new and different element in God's speaking to Job. It begins with a kind of questioning whether it all boils down to: if the one is right, the other must be wrong and vice versa. It may surprise you, but I believe the theme of verses 6–14 of chapter 40 is the justice of God.

God continues to reveal his power, but now focuses on his justice. He does this by inviting Job, and every other person for that matter, to do all he can within his power in order to settle the question as to what would happen if people directed everything. This would become evident if God gave free rein to human power. If humanity could make it work, he would praise them because their justice would have saved them. In fact, God proposes three things to people in this text. First, to overturn God's judgment and to put God in the wrong for having declared himself as right; second, to punish everyone who is wicked; and, finally, to save themselves. If people succeeded, they would be like God; and with this the text reflects what we encountered in the book of Genesis. In fact, in these six verses we encounter three times the expression translated from the Hebrew as 'like God.' 'Do you have an arm like God's?' 'Do you have a voice like God's?' 'Can you be like God, overturn his judgment, punish the wicked, and save yourself?' In each case, the Hebrew term is exactly the same as the one used by the serpent in Eden. Job has end- lessly spoken of justice and declared himself to be just. He discerns justice. For Job, this justice had to do with saving the poor and address- ing all manner of poverty and misery. However, God reminds Job of another aspect of justice, namely, the justice that destroys the wicked (those who are not just). Is Job, or any other person for that matter, able to judge injustice and to punish it? Does Job have a sufficient discern- ment and an adequate power to establish this justice? Job has to learn that beyond his justice and beyond his merit, so to speak, there is an aspect of justice that is completely beyond his (human) reach. In our world this is almost self-evident. Our individual justice counts for little because we can do all we like and follow Jesus' advice to the rich young ruler and sell everything we have to give to the poor, but all this amounts to nothing in the face of the misery of the Sahel, the suffering of the Cambodian people, or the distress of the Vietnamese people. Just as in Protestantism we have reduced salvation to a purely individual matter, Job has reduced justice to what concerns himself, as if that is all there is to evil. What God is showing Job is that there is evil in the world, and this evil is much greater than what has threatened him. We must transcend Job's situation and consider evil in the world as a whole. In a sense Job has paved the way by insisting that if he as a just person was condemned, then the entire world was called into question. God's reply is that if Job succeeds in calling him into question, then the powers will reign. If we challenge God's justice and power, then Behemoth and Leviathan take over. In other words, this completely overshadows Job's and our individual concerns. I believe that this is the perspective created by verses 6–14 of chapter 40.

In response to your questions: I believe that Christians for far too long have approached others with a view to imposing what they hold to be certain. In contrast, we ought to enter into the situation of others. We should not engage them on our terrain but on theirs, in order to enter into their way of thinking and their way of understanding the world. One of my close friends put it very well. The more certain we are of the Truth that has been revealed to us, the more flexible we can be in our relations with others. This makes it possible to accept others as they are without judging them. The less certain we are, the more we tend to harden ourselves and invent a shield against them. It is clear that Jesus himself was extraordinarily flexible in his behaviour toward others. Moreover, anything negative was always encapsulated in a promise and a message of hope and forgiveness.

We will now examine more closely the text regarding Behemoth and Leviathan. Within a positivistic perspective, these are often translated as the hippopotamus and the crocodile. It is argued that these exceptional animals were part of the Egyptian animal kingdom and highly characteristic of the Nile. This ought to come as no surprise because the text is originally an Egyptian poem. The translation is further justified by the exceptionally realistic descriptions of these animals. You can almost see them in front of you.

Nevertheless, such a translation fails to resolve some serious difficulties. First of all, if it were just a question of two more animals, everything would have already been said. What do these two animals add to the descriptions of the bison and the lion? Why were these animals chosen over the elephant, which was known and used by the Egyptians during the time of this text?

A second difficulty is particularly embarrassing for those who would argue for a literal interpretation. The verses that ask whether this is the way you would go about catching a crocodile accurately describe how this was done. As a result, these verses would not mean anything at all, and this is hard to believe since Job knew the Nile. Hence, it is difficult to accept that the Leviathan is simply a crocodile.

The third difficulty stems from the fact that this book, although very poetic, is carefully structured and shows great intellectual rigour. It is difficult to accept that the author inserted a passage that adds nothing to what has already been said between two magnificent poems. To me it is unthinkable that the last editor of this book could have done such a thing. It is for these reasons that these two animals must be interpreted in a different way.

The name Behemoth means powerful beast, and the root of this name means being fortified and surrounded by walls. I believe it represents the power of living matter as a kind of blind force. The wording of the text must be taken seriously. For example, when the text declares that it is the first of God's works, it could not possibly be referring to the hippopotamus. The text would make sense if Behemoth referred to the power of matter, because it was created first. It was created as the tyrant among its companions, which means that everything in our world depends on the power of that matter. This is why I would translate it, 'its power is its secret' (instead of literally, 'in his loins,' according to the text), because the power of matter is indeed fundamental. We are busy attempting to discover this secret, and it may well cost us dearly. Once again, if the text simply spoke about the hippopotamus, it is impossible to make any sense of the mountains paying tribute to it. In his commentary, Rashi states that the mountains represent inanimate matter and Behemoth the power of animate matter. For Rashi, this text means that inanimate matter is subjected to animate matter. This interpretation goes back to the fourth century. In other words, we either take these verses as poetic hyperbole that has no meaning, or we accept that there must be a meaning, given that it is a revealed word. In the latter case, we are led to the interpretation that Behemoth represents the brute force of matter that may be unleashed.

Concerning the meaning of the Leviathan: I have already noted that it cannot be a crocodile. It is better interpreted in the context of a series of texts. The Leviathan was already mentioned in Job 3:8, where it refers to some kind of power that may be awakened to do terrible harm. In Psalm 104:26 we again encounter the Leviathan and, once again, it cannot be a crocodile because it lives in the sea. In Isaiah 27:1 we see the Leviathan as a monster in the sea, representing a hostile power. In fact, in the Jewish and Christian traditions the Leviathan has always been interpreted as the monster of chaos, the destructive power of evil, and the enemy of God. Of the Leviathan it is said that the pagan gods are afraid of his majesty, as the king of everything that destroys. It is the beast of the abyss.

The Leviathan designates spiritual powers and not merely material powers. To clearly see this, we must remind ourselves that we are talking about Egypt. The Hebrew word for Egypt means the land of double anguish, since for them it was the land of slavery. Moreover, the hippopotamus and the crocodile were Egyptian gods. All this represents a world which is the enemy of God and Israel and which is ruled by a king named Leviathan, according to Ezekiel. Ezekiel 29:3–6 describes the Leviathan as the king of the kingdom of slavery and hence as the power opposed to God and Israel. However, God is more powerful than this Leviathan. In Psalm 74:14 we read that God has crushed Leviathan's head and given it as nourishment to the people of the desert. The previously mentioned Jewish commentator Rashi holds that this represents the communion meal following the resurrection. At this meal, we will all eat the power of evil. All these texts converge on the Leviathan's being much more than a mere crocodile. What we have here is evil, represented by the attributes of the beast and the dragon.

It is impossible to speak directly about this evil that has entered into the world. It can only be spoken of indirectly by comparing it to the hippopotamus or the crocodile. This impossibility is somewhat similar to the well-known psychological phenomenon of not being able to re-member great pain. All that we can say later is that it hurt a great deal. You can only speak of it allegorically or symbolically, and this is also true for evil. It is possible to speak of someone who does evil or of an evil experienced by someone, but not of evil itself, except indirectly by comparing it to something, such as a hippopotamus or a crocodile. It is here, I believe, that we reach one of the high points in the book of Job. The evil in the world is not something real, a being as a phenomenon (to use a philosophical term) that can be logically defined or circum-scribed. This is what Job's friends attempted to do all along by arguing that everything was perfectly coherent and logical, and evil was this or that. However, with the appearance of these two animals it is revealed that evil exceeds this by far in its horror. It is simply horrible, and that is all we can say about it.

This brings us to what God reveals after posing Job some questions. If he stopped keeping these powers under control, everything would return to chaos and no one would be able to do anything about it. You can catch a crocodile, but nobody in the world is able to trap the Leviathan. God reveals his love by showing that he prevents the ma-terial powers of Behemoth from becoming the tyrant of creation. God prevents the domination of everything by that material power. He pre-vents the unchaining of the chaos of the Leviathan.

Hence, Job receives a kind of response. He had asked who was the cause of all this suffering and concluded that it was all God's doing. God replies to Job in the negative. It is Behemoth and Leviathan who did all this. The evil is there, Behemoth and the Leviathan are present. It is no longer a question of Satan because each one has its specialty. Satan is the accuser, who, at the beginning of this book, plays a different role. It would not help Job to tell him all about the history of Satan. It would not help him go further. What God does is show him his assail-ants, namely, Behemoth and Leviathan. They are the source of his mis-ery, but it is a misery that God holds in check. God reveals himself as the One who limits the powers of matter and prevents chaos.

Although the Leviathan is not directly referred to, Psalm 22 consti-tutes a very important text. It begins with what Jesus cries out on the cross, namely, 'My God, my God, why have you forsaken me?' In verses 12 and 13, it does not directly refer to Behemoth and Leviathan but to monsters nevertheless. 'Numerous bulls surround me, the bulls of Bashan surround me, and the lions open their mouths against me, like the lion which roars and tears its prey.' I believe that the presence of monsters in this psalm, which Jesus cites on the cross, is highly significant. Jesus is attacked by monsters and it is God who limits their powers. This is not all. For me it evokes the beast and the dragon in the book of Revelation (chapters 12, 13, and 19). The dragon in the heavens is waiting to devour the Son, and the beast rises up from the earth to dominate him. However, both the dragon and the beast are conquered and eliminated. Throughout the history of creation, God limits the extent of evil and promises us that everything will end in victory. However if this victory were a victory of God's power alone, it would be entirely foreign to us. In other words, if the story of Job ended here and we did not see in it a prophecy of Jesus Christ, then all we would have learned from this is that God is more powerful than the monsters. It would leave us entirely out of the picture. If, on the other hand, the book of Job reveals to us that the dragon and the beast are conquered in Jesus Christ, then it is the union between God and humanity that brings about this victory. In this case we are completely in the picture, and it profoundly concerns us since we participate in this victory in Jesus as a fellow human being. All this is very clear from what we are told in chapters 12 and 13 of Revelation. It is now clear that because of this, humanity may be fully consoled.

All this is in sharp contrast with what we find in the Babylonian theogonies, where human beings are the objects of a struggle between the power of good and the power of evil. However, they play no part in this whatsoever. In contrast, the beast and the dragon are conquered by a God who incarnated himself, that is, by a God who became a human being. Here we encounter the third prophecy of Jesus Christ in the book of Job. Consequently, these two chapters in Job are very important.

In response to your questions: I would like to emphasize that, although the monsters are a part of creation, nowhere in the Bible does it state that God created them, with the exception of Behemoth which, as matter, is the first of God's creations. However, when everything is reduced to matter, resulting in its domination, evil makes its appearance. Adam was created from clay and from God's spirit, but when he becomes nothing more than clay, evil appears. Chaos is not one of God's creations. However, everything is at risk of becoming chaos again. This is the reason why in Leviticus there are all these prohibitions (which to us appear to be ridiculous), against mixing things such as threads of linen and wool. The underlying idea was that if you begin to mix things, the chaos begins.

In the same vein, we have gradually discovered that it is impossible to do real justice. From our experiences with prisons we have learned that the imposition of a punishment often brings with it a much greater punishment. Hence we are caught in a dilemma from which there is no escape other than God's grace. To send someone to prison is to inflict an evil as well. It simply is impossible to consider yourself just when punishing someone who has done evil. A society has no choice but to punish someone who violates its laws, but we should have no illusions about what this means: it is a necessary evil.

The Leviathan is a power of chaos, which means that the order of the world is fragile indeed. It does not mean that God created this chaos, but that from it God draws something that is alive and livable. However, this is constantly menaced by chaos. In other words, life is a miracle, another day to live is a miracle, the world in which we live is a miracle, and so on. In a sense, this is not normal. On the one hand, God ensures that what he has created is not called into question to the extreme; and on the other hand, he asks us to live in the knowledge of this threat. Our responsibility is that everything does not become chaos once again, and this involves our freedom. Similarly, God created matter. It was the point of departure, but it would be terrible if everything were enfolded back into it. In other words, we can never content ourselves with the power of matter or with becoming clay again. We live in God's creation, which is not evil in itself but which we can make evil. Here we encounter the difficulty faced by our civilization, which is accumulating an ever greater material power thanks to *technique*, without having the spiritual maturity to go with it.

Every generation has to confront the horror of evil. For example, the Medieval civilization had its year of the plague in 1349, during which one third of Europe's population died. In Limoges there were about ten thousand inhabitants in 1347, of whom only six people survived the plague. It is impossible to imagine the mental state of these people, who saw everyone else die within a year. It is the horror of absolute evil, of the kind we have also witnessed after the dropping of the atomic bomb. The worst a generation can do when confronted with the horror of evil is to deny it or to explain it away. This was in fact the terrible error of Job's friends, who rationalized evil. The Bubonic Plague may have been taken as a sign from heaven, but this hardly detracts from the fact that the rats arrived on the trading ships of Venice and Genoa. Given that our material means are the most powerful ones in human history, it simply means that our responsibility is even greater. On another note: when, while having a discussion with Jews in Israel, I reminded some people that they were the elected people, I received the reply that if being God's people meant being persecuted and massacred for twenty centuries, then they would rather no longer be that people. This horror also must be taken very seriously.

10 Job's Conversion (Chapter 42)

Next comes the second of Job's confessions. In the first, Job appears to be beaten but not convinced. The situation is now very different. Job now recognizes that there are wonderful things that were beyond him, that he didn't know existed, and that he did not understand. He had heard God being spoken of, but it is different for him now. In other words, a change has taken place between the first confession, in which he acknowledges that God is the stronger, and the second, in which Job marvels and acknowledges that he has to repent. As Maillot[1] and others have pointed out, the reason for this change cannot be explained, as is the case for any conversion. Nevertheless, there are a number of elements in this conversion that we can probe.

Job's first confession was in response to the presentation of God's works. It is God's speaking to Job about these works and revealing the most profound mysteries of his creation that makes all the difference. What appears to convert Job is the fact that God speaks to him. Karl Barth notes that the mystery that leads Job to repent is identical to that of the revelation, that is, the election and history of Israel, the cross, and the resurrection of Jesus Christ. In other words, when God speaks, when there is his Word, all this is involved. We will see this more clearly when we examine the first two verses of the gospel of John, where we learn that the Word already was in the beginning.

Barth adds that if Job, through God's works, had not been able to contemplate that most excellent one, namely God's Word, how could we possibly understand Job's conversion, repentance, and this insight,

---

1 Alphonse Maillot, *Pour rien ... Prédications sur le livre de Job* (Lyon: Cahiers de Réveil et Éditions SNPP, 1966).

which he did not discover by himself and which his friends did not help him find? What Barth means is that when God speaks, he speaks of the totality of his revelation and that, as a result, this Word places us within the totality of the history of salvation. I believe this is fundamental when we read any text in the Bible and meditate on it together.

When Job hears this Word which contains everything, he recognizes that we cannot know anything about God. We cannot have any idea of God, nor a true philosophy or theology. Job recognizes that it is not sufficient to have heard others speak of God. A person can participate in studying certain texts, engage in philosophy or theology, and even if all this is true for that person, what people say is of no value unless God himself intervenes. To bring about a conversion, God must himself descend to us in order to reveal himself. Nothing happens without such a personal encounter. Following it, Job declares that now he sees God with his own eyes. This is rather astounding since no one has ever seen God. For example, we are told that on Mount Sinai God spoke to Moses as to a friend, and yet between them was the cloud that hid everything. When Moses asks God at their second meeting whether he can see him, God replies that this is impossible. However, he will put Moses into the cleft of a rock and shield him with his hand until he has passed by. When Elijah speaks with God at the cave, he wraps his cloak over his face so as not to see him!

What Job has seen is the reflection of God in his works. Now, there is a direct relationship with God, as opposed to Job having heard others speak of him. There is now a true and personal knowledge, but it means much more. The Bible opposes hearing and seeing.[2] Seeing refers to the end of time, when we will truly see because reality and truth will be reunited. In the Bible, sight gives us access to reality while hearing gives us access to the truth born of God's Word. In our world, reality and truth cannot be reconciled. These two domains are distinct, and we must take care not to confuse them. In science we often take reality for truth, but science only gives access to real phenomena. The same confusion reigns in daily life when we ask a child to tell us the truth. What we really want to know is what the child has done, which regards reality and not truth. Only the word belongs to the domain of truth, and the opposite of this truth is the lie. The only time reality and truth came together in our world was in Jesus Christ. In the incarnation the Word

---

2 Jacques Ellul, *The Humiliation of the Word*, trans. J.M. Hanks (Grand Rapids, MI: Eerdmans, 1985).

becomes flesh, and that is why the gospel of John as well as the epistles of John insist on people having seen that Word. It is the only time that the truth has been seen in reality. At any other time, a reference to seeing is always eschatological in character, pointing to the end of time. For example, when Ezekiel sees God with the seraphim, the wheels, and the earthquakes, he sees a vision of the end of time. When the Apocalypse speaks of what John sees, it refers again to the end of time. Seeing God is always related to the end, and places us in the dimension of the last judgment and the resurrection. This is the significance of the reference to seeing in Job 42 as well.

When Job gains a knowledge of the Word and the revelation of God, he repents and humbles himself, which until now he had refused to do. Moreover, he begins to understand that it is impossible to receive the revelation without repentance. There are many examples of this in the Bible. When John tells the story of the disciples arriving at the empty tomb, he notes that the first one bowed. This was not simply a question of stooping to get into the tomb but of humbling oneself before God's truth. When Job learns of how God, in his love for him, protected him from Behemoth and Leviathan, he discovers his own guilt. The text explains the precise nature of this guilt. Job recants and relents, and repents of having attempted to uncover the mystery of God on his own by endlessly asking why God did this or that. Job had demanded that God explain his motives. We all constantly seek to understand God's reasons, and we all find it difficult to accept the definition Kierkegaard gave of God, which is that he is the One who is not conditioned. What Kierkegaard means is that God is not conditioned by anything – he is who he is. We find this next to impossible to accept.

There is more. Seeking to penetrate God's will exactly constitutes the temptation Jesus encountered. The devil constantly suggests that Jesus unveil God's truth: 'If you are the son of God, why not do this or that?' Jesus always responds with, 'It is written.' Jesus refuses to penetrate the will of his Father by asking him to account for it, but restricts himself to what has been written. What this means is further clarified by what Jesus does when people ask him for a miracle. He replies that no other miracle than that of Jonah will be given: either you believe what is written regarding the miracle of Jonah, or you do not believe it. In the latter case, I could perform any miracle you ask, but your belief would not be any greater than it is now. For the same reason, Jesus never asks his Father any questions, except on the cross. He obeys without questioning. On the cross Jesus asks why his Father has abandoned him, but we must remember he is simply citing what is written in Psalm 22. Having said this Word, Jesus could say that everything had been accomplished, including asking this question. Jesus then places his spirit in God's hands – and here we are back to Job. Job understands, humbles himself, and puts himself in God's hands.

The Targum makes two remarkable observations regarding the sixth verse of chapter 42: 'I recant and relent ...' This Hebrew interpretation implies that it is not a question of Job condemning himself but, in a sense, of condemning what he has. Hence, the Targum observes that Job condemns all his riches. Of course, I recognize that this is but one interpretation of what is next to impossible to translate. The Targum also concludes that Job repents on the dust and ashes of his children, which means that he consoles himself about his dead children (who are now only dust and ashes). This is arrived at after five pages of commentary, showing the seriousness and depth of Job's repentance. Job has forgotten nothing of what he has lost, but he rejects his riches and consoles himself about his children. As an interpretation, it has the merit of making everything Job has lost reappear. Even though he has new sons and daughters, his earlier children are dead. According to this interpretation of the Targum, it is because Job has seen God that he can say he is consoled about his children. This interpretation is a good example of the Hebrew style which is extremely thorough, examining every detail (including each letter) right up to the grammatical structure of the text.

In response to your questions: The great miracle of Elijah in confronting the prophets of Baal did not convince anyone either. It failed to convince the Jewish people. It is true that miracles accompany the Word of God (as we see in the Acts of the Apostles) as a manifestation of the power of the Holy Spirit, but the miracle by itself has no value or meaning. Jesus performs a miracle because he is moved with compassion toward a particular person he encounters.

Those who bring God's Word have an important role to play in human history. If they do not announce God's grace and pardon, people will not know there is a God who pardons and extends grace. It is for this reason that God selects a number of witnesses, a people, and a church – so that there is a mediation between God and all people who search and ask questions. Hence, I believe the important question is not whether I have faith or not but whether I have received a Word, and whether this has created something new in my life. However, when

God does not reveal himself, it is a human greatness and privilege to be able to question him. What we have learned is that at no point is Job condemned for questioning God. As we shall see, Job's friends are condemned for claiming to have answers to all Job's questions.

11   Reconciliation (Chapter 42)

We now come to the last section, which is in prose. It contains God's reply, followed by an account of what happens next. We immediately encounter God's anger against Job's friends, who are rejected for not having spoken the truth. I think that the reason they have not spoken the truth is that they claimed to have answers to Job's questions. They thought they could explain the mystery of God's will. Biblically speaking, one is better off to ask questions than to provide answers. The Bible is there to question us and not to provide answers and security. For example, in Ecclesiastes we read that the writer found nothing to make his wisdom worthwhile. It did him no good in the end. Luther put it well when he said that we make God unjust when we claim to be able to explain his justice with our own concepts of justice. In other words, the more we explain justice the more we obscure it. This is exactly what Job's friends were doing.

However, it is not simply the question of having claimed to possess the mystery of God. What is even more important is that the friends fail to bear witness to God's love. If God is love they have not spoken of him in truth, worse, they have told lies about him. They condemned Job who, in the end, was not condemned by God. I believe there is an important lesson here when we engage in scientific thinking without love. All this begs the question: Why did Job speak the truth? To begin with, Job was a prophet who, in his own life and suffering, announced the presence of Jesus Christ. Moreover, Job was entirely honest and in his heart not divided. To use a modern term, Job was authentic. He spoke what he lived. He knew that only God could answer him and that he was the Living One. In other words, Job did not trap God in theological, philosophical, or moral categories. Nor did he make God into an idea, a concept, or a theory. Job recognized that his relationship with God was one that is lived.

The judgment pronounced by God against Job's friends raises a question that concerns all Christians, namely, that of being right or wrong. In biblical thinking, no person is ever right. It is essential to remember this in any church affair. It is simply impossible for us to say that we are right and the others are wrong, the reason being that everything ought to be done in the context of a relationship of love with God and our neighbour. Hence, it is impossible to be right against someone else. If I am right in opposition to someone else, I do not love him or her. If I say the other is wrong, I do not love that person. We have here the exact opposite of all non-Christian wisdom, well summed up by the beautiful Latin expression: Cato is my friend, but the truth is even more so. For Christians it is the exact opposite: I love the truth, but love for others is more important. I must love the other more than truth. Or, to put it more accurately, I should know that there is no truth if there is no love of God and the other. Hence, there can be no question of being right or wrong with regard to one's neighbour.

God makes Job the mediator and intercessor. The friends have to go to Job, who is to offer a sacrifice on their behalf; and Job, as God's servant, is to intercede for them. Job has to pardon these friends for having been the Devil to him by attempting to separate him from God. In this, they have greatly added to his suffering. Hence, it is indispensable that Job forgives them just as he has been forgiven. It is the consequence for others of Job having been forgiven by God. For this Job is called God's servant, which is very important because it means that he bears God's will on earth. Job is the image of the suffering servant in Isaiah.

The friends must offer a sacrifice of seven bulls and seven rams. It is a sacrifice that we encounter several times in the Bible, such as the great sacrifice of the restoration of the Passover in Ezekiel. When the Jewish people were dispersed, Passover was no longer celebrated. When the people returned to their land, the Passover feast was restored in Jerusalem, with the same sacrifice. There can be no coincidence about this. Job is present at this sacrifice as a priest, and it is in Job's name that God forgives the friends. The text is very specific on this point. God then answers Job's prayer for his friends. Here again we have the image of Jesus Christ as the suffering servant, the intercessor, and the priest who offers the sacrifice.

This brings us to what happens at the end. I believe this ending must be read symbolically and, in any case, I have been unable to find any other satisfactory explanations. For example, Steinmann,[1] who I have frequently criticized, explains that people come to the rescue in anticipation of Job's future riches. I think this completely misses the point of this whole text. Even Roland de Pury,[2] whose commentary I appreciate, finds himself in a very awkward situation because all along he has argued that the book of Job is all about serving God for nothing. Then, in the end, he has to deal with the fact that Job (who served God for nothing) now receives everything again. He tries to extricate himself by concluding that once Job's testing is over, God has the right to once more shower Job with blessings. I would hardly want to argue that God does not have the right to reward those who love and follow him, but I find this a highly unsatisfactory and weak conclusion. The reason is obvious. This was exactly the thesis of Job's friends, which they kept telling him: repent and everything will be well.

I believe we need to interpret the end symbolically. Particular attention must be paid to verse 10, which appears to allude to the last judgment and the resurrection. In fact, the Hebrew text is very complex and almost untranslatable. It literally says that Yahweh gathers what ceased to be of Job. To make good English out of this loses the meaning. The text appears to refer to a passing through death and a re-creation. This is confirmed by the Talmud, which concludes that this ending of the book of Job occurs after his death. Hence, for the Talmud it is about the resurrection. For St Jerome and St Augustine it meant exactly the same thing: it is after his death that Job is showered with God's gifts. For St Jerome in particular, because he worked directly from the Hebrew text, it is entirely possible that he took this verse as dealing with the resurrection itself. In other words, a number of traditions have interpreted the ending of the

---

1 Jean Steinmann, *Le livre de Job* (Paris: Éditions du Cerf, 1955).

2 Roland de Pury, *Hiob, der Mensch in Aufruhr*, 1957. Barth records a very interesting passage from this commentary: 'The remarkable thing about this book (Job) is that Job makes not a single step of flight to a better God, but stays absolutely on the field of battle under the fire of the divine wrath. Although God treats him as an enemy, through the dark night and the abyss, Job does not falter, nor invoke another court, nor even appeal to the God of his friends, but calls upon this God who crushes him. He flees to the God whom he accuses. He sets his confidence in God who has disillusioned him and reduced him to despair ... Without deviating from the violent assertion of his innocence and God's hostility, he confesses his hope, taking as his Defender the One who judges him, as his Liberator the One who throws him in prison, and his Friend his mortal enemy.' (Karl Barth, *Church Dogmatics*, vol. 4, part 3, first half [Edinburgh: T. & T. Clark, 1961], 424).

book of Job, not as one of material success as it were, but as an announcement of the resurrection.

In the same vein, we have already noted that Job's friends offer the sacrifice of the reinstatement of the Passover, and hence the sacrifice of the resurrection. Of course, all these are interpretations, and there is no guarantee that this is exactly what the text says. However, we are probably on the right track.

Another aspect of this idea of the resurrection is forgiveness. When God forgives everyone, a reconciliation is achieved. It is the reconciliation between Job and his friends, between Job and God, and between God and the friends. When this happens the resurrection is a certainty because it is a reconciliation of God with everyone, and of everyone with everyone else. Hence, what is created as it were and given to Job (the camels, sheep, and so on) is not a reward but a sign of the resurrection and of plenitude.

This is not all. The pardon has another dimension that is rarely considered and which we find difficult to accept. Job has pardoned God. He has endlessly complained that it was God who sent everything that made him suffer. When Job bows before God, repents, and stops his protests, he has in effect forgiven God. I believe this is a fundamental part of our relationship with God. We always expect forgiveness from God, but God in his weakness (of the incarnation) also awaits our love for nothing, that is, our forgiveness. Even when we think God is unjust, even when we think he persecutes us, it is all the more important that he awaits our forgiveness and our justification of him. In other words, God is right because of Job. It is hard to believe that we can contribute to God's being right. However, there was that wager between God and Satan, and whether God was right or wrong depended on Job. It is in this sense that Job justified God.

The last sign of this complete union is that everyone comes to eat bread in Job's house. This succeeds the Passover sacrifice and is clearly the meal of communion.

What remain are simply some purely symbolic signs of the benediction, namely, the sons, daughters, and livestock. Of particular interest are the names of the three daughters: Jemimah, which means dove, Keziah, which means camphor, and Keren-happuch, which may be translated in two different ways. It could mean a stick of makeup (kohl) but it could also mean a sparkle from a carbuncle (a bright red gem). Almost everyone agrees that these names are symbolic. For de Pury, the dove obviously represents God's spirit, camphor is a perfume that symbolizes the prayers of the saints, and the stick of kohl, as found in the Song of Songs, symbolizes the finery worn by the bride awaiting her groom. For the Talmud the meanings are not exactly the same. The dove is the sign of reconciliation based on the dove in Noah's ark. The camphor is related to Psalm 45, which speaks of a perfume exclusively used during specific services and which is consecrated by God himself. It is the perfume of perfumes. For the third name, the Talmud chooses the second translation, the sparkle from a carbuncle, which is the light of Egypt. Whatever the differences, all these interpretations of the names refer to God, as images of the Divinity.

The daughters receive their share of the inheritance, which for that time and culture was unthinkable if not downright scandalous. It means that the woman will be restored to her full place in the new creation and God's truth. I believe this is absolutely fundamental, because this place is of the utmost importance. I have never been able to understand how, over the ages, people have been able to draw from the Bible a theology that is anti-feminine. It is undoubtedly the result of reading the Bible through cultural frameworks that were anti-feminine.

Job lives 140 years, which is 7 plus 7 multiplied by 10. The number 7 is the number of fullness which is added to fullness and taken to the absolute, as indicated by multiplying by 10. It should be remembered that numbers in the Bible are always symbolic. Job has 4 generations of descendents, and 4 is the number of creation. Job is present in the whole of creation, which he sees in the four generations that descend from him.

Finally, we see Job clothed in God's light, and the completion of God's works in their fullness. We have also seen Job gradually appearing as mediator, servant, and intercessor, hence it is a prophecy of the Messiah. This ending of the book reveals Job as an image of the Messiah who is to come.

In concluding this study of the book of Job, I would like to add that this book ultimately guides us toward taking a different perspective. If we see God and this world with our own intelligence, we only see scandal, absurdity, incomprehensibility, and so on. Job's entire life story shows that we must change the way we look at things and recognize the mysterious presence of God in our lives and in our world. The mystery stems from God being, at the same time, the One who is all-powerful and the One who does not take advantage of this power. It is not simply a question of God not using his power with regard to Job, but neither does he do so in regard to the powers of evil, including the Behemoth and the Leviathan. He only restricts them but never uses the totality of his power. Instead, God waits for Job to justify and pardon him. I believe this is fundamental for our faith.

In response to your questions: I would like to add that the Bible has always been a book of questions and not one that provides pseudo-answers to help us feel secure. Throughout the ages, orthodoxies have tended to transform this Bible into security blankets of one kind or another. For example, in the Protestant tradition the theology of Karl Barth was transformed from one that constantly questioned into its opposite: a closed system that could explain everything. It is these kinds of transformations that I consider the most scandalous within Christianity. A faith in a God who humbles himself and even allows himself to be crucified is transformed into a kind of armour against others, if not a means for crushing them. It is the most dreadful way of turning things inside out and upside down.

PART THREE

The Culmination of Judaism:
The Kingdom of Love

Those who knew the law and the prophets lacked one dimension, namely, a teaching of the kingdom of heaven. This kingdom was not announced in what we call the Old Testament, but revealed through the orientation and teachings of Jesus. What had been announced was the triumph of the kingship of David on this earth and, for the sects who believed in it, the kingdom of God to be established at the end of time. What Jesus revealed in his teaching was the kingdom of heaven hidden in the world. It was entirely absent in the Jewish perspective on kingship up to that point, but it nevertheless completed what the Jews already knew. What we learn is that the kingdom of heaven appears on the earth with Jesus. As we will see later, the kingdom of heaven is there for the king and does not exist until he is born. Everything the Jews knew as Word and doctrine is now being realized, but in a way that is hidden. The kingship of David that would be triumphant is now in the world, but it is not apparent. Also, the kingdom of God that would come at the end of time has now come, but as the hidden kingdom of heaven. In other words, the two dimensions of kingship and the kingdom that we find in the Old Testament are being realized through the presence of Jesus. The kingdom of God remains eschatological, but there is now a hidden presence. The kingship of David triumphs through the service of the Son of God. This accomplishment permitted the authors of these texts to rediscover the treasure, which is the love of God, thanks to what they already knew from the prophets regarding the double royalty and from the kingdom of heaven fulfilling these prophecies. What had been announced was now fulfilled.

This message confronts a fundamental misunderstanding. The laws were never intended to dictate and impose a certain behaviour. Instead, the laws had a double dimension. They traced the limits of life and death, thereby serving as a warning: if you are within the law, you are alive, and if you transgress, you will die. The laws also indicated a separation which is of the order of holiness. I am referring to all the laws, including the Decalogue as well as the Sermon on the Mount. People and their lives were set apart by God as a holiness: to live in love within these laws. In other words, the laws were never meant to be executed point by point and letter by letter, which leads to all kinds of insoluble problems such as whether telephoning on the Sabbath is lawful. When people begin to go down this road there is no escape, as is evident from a whole moral and theological interpretation within Judaism. What the parables of the kingdom of heaven teach us is to get away from the endless interpreting and reinterpreting of the laws in order to rediscover the intended orientation of love.

The Kingdom of Heaven and the Kingdom of God

A distinction must be made between the kingdom of heaven and the kingdom of God. Only the gospel of Matthew speaks of the kingdom of heaven. The gospels of Mark and Luke essentially only speak of the kingdom of God. This must not be taken as an opposition between these gospels. The gospel of Matthew also speaks of the kingdom of God, but when it does it is not by means of parables. This is crucial. For example, the Sermon on the Mount speaks of first seeking the kingdom and justice of God and everything else will be granted. There are several texts of this kind in Matthew, but they are never embedded in the parables. In these parables it is always a question of the kingdom of heaven.

In the gospels of Mark and Luke we find parables referring to the kingdom of God, but the equivalent text in the gospel of Matthew refers to the kingdom of heaven. For example, in Mark 10:15 we read that whoever does not receive the kingdom of God like a child will not enter it. Almost the same phrase is found in Matthew 18:3: unless we become like children we will never enter the kingdom of heaven. When we do encounter the kingdom of God, whether in Matthew, Mark, or Luke, it is always related to the end of the world, the return of Jesus Christ, or the last judgment, and always has a 'final' dimension. In contrast, the kingdom of heaven is always related to the present.

Both the kingdom of God and the kingdom of heaven affirm that God is the king. Nevertheless, there is a distinction. In the one case, it is the kingship of the Creator and the Father which affirms itself from heaven on high and is associated with eternity, the beginning and the end. The kingdom of heaven is the kingdom of the Son who incarnated himself and came to us on earth, where his kingdom is now present.

It is helpful to recall that in our study of Genesis, the heavens referred to the abode of God, who is the entirely Other and absolutely different from us. We also learned that the heavens are separated from the earth and that there cannot be any permanent contact or relationship between them, except through an occasional mediation by an angel. What is radically new with Jesus is that the heavens are now present in this world. This is what the term 'kingdom of heaven' means. What was absolutely other and beyond is now present in this world, and he who is at the centre of this different world is regarded as a king. This kingdom of heaven is associated with the duration of the presence of its king on earth and with the period between his ascension and his return, thus giving it a temporal character. A number of texts imply that this kingdom of heaven belongs to a time in history, and that it will be transformed into the kingdom of God at the end of time.

The kingship of Christ is founded on a past victory over the powers and principalities, as explained in the epistle to the Colossians. In chapter 1:13 we read that God has delivered us from the dominion of darkness and transferred us to the kingdom of his beloved Son. This revelation of an act in the past, which makes it possible for us to be in the kingdom of his Son, raises many difficulties similar to those encountered with the incarnation. What is meant by the heavens being present on earth? What is this truth hidden within reality? Why do we endlessly confuse the reality that we can see with what can only be discerned through faith? What, for example, is the relationship between the kingdom of heaven and the church? These kinds of problems will surface soon enough when we begin to work through a few of the obvious distinctions between the kingdom of God and the kingdom of heaven, which may be expressed as follows. The kingdom of God is of the order of what is promised and its fulfilment. It is thus proclaimed and is the subject of the good news. The kingdom of heaven, on the other hand, exists in the present and is of the order of service, involvement, responsibility, and hope. All this represents two very different dimensions of the Christian life.

Although the kingdom of heaven present during this period of history becomes the kingdom of God, we cannot interpret the one following the other as a succession in time. It is not linear and there is no 'before' and 'after.' We are confronting the same difficulty when we attempt to understand the relationship between time and eternity. It is impossible to consider the latter as 'after' when we speak of the Eternal One. It is impossible to think of this as a kind of passing from the past to a future because the movement is in the opposite direction. When certain texts tell us that the kingdom is coming or that Christ is coming, we must recognize that they are coming from the future and moving toward the present. The movement is opposite to the one we regard ourselves as being engaged in, that is, we are not moving from our present situation toward the one where we enter the kingdom of God. On the contrary: the kingdom of God comes toward our present; it is the one that is coming to us and not we that are coming to the kingdom. We might say that the kingdom of heaven is this movement of the kingdom of God toward us. It is very difficult for us to think this way because we are so used to living each year as a step closer to the end of time and hence to the kingdom of God. Nevertheless, from a biblical perspective the presence of the kingdom of heaven is the presence of the kingdom of God that has already been established and which is coming into our time, and thus the end of time is already present. If this were not complicated enough, we are only at the very beginning of understanding the relationship between the kingdom of God and the kingdom of heaven.

I would like to introduce another question. Why it is only the gospel of Matthew that speaks of the kingdom of heaven, and why does it only speak of it in parables? From an exegetical perspective, the distinction between the kingdom of God and the kingdom of heaven can be explained. Among the three synoptic gospels, Matthew is regarded as having been written last and thus had as sources the other two gospels as well as other documents. It has become widely accepted that some texts may have been reinterpreted because of the unexpected delay in the return of Jesus Christ. Some exegetes even suggest that Jesus contributed to this problem by believing that the end of time would come very quickly, and he may have passed this on to his disciples and followers. This plunged the early church community into a crisis because human history continued longer than expected. This delay appeared to make little sense because Jesus himself had said that the end of time is here, and that in him everything had been accomplished. According to this explanation, a number of earlier texts were reinterpreted and rewritten in order to explain the situation. As usual, many historians regard these texts as little more than justifications and hence of little value: the poor early Christians were frustrated because they didn't see the end of the world, and so they set out to explain it as a kind of psychological adaptation to the situation. If this were true, then the gospels of Mark and Luke speak only of the kingdom of God as the final kingdom because it would come almost immediately. By the time the gospel of Matthew was being written the kingdom still had not come, and attention was thus paid to certain affirmations of Jesus that the kingdom of God is among you and that he did know the hour of his return. Matthew had to face the possibility of a difference between an enduring presence that clearly was not the kingdom of God in all its fullness and what was still to come. From this situation, the notion of a kingdom of heaven was born.

If we are willing to accept that this is possibly what happened (personally, this would not upset me because it cannot be ruled out), the real question is: Is it a problem that certain texts are not 'original'? From the perspective of faith, I would say that everything that the gospel of Matthew reveals regarding the kingdom of heaven is rigorously and astonishingly in conformation with the Old Testament. What we find in the parables about the kingdom of heaven is the same interpretation, perspective, and understanding of, for example, the actions of God in history; and we will see this when we study the texts. Hence, these parables are not 'gratuitous' to explain a problematic situation because, whatever explanation of their origin we may prefer, these texts remain exactly in line with the revelation of the Old Testament and hence conform to its fulfilment in Jesus Christ. This is the first observation I would like to make. I believe it will be borne out when we examine these texts in some detail. The second remark that I would like to make is that, as a believer, I accept that the Holy Spirit is at work (which does not mean at all that the Holy Spirit literally dictates the texts), and that this Spirit conducts us in the whole truth, as promised in the gospel of John. If the entire truth is in Jesus Christ, then we certainly will not know it in an instant with one stroke.

I believe that we should interpret the whole situation as follows. By the delay in the return of Jesus Christ, God questions those who believe. It is part of what God calls the testing of our faith. It is our responsibility to respond to this questioning and testing. When we are confronted with this situation, we must not expect that God will immediately furnish us with an answer. It is our responsibility to respond, and that was equally true for the first generation of Christians, including the apostles. Their responses to many challenges are found in these parables of the kingdom of heaven.

I began by examining some of the differences between the gospel of Matthew and the other gospels to introduce the distinction between the kingdom of God and the kingdom of heaven. Next, I examined the relationship between the two kingdoms. My third set of introductory remarks relates to the kingdom of heaven not being characterized by an organization, nor by the establishment of limits or boundaries. What first and foremost characterizes the kingdom of heaven is the presence of its king. In conformity with the Old Testament, there is no question of the existence of a kingdom independent from the king. It is because Jesus Christ is revealed as a king that the kingdom exists. Where he is, there we find the kingdom and nowhere else. It is made up of people who follow Jesus Christ.

Jesus' presence raises other questions. Just as he remains hidden in the incarnation, so also his kingdom adopts the same kind of presence. Here, once more, we are confronted with many difficulties not unlike the ones mentioned above. The one we will constantly encounter is the relation and opposition between this kingdom of heaven and the church. There is opposition because the kingdom of heaven has no institutional character, and neither claims nor exercises any power whatsoever. As far as the relationship between the kingdom of heaven and the church is concerned, I believe that the relationship is between this kingdom and the body of believers because the latter cannot be equated with the church. Just like the kingdom of heaven, the body of Christ (which is made up of all believers) is a way of his being present, as Christ was once present on the earth. This kingdom as the body of Christ is a hidden affirmation of his lordship. For the members of this body it implies a responsibility and a role to be played in it. This responsibility is very well explained by Paul.

There is never any question of limiting the membership in this body in the way an institution separates members from non-members. It is always a question of being present in the world the way Jesus Christ was present; and this takes us back to the many difficult issues that confront us when we seek to understand the incarnation of the king, which have a direct bearing on our understanding of the presence of his body of believers.

Finally, when continuing our study of the parables of the kingdom of heaven, we will encounter the following characteristics. First, the kingdom of heaven is a force in action. It is certainly not a place or some kind of territory where you can establish yourself.

A second characteristic of the kingdom of heaven, which we have already noted, is that it is a hidden power, thus implying a kind of weakness. A third characteristic is its being a combination of the actions of God and the actions of people. However, this combination is extremely complex: it is not simply a cooperation between the two parties; it is not the sum or combination of their actions; it is not a use God makes of human actions or anything like these. It is a coming together of the actions of God and the actions of people in a manner that is clearly explained in the parables. A fourth characteristic of the kingdom of heaven is the relationship it establishes between justice and love; and we will see that this raises some rather fundamental questions. A fifth characteristic (and this is possibly the most astonishing of these parables) is that its 'laws' are diametrically opposed to the laws of the world. These characteristics summarize what I believe are the most important themes of these parables, but there are certainly others as well.

To reply to some of your questions: I will briefly revisit the impossibility of a dualism. The Bible is not dualistic. For example, it does not present us with a neutral world as a kind of stage on which the powers of good and evil do battle. I would say that such an interpretation is entirely anti-biblical. We are not presented with a world (neutral or sacred) but with a history. This history is made up of an ensemble of forces that interact with each other, and among them we find the force in action of the kingdom of heaven as the body of Christ, that is, the Word of God borne by people. It is not independent from all the other forces. This kingdom has meaning only if it is present in the world, relates to the history of the world, and helps make that history along with the other forces. It would be a mistake to think that on the one hand there are the communists who make history and build the secular city, and on the other, we are in the kingdom of heaven. It would be equally wrong to believe the reverse: that we as Christians make history and that the rest has to do with the kingdom of this world, which will pass away and of which nothing will be left. What the Bible reveals is a history as an interplay of elements brought by people, including the power associated with the bearing of the kingdom of heaven. This element is hidden and unknown to others, but it is nevertheless essential for the whole ensemble to function. This is very clear from the parable of the yeast and the dough: without the dough, the yeast has no function whatsoever. It goes without saying that the church is one of the human components of this history.

In that history there are also forces that can be discerned only by faith. They cannot be accounted for or grasped in the ways we deal with reality. These are of the order of truth, but this does not mean that they can be dissociated from the rest.[1] Attempting to do so is as vain as seeking to determine what in Jesus is human and what is divine. Centuries of debate over this question have led nowhere because the very question was ill-conceived.

One of God's actions in this history is the election of certain people, but this is not an election to salvation or damnation but to carry out a particular mission. In other words, this election is a point of departure – it puts someone 'with their back to the wall' to take charge of something of the kingdom of heaven since no one else will take care of it.[2] It is essential to recognize that a Christian is not someone who is privileged above others by reason of being saved, being better than others, or for some similar reason. A Christian is simply someone who is charged by God to perform a particular function and role, and that is the only thing that distinguishes him or her from others. Christians do not have an advantage over others. In fact, because they have been given something, much more will be demanded of them; and that is why the judgment begins with the church.

The Kingdom of Heaven as Mystery

The fact that Jesus speaks of the kingdom of heaven exclusively through parables is important for the interpretation of these texts. When instead he speaks of the kingdom of God, he does not speak of it in terms of parables, but does so quite openly. To return to our earlier example of Matthew 6:33, where we are told to first seek the kingdom and the justice of God, there is no parable. Similarly, in Matthew 19:24, there is no parable either when Jesus speaks of it being easier for a camel to pass through the eye of a needle than for a rich man to enter the kingdom of God. I think that the reason why Jesus speaks openly of the kingdom of God is because there is nothing to know about this kingdom other than that we await its coming. It is simply of the order of what is promised and what will be fulfilled. No description is ever given of the kingdom of God or of paradise. All we need to know is that it is God being 'all in all.'

---

1 Jacques Ellul has dealt with the complex relationships between reality and truth in his book *The Humiliation of the Word*, trans. Joyce Main Hanks (Grand Rapids, MI: Eerdmans, 1985).
2 Jacques Ellul experienced such an election in his own life resulting from an intervention of God. He wrote a book about it, which he destroyed prior to his death.

In contrast, the kingdom of heaven is the kingdom of Jesus in the present – one in which we are called to participate. Doing so means living according to this kingdom, and that means we had better know something about it. The trouble is that we cannot know it directly, since the texts about this kingdom tell us several times that it is a mystery. When the disciples ask Jesus why he is using parables to speak to the people, he answers that it is given to them to know the mystery of the kingdom of heaven. Revealing it as a mystery makes it impossible to speak of it directly. This has nothing to do with Christians having been reproached (quite justly) that every time they could not explain something they called it a mystery. In the Bible something is a mystery only when it cannot be explained rationally in a direct manner. It means that there are other ways to search for understanding and to attempt to know everything that can be said about it. We encounter such attempts in mythical thinking, which deals with things that are extremely fundamental to human life even though they cannot be grasped rationally. In other words, mythical thinking always expresses a mystery that cannot be the subject of a systematic teaching. It nevertheless transmits a knowledge of a certain kind via the intermediary, for example, of a parable involving some kind of comparison.

We cannot treat these parables as some kind of enigma that can be decrypted by finding the hidden meaning of each word. Many commentators have pointed out that the story of a parable makes a single point, and in this sense has the single objective of revealing one truth. This has important exegetical implications: a parable does not describe a certain reality and it does not teach a moral lesson. For example, it is almost exclusively in the parables that we encounter a hell, but none of them involve a teaching about it. Nevertheless, some exegetes have deduced from this the objective existence of a real hell, even though not a single parable has anything to do with this hell and each one is meant to reveal something entirely different. It would appear, therefore, that to read into any of these parables a teaching about hell is simply to miss the point it seeks to make.

It is equally impossible to interpret a parable as if it were an allegory. In an allegory, every word or term corresponds to something else from which comes its meaning. Some church fathers have attempted to interpret the parables in this way, which results in a complete distortion of these texts. Ultimately, they can be made to say almost anything.

By stressing that the parables have a clear story with a single point, we must not overlook the fact that collectively they have an overall significance. They are not simply beautiful poetic images which Jesus chose for their pedagogical value, but they reveal something very fundamental about how this revelation proceeds. It does so by simultaneously unveiling (revealing) and veiling; and this interplay is at the centre of the flow and development of these parables. In fact, the entire revelation regarding God involves an unveiling and veiling, in the following sense. People by their own means form an image of God. There have been hundreds of these images, and they are all false ones. After all, if God is God then human beings cannot understand or take hold of him by any or all means at their disposal, even though we are convinced it is entirely within our grasp. However, what we grasp are simply our own ideas of God and nothing else. The Bible tells us that when God reveals himself to us, he shows himself as the unknowable One, beginning with his name, which no one can pronounce. We learn that we cannot grasp or know him in any way. Consequently the only possible relationship with God is one of faith, trust, and love. Recall that when God finally reveals himself, Job responds that he thought he knew, but now he recognizes that he was mistaken. Here we see clearly that what God reveals of himself to us is that he is a hidden God. We constantly think that with our intellectual means we are able to explain God, but we cease to think this the moment we encounter the true revelation of the hidden God. We learn that he and his revelation are inexpressible. A distance is thus created between the biblical texts and the revelation we may receive from them. When we read these texts, analyse them, and understand them, we have not necessarily created a revelation. When it does become a revelation for us, we cannot explain what happened. All we can do is bear witness to this and invite others to 'come and see' (John 1:46).

With regard to the parables, all we can intellectually accomplish is to construct what has been referred to as a negative theology. This means that all we can intellectually discern is what God is not. The only other theology is that of God revealing himself in Jesus Christ as relived through the witness of the apostles, and this includes the parables. Human beings by themselves cannot understand this revelation. The parables reveal at the same time as they veil, and they veil as they reveal. When a parable reveals something it does so within an account which, if we are not fully committed to Jesus who speaks, it may fascinate us but it will also turn us off. For example, some exegetes were excited by the many possible allegorical interpretations of the parables, but in the end the results were void of meaning. Others have been interested in their social and political implications, with similar disappointing results. To me all this suggests the process of veiling and unveiling. Only by faith can the mystery of the kingdom of heaven be heard and believed.

Does this mean that expressing the kingdom of heaven by means of parables amounts to an injustice? I believe the opposite is the case, in the sense that it represents a kind of safeguard. The parable only speaks to faith. When this Word is received in faith, it becomes a living truth. It is important for people who do not live by faith to be unable to understand this Word, an understanding which would make it impossible for them to refuse this invitation to participate in the kingdom of heaven. The parables protect them from this danger. I believe this is the crucial point. Once again, this has nothing to do with the fact that there are those who are privileged and those who will be left out. There are those who listen in faith, who receive this Word, and who participate in the kingdom of heaven. For everyone else this message would be dangerous because it might put before them an impossible choice: whether or not to enter. It is a choice God never demands of anyone. God loves us too much to put anyone in such a situation. Hence, I believe that parables are the only means for dealing with the need to simultaneously reveal (unveil) and to mercifully veil the message, in order to prevent people from refusing a revelation. These parables teach us that the kingdom of heaven works on behalf of everyone, but only a few know that this is the case because they have been called for service. It is part of a situation in which God's Word creates something new and where he leaves his creatures some autonomy because of his love for them.

There is, of course, much more that can be said about these parables of the kingdom of heaven. I have limited myself to what I believe to be the most essential questions.

13 The First Three Parables
(Matthew 13:1–43)

The parables of the kingdom of heaven are often arranged in pairs. The first pair likens the kingdom of heaven to a man sowing good seed and to a grain of mustard seed. It is followed by a third parable comparing the kingdom of heaven to yeast. It will become evident that the third parable is joined to the second, since they both compare the kingdom to a thing. Each pair presents us with an act of God along with another form of action, which appears to signify a correlation between the actions of God and those of human beings. The kingdom of heaven is where the king and the people meet, where the actions of God interpenetrate with those of human beings, and where the latter extend the former.

Beginning with the first parable, we encounter two separate texts: the first is the parable itself (verses 3–9), and then in verse 18 begins what appears to be an explanation. It is this explanation that presents us with several difficulties. First, it is allegorical in form: he who sows the good seed is the Son of man, the field is the world, the good seed is the children of the kingdom, the enemy is the devil, and so on. I have already noted that this explanatory approach was used by some of the church fathers and others to find similar correspondences. I have also noted that many believe that this is not a good approach to interpreting the parables because each one focuses on a specific teaching and not on a kind of general panorama of the world (such as the allegorical explanation found in the text). In fact, when we compare this explanation with the parable itself, it does not correspond very well. The parable teaches about the kingdom of heaven, whereas the explanation warns against hasty judgments and tells us to let things be until the last judgment. The parable has to do with the kingdom of heaven, and not with the final judgment of which the explanation speaks so much. For these reasons some believe that the allegorical explanation, instead of coming from Jesus, represents a later interpretation possibly given by the disciples or others belonging to the first generation of Christians. Matthew (initially as a kind of footnote) may have incorporated this into the text of the gospel. I realize this may shock some readers, but there are some difficulties we need to face.

In the allegorical explanation, the intent of the message of the parable has completely disappeared: there is no teaching about the kingdom of heaven and no exhortation to be patient and not to judge. In addition, there are some linguistic matters, including the reference to the angels of the Son of man in the allegorical explanation of the second parable (13:41). These words could not possibly have come from Jesus himself because his use of the term 'Son of man' is always a reference to the incarnation of God as the God-man as well as to the humanity of God. This rules out any possibility of the angels of the Son of man. In the same vein, it is impossible to refer to a kingdom of the Son of man: there is a kingdom of heaven, which is entirely different. There are also grammatical reasons that make it unlikely that the allegorical explanation came from Jesus himself. It is interesting to note that the gospel of Thomas, which has recently attracted considerable attention, includes the parable almost word for word but without the allegorical explanation. Having said all this, I wish to make it quite clear that the possibility that the allegorical explanation may have been added by Matthew does not in the least imply that we should not take it seriously. Even if it did not come directly from Jesus himself, or did not constitute Jesus' interpretation of the parable, we are still confronted with a text that represents an authentic witness of the first generation of Christians and which can become a Word of God. After all, such a witness is no different than the epistles of Paul or John, for example. We should not establish different levels of authority within the gospels or between parts of the New Testament.

Keeping in mind this difficulty, I would like to draw four principal teachings from this first parable. The kingdom of heaven is likened to a man who works in his field, much like a king does in his kingdom. In other words, we are presented with the power associated with a person who works in a field or a king who rules in his kingdom, thus depicting the kingdom of heaven as an action involving decisions and interventions. It is not a place, a point of assembly, a country with open borders, a party receiving adherents, or the like. I believe this identification of the kingdom of heaven with the person of the king who works in it is very important.

As a second teaching, the parable presents us with two actions that intervene in the world: one from the prince of this world and one from the Lord of the kingdom of heaven. There is a kind of duality when Christians think of the world as the kingdom of Satan and simultaneously regard Jesus Christ as Lord. It comes from a tendency to interpret things in terms of institutional forms. For example, in the political domain we accept that if Mr Smith is the president of a republic then it cannot be Mr Jones; or alternatively, you cannot have a king and an all-powerful dictator at the same time. The parable of the kingdom of heaven does not present us with a kind of competition between two institutionalized authorities. Its perspective is that of two actions intervening in history, where they mingle. It seems to me that the parable is very clear on this point: there is the one who sows the wheat and the one who sows the tares. It is also evident that the world is not the kingdom of heaven. This corresponds to one of the elements of the allegorical explanation, where we are told that the kingdom of heaven is a person who intervenes in this world. It also means that the kingdom of heaven cannot exist apart from this world: it is not in heaven, it is not a spiritual kingdom, it is not something abstract or theoretical. All this will be confirmed by the second parable.

The presence of the kingdom of heaven in the world has a double aspect. There is the person who sows the seed as well as his servants, who should be watching on behalf of their master but who have fallen asleep. We might say that the evil or non-kingdom of heaven comes about precisely when the servants sleep. It reminds us of the constant calls to be awake and to remain vigilant.

A third teaching of this parable is the impossibility of clearly discerning what is of the domain of Satan and what is of the domain of the kingdom of heaven. We must not attempt to judge these things in order to split them up. Even if it were given to us by the Spirit to discern the wheat from the tares, we cannot anticipate the Judgment and bring about the harvest. This implies four things. First, each and every one of us has the wheat and tares within us, and none of us is completely one or the other. The parable tells us, in fact, that the wheat and the tares are so completely mixed that no one can dissociate them. It should be remembered that the kinds of tares found in Palestine and the Near East do not in the least resemble the ones we find around here. They look almost exactly like wheat except that their seeds are poisonous. When wheat and tares are mixed, their root systems are so completely intertwined that one cannot be uprooted without uprooting the other. A second implication is that this is not only true for people individually but also for the world. It too closely intertwines the Word of God and what might be called the works of death. Each institution, each situation, and everything else bears a justice that comes from the love of God but also bears an evil inseparably bound up with it. The third implication is that our actions and interventions cannot possibly hope to bring about a Christian order that entirely conforms with the gospel, or create an ideal society. A final implication is that we by ourselves must not separate good people from evil ones and take on the role of the last judgment, where the harvest will be decided. Only God can do this, and this poses a troublesome ecclesiastical problem for the church. It can never establish a boundary between itself and the world and say to people on the one side, 'You belong,' and on the other side, 'You do not belong.' It is impossible to create a pure church. Remember that this parable is addressed to believers.

A fourth teaching relates to the last judgment. The parable only hints at it but does not speak of it directly, leaving it to God's sovereignty. In contrast, the allegorical explanation addresses the judgment directly, thereby raising the question whether verses 41–3 affirm the existence of a last judgment and the condemnation to hell of those who have done evil. In order to understand these texts, we must first of all remind ourselves that the parable is a teaching about the kingdom of heaven and not about hell. Hence the texts that speak of a hell are in a sense peripheral, and in any case they do not present us with a description of hell but with a warning. The usual translation of verse 41 is that the Son of man will send out his angels, and they will weed out of his kingdom all that provoke offence and all who do evil and throw them into the blazing furnace, where there will be weeping and grinding of teeth. This is not at all what the Greek text says. It first speaks of what gives offence and does so in the neuter, thus referring to things and not to people. Moreover, the text does not speak of those who do evil. Literally translated, it refers to the creators of *anomia*, which means the absence of laws. In popular Greek thinking of the time, this did not mean anarchy or disorder but a condition of life devoid of any type of meaning. The law was expected to provide human life with meaning, and its absence would therefore rob it of meaning and make it impossible for people to conduct their lives. Existentially this would be the equivalent of being in a thick fog, excluding any possibility of finding a good direction for one's life. This is what the absence of *nomos* means. A consequence of such a condition of life would be the inability to trust any other human being, thus making human relations impossible. It is evident that the usual translations are incredibly superficial. When I reread the explanations of this condition of life given by the stoic philosophers, I was struck by the fact that it is the exact opposite of faith, hope, and love. In *anomia* (what we refer to as *anomie*) it is impossible to place your trust in anyone, which is the opposite of faith. It is a condition of life without any meaning and hence without any possibility of a future, which is the opposite of hope. Finally, it makes any true relationships unliveable, which is the opposite of love. It is precisely the creators of *anomie* that are being weeded out of the kingdom of heaven, according to the Greek text. I do not believe that this could possibly refer to people creating this condition of life because *anomie* reaches far too deep.[1]

All this corresponds to what is revealed in the book of Revelation. Since I have examined this in some detail elsewhere,[2] I will simply point out that in those texts hell is prepared for the Devil and his angels, but not for people. We can therefore be fairly confident that in spite of the translations, what will be eliminated from the kingdom of heaven is everything that provokes offence, anything that creates a trap or 'stumbling block' for people, and any kind of life without hope, faith, and love. There is no question whatsoever of separating humanity into those who are saved and those who are damned.

Another text that makes this very clear is in 1 Corinthians 3:11–17, which shows that the judgment passes through the whole of our lives as it separates the tares destined for destruction from what we are before God as sons and daughters of the kingdom of heaven. We are persons with a history and a life. This life is referred to as our works

---

1 Jacques Ellul set out his view of the role of legal institutions in human history in a doctoral course he gave at the Faculty of Law at the University of Bordeaux. Essentially, this course sought to understand the universality of legal institutions as a response to difficulties any human community must surmount. Since Jacques Ellul had published only parts of this course, and since it fit extraordinarily into my analysis of the role of culture and individual and collective human life, he gave me permission to include a summary of this course (which I attended during my five-year stay in Bordeaux) in my book *The Growth of Minds and Cultures* (Toronto: University of Toronto Press, 1985), 272–8.

    The theological implications are clear. Human laws have little or nothing to do with justice but instead with making it possible for people to live within a community. In contrast, the laws of God judge the human heart, which is something entirely beyond the scope and intent of human laws.

2 Jacques Ellul, *Apocalypse: The Book of Revelation*, trans. George W. Schreiner (New York: Seabury, 1977).

because it is built up from the many things we do. Our works have nothing to do with morality. In the end, we will come to see what that life is and whether or not it stands. In other words, we will see whether all that we have done, thought, valued, and otherwise lived can make it through God's judgment and the fire of his love. If nothing can pass through that fire, nothing of that life remains; but we ourselves will be saved nevertheless. What God saves is what he alone knows of us. This perspective makes many of the traditional questions regarding the resurrection irrelevant. For example, it is not a question of whose wife we will be in eternity if we have remarried after the death of our first husband. We are told that there is an 'us' that only God knows, and that is whom he loves and saves. As far as the rest is concerned, the text is very clear. It will be extraordinary if anything of our lives survives the fire of God's love and judgment; if so, it will be our reward for having accomplished something that merits being incorporated into eternity. Remember that the book of Revelation makes it very clear that God respects his creatures, to the point that whatever out of all of human history is 'unto life' will be incorporated into the new creation.

The references to fire in these and other biblical texts would have been very clear to the people of that time. Gold was purified by the use of fire in order to bring the impurities to the surface of the molten mixture. This made it possible for them to be removed, leaving behind the pure metal. An equivalent modern image might be that of a surgeon saving someone's life by removing every last bit of cancer from his or her body. This is why the fire of judgment is also the fire of God's love, which saves us by removing everything that is 'unto death.' If something makes it through the fire and merits being brought into eternity, then this is the reward Paul speaks about.

In the second and third parables, the kingdom of heaven is no longer compared to a person but to a grain of seed and to yeast. However, as before, these are at work: the grain of seed grows and the yeast makes the dough rise. Once more, the kingdom of heaven is likened to a force. There is another important link as well. In the first, a master sows the seed and in the second, the grain of seed has been sown. These two actions show us something else about the kingdom of heaven. The king and his action, the Spirit and the people who bear it, belong together and are inseparable. For example, in the Bible there is no Spirit of God apart from those who bear it. All this together designates the kingdom of heaven.

Another point on which many exegetes agree regards the eschatological character of these two parables. For example, the reference to the birds of the sky coming to nest in the branches of the tree is found in many texts of that time as well as in older texts, and it always refers to the same thing, namely, the incorporation of the pagans into the people of God – which is clearly eschatological. Another such aspect comes from the enormous exaggeration of the size of the mustard tree, which in reality grows no taller than about six feet and therefore is not really a tree at all. The same kind of exaggeration is found in the three measures of flour which make enough bread to feed one hundred people. It is impossible that a woman can knead that much dough in her bowl. Anyone of that time would have known this, hence there is a deliberate exaggeration to give the text a kind of eschatological depth.

I would like to mention four things about the second and third parables. First, we are shown a power at work in secret. The seed is in the soil and the yeast is in the dough, and their actions cannot be observed from the outside. It is quite understandable, therefore, that non-Christians have argued that twenty centuries of Christianity have not brought much improvement. We cannot expect a sort of progress in the kingdom of heaven during the course of history. It is impossible to measure any kind of effectiveness of how well it works. Both the seed and the yeast are hidden in something much larger and work in secret.

Second, the kingdom of heaven seeks to transform the world, like the yeast that transforms the dough. It does not seek to infiltrate the world, nor does it seek to withdraw a certain number of people from that world and then conduct it towards its destruction. The world is not moving toward the last judgment, as is clearly shown by these parables of the seed and the yeast. They teach us to wait for the seed to germinate and produce a tree and for the yeast to make the dough rise. This contradicts any interpretation of the verses that follow (Mathew 13:41–3) as referring to a movement toward a destruction of the world. It is not a question of the destruction of the dough but of the transformation of the dough and the yeast together into something new through the process of fermentation; but this is apparent only when the process is completed. So also, the workings of the kingdom of heaven end up producing a kind of mutation of the world. The theological implications are far-reaching. There cannot be one history of God and another of humanity, one history of salvation and another of the rest. It is not the kingdom of heaven that by itself becomes the kingdom of God. It brings along the human world in a process that makes all things new. It is the same image as the followers of Jesus Christ being referred to as the salt of the earth. The yeast as such disappears during the rising of the dough and the baking of the bread, and the salt as such disappears when it accomplishes its purpose. Karl Barth has often reminded us that in the kingdom of God there no longer is a church. Everything else is there but the church, because it will have performed its function in the process of making everything else new.

Third, these two parables make it very clear that, although the kingdom of heaven begins as something very small, in the end it becomes enormous. A contrast is drawn between its beginning and its end, like one of the smallest grains of seed growing into a large tree or a tiny pinch of yeast making a large quantity of dough rise to make bread. In order to grasp the full significance of this contrast, it is essential to draw attention to a fundamental difference between western and oriental thinking. The former is preoccupied with how such a small beginning becomes so enormous and seeks to understand the intermediary stages of transformation. This is clearly manifested in the western scientific orientation, which would want to know how a seed becomes a plant. In the oriental thinking reflected in these parables, this is not at all what is important and interesting. What really matters is the point of departure and the point of completion. What comes between is much less important. Hence, the opposition between the beginning and the end is one of two very different realities. We encounter this kind of approach in other texts as well. For example, Paul uses this image of the seed when he speaks of the body born corruptible but resurrected incorruptible. There are also the well-known texts about the seed that must die. In each case, there is an opposition between the point of departure – the seed that disappears – and what comes of this, namely, the plant. It is the image of the opposition between death and life. The seed in John and Paul is a symbol of the resurrection, thus opposing two situations that have nothing in common. Our usual curiosity about how exactly the resurrection will work is entirely outside the biblical perspective: there are simply two different and opposite realities. In these two parables, there is an opposition between the beginning (with the weakness and non-power of Jesus) and the outcome (when the kingdom of God encompasses the totality of human history in the world). In other words, what these two parables teach us is that when we judge in terms of success we will almost certainly be mistaken. This Jesus, who has no power, status, authority, or anything else of the kind, is the one who transforms himself and the kingdom of heaven and who will make all things new. There is a complete opposition between the two, without any connection or any intermediary passage from one to the other.

Understanding this means that we can only receive the kingdom of God as a promise. We are obliged to face the question of faith: are we able to believe this? If we do, we must conduct our lives with the same orientation and perspective. Instead of judging like the world, with the belief that great results can only be obtained with the greatest means, we must recognize that the realization of the kingdom of God is indissociably linked to a choice based on an absence of means. We must choose as Jesus chose: the smallest grain of seed and the pinch of yeast. A decision to do this can only be based on faith; choosing what is weakest and the means of non-power is an expression of hope.

Fourth, when Jesus chooses these two parables, he completely turns on their heads the traditional images and stereotypes of his time. In Jewish thought (and we see one aspect of this in the book of Daniel), a big tree was the symbol of political power. Also, in all the Jewish writings of that time, yeast was the symbol of everything evil. Jesus thus takes these two negative images to show that the real power is not political but instead the eschatological dimension of the kingdom of heaven; and similarly, he withdraws the yeast (as the symbol of evil) from the power of Satan in order to redefine it in relation to the kingdom of heaven. To turn things upside down in such a fundamental way must have been so offensive to the people of that time that only someone with the authority of Jesus could undertake this. For this reason, I cannot imagine that these parables could have come from anyone but Jesus himself.

14 The Second Set of Parables (Matthew 13:44–50)

Many commentators have concluded that the parable likening the kingdom of heaven to a treasure hidden in a field is essentially identical to the one comparing it to the merchant finding an exquisite pearl. I was a little taken aback that even Karl Barth came to that conclusion, but I believe he may have been influenced by the German translation of the text. The argument holds that the first parable describes a person who has found a treasure and the second a merchant who has found a beautiful pearl, and that this amounts to more or less the same thing. However, this is not what the texts say. Once more, we will discover that these two parables are joined as a pair by what they reveal about the kingdom of heaven.

The first parable likens the kingdom of heaven to a treasure hidden in the world. Even though it is invisible, someone finds it in one of the most ordinary settings of daily life, namely, a field. In other words, it cannot be obtained in a specific place, from a particular institution, or from a designated person. For example, it is not by going to church that we necessarily encounter the kingdom of heaven. We are likely to find it in a place we work or some other daily life setting as represented by the field. Even though it has no special place and is hidden where we work and live, it has never been discovered until now, but the moment it is discovered everything changes.

The discovery of the treasure is highly personal as a unique encounter between someone and the Lord of the kingdom of heaven; and for this reason the person hides it from others, even though it evokes a great joy in his life. I believe this is the fundamental point instead of the business of selling everything to purchase the field. Placing the emphasis on the latter, as many commentators have done, implies that this may be very difficult to do and possibly involves a sacrifice or duty. It would all but eliminate the joy that the text speaks about, which devalues everything else in comparison. In other words, Jesus is not demanding a decision here. The decision is triggered by the joy of the discovery. This point is taken up again and again in the New Testament. If we do not live the good news in joy and in freedom, we quickly turn it into a constraint, an obligation, or a law, which is the exact opposite. The moment someone has lived the experience that the kingdom of heaven is more important and beautiful than anything encountered before, it puts everything else in a different light. This includes possessions, ideological commitments, spiritual orientation, or anything else that is part of the context of our daily life.

Nevertheless, the business of selling everything to purchase the field raises important questions. For example: Must the kingdom of heaven be paid for somehow? Does this justify a theology of good works, which means that a person must do a certain amount of good to qualify for the kingdom of heaven? I would like to remark on two things. First, there is no mention of a price demanded by the keeper of the kingdom of heaven, nor even that there is such a keeper. All we are told is that the treasure is at the disposal of the finder, thus implying a prior act that makes this possible. The king demands nothing. It is the person who finds the treasure who is happy to give up everything else for it, but that is not the equivalent of a price to be paid.

Second, the parable clearly tells us that it is not the treasure that is bought but the field in which it is located. In other words, the person who finds the kingdom of heaven does not purchase it but instead the world in which it is hidden. The price of the field is not paid to God but to the prince of this world, that is to Satan or Mammon, for the piece of this world in which the kingdom is hidden. It is not a question of rejecting the world in order to gain the kingdom of heaven. Such a perspective, of having to choose between the world and the kingdom, continues to mislead the Christian community. It is also contrary to many other texts, including the well-known one which says that God so loved the world that he gave his only Son ... The parable rules out any possible rejection of the world, since it is there where the treasure is found. Instead of rejecting the world, we must penetrate it in order to find the treasure. We encounter the same orientation in the gospel of John, where Jesus says that he is not praying for his disciples to be withdrawn from the world (John 17:15). The implications for Christians are clear, in spite of what has happened most of the time. We must not withdraw from the world to take refuge in a separate kingdom of heaven, but instead we are called to 'buy back' parts of the world where the treasure is found in order to keep the kingdom associated with the world. This teaching complements and reinforces what we have learned from the parables of the seed and the yeast. The seed must not be removed from the soil, nor the yeast from the dough. The kingdom of heaven cannot be obtained by a withdrawal from the world. This parable could not be clearer on this point. The person who finds the treasure does not dig it up, remove it from the field, and run off with it. Apparently the value of the treasure cannot be commercialized. The person buys the field with the treasure in it, which corresponds exactly to God's associating the kingdom of heaven with the world. It is a work of redemption, not just of ourselves and some others we may be concerned about, but of the entire world – as other texts, such as Romans 8, tell us. Christians are to participate in this work of redemption, this work of buying back the world from its prince, piece by piece and activity by activity. We are told specifically, for example, to redeem the time for the times are bad (Ephesians 5:16). In order to participate in this work of buying back the world we must abandon everything, beginning with our egotism.

In the second parable, the kingdom of heaven is compared to a merchant, that is, an active power that intervenes in the world. Of all things in the creation, the pearl of great value is the humanity God loves. Nothing is more precious, to the point that God is willing to give up everything for humanity. The price he paid was the most precious thing he had, namely, his son Jesus Christ. Particularly in the fourth century, Greek theologians had the conception of a humanity enslaved by Satan, and God's buying back this humanity by striking a deal of sorts with Satan by paying him the price of his son – except that Satan was not strong enough to hold onto him, so that he escaped. Most of us would probably be very uncomfortable with this idea of deal-making, and it certainly does not add up. Nevertheless, it seeks to make two things clear: that God accepts to give everything, and that Satan demands a price for humanity.

The reciprocity between these two parables is now obvious. In one parable, God gives up everything to gain the pearl of great value, namely humanity; and in the other parable, people give up everything because they find the kingdom of heaven. When they discover the enormity of God's love for them, everything else pales in comparison. The possibility of letting go of everything is in fact a criterion by which we can judge how much we have understood this love. It is exactly what Kierkegaard suggests: when it is difficult to let go of something, we have not yet fully understood how much God loves us. It is a criterion of the extent to which we are able to live by God's love. There is a striking reciprocity in the two parables of the sacrifices that are made to re-establish the love between God and humanity.

It should also be noted that in both parables the price is paid to Satan. In the one case, people pay the extreme price to buy back a part of the world; and in the other, God pays it to redeem humanity. I think this is very symbolic because it highlights the completely opposite approaches of God and Satan, and of what might be called two different economies. Satan is the one who sells. In a later parable, he is referred to as the Mammon of iniquity because everything needs to be paid for and nothing can ever be a free gift. It is for this reason that the world of money is so important in the Bible and why it is the very sign of Satan, the Devil, and Mammon. There can be nothing neutral about money. It is, after all, a means of exchange for buying and selling, thus excluding any possibility of a free gift. In contrast, God leads us to where everything is gratis because everything is a gift. God never demands anything in exchange for what he gives freely and in love. I believe this is the second link between these two parables, which makes them a complementary pair.

The comparison of the kingdom of heaven to a fishing net presents relatively few problems. The kingdom of heaven is in the world and integral to the course of history, where it catches what we may judge to be the just as well as the unjust, but they all belong to this kingdom. In any case, most people are neither completely one nor the other. It is not a question of dividing humanity into those who go to church and those who do not, into the Christians and the pagans, or those who are saved and those who are dammed. After all, this parable clearly addresses itself to those who regard themselves as believers. We are warned that the judgment of God may well be painful for us. The previously discussed text from the first letter to the Corinthians speaks of the fire of God's judgment and love passing through everything we have done and lived, causing the separation of good from evil to pass right through our lives. Hence, it is a warning first given to the disciples but which concerns all believers, namely, that this judgment awaits us all. Once again, this has far-reaching implications.

Unfortunately, the church continues to reach out to others by preaching hell and damnation. Such an approach is the exact opposite of the one we find in this parable. Any preaching regarding judgment must stay within the church as a warning to those who live by the Holy Spirit and by grace. They alone can take the warning of the coming last judgment seriously because they alone are able to hear this message, situated as it is within their discovery of how much God loves them. It perfectly links together these three parables. Only Christians can understand and existentially bear a revelation that warns them of passing through the fire of God's judgment because they know that, whatever happens, God loves them to the point of giving up his own son. To be sure, they are the pearl of great value, but the merchant who finds it tests it very carefully to see if it is truly that pearl. To preach hell and damnation to those who have not yet discovered that they are loved is destructive and suicidal. It cannot be a call to repentance except by exploiting people's fear and weakness, which turns it into the exact opposite of preaching the good news of God's love. I take this to be a fundamental implication of these parables.

They also have an ethical character, in the sense that they provide a certain orientation for our lives that flows from the proclamation of a message that concerns us. You are loved, you have discovered that you are loved, you may enter into this work of redeeming the world, you discover how deeply God loves that world through a particular engagement, and you buy back the corresponding part of that world. These parables thus announce a message as well as providing a certain orientation for our behaviour.

Finally, it has often been said that the parables are short poetic stories intended to make clear what otherwise may not be understood. What strikes me is that real people would never behave like the people in these parables. For example, when you find a treasure in a field it is not likely that you will sell everything that you own to buy the field, because we are all tempted to simply take it. The things that are drawn from daily life are somewhat reoriented, made less likely and even somewhat improbable. It fits the message that this is what the kingdom of heaven is like, in that it belongs to and is inserted in our daily-life world but that it also veers away from that world. This kingdom leads to behaviour that is somewhat strange, and foreign to what we would normally expect. I believe that is what the unusual behaviour of the people in these parables means.

15   The Parable of the Debtors
(Matthew 18:23–35)

I would like to start with four preliminary issues. Once more the kingdom of heaven is presented as an active power intervening in our world and our history, in the form of a king calling his servants to account. Second, I believe it rather forcefully poses the question of the relationship between justice and love in the kingdom of heaven. There clearly is a conflict between this justice and love, in the sense that when the just king exercises his rights, the results are opposite to those of showing his love. The solution appears to be a transcendence of justice by love. Here Jesus reveals an orientation that is the inverse of what was customary in Judaism at that time. The rabbis taught that God had two measures for governing the world, namely mercy and justice; but this would change with the last judgment, when justice would reign and mercy would disappear. Jesus turns this around by making God's judgment a matter of mercy. The king extends grace and forgives the entire debt, and he expects people to do the same for each other. It is the opposite of justice; and this has far-reaching consequences, as we will see. A direct intervention of the king is required to transcend justice through love.

Third, this parable introduces a certain logic or modus operandi of the kingdom of heaven, which we will encounter in all the subsequent parables of this kingdom. It begins with a debtor whose debt is forgiven, which has repercussions for another debtor. It goes without saying that this logic is not the one by which people and communities normally operate and live. Finally, this parable emphasizes the sovereign independence of the king, who decides to cancel the debt and to condemn the servant who has no pity on others. God alone decides what he will do.

I would like to draw your attention to a few historical details in this parable that were almost certainly drawn from Egypt rather than from Judaea. For example, the word in the original text normally translated as servants really refers to a king's functionaries, of the kind found in Egypt. Also, the Jewish laws of that time permit the selling of a debtor but not his wife or children. Egyptian law did permit the selling of a debtor's wife and children, with the result that the parable speaks of a situation that could happen in Egypt but not in Judaea. Finally, the sum of ten thousand talents was unthinkable even for the biggest Jewish banker of that time, but it might have been possible for some of the highest functionaries in Egypt. Given these historical details, some exegetes have concluded that the protagonists of the story were almost certainly Egyptians or, in any case, pagans. I believe, however, that these are secondary details.

The three central questions dealt with by the parable are the debt and its forgiveness, the repercussion this forgiveness has on others, and the judgment. We have already seen that the kingdom of heaven is in the world, which in this parable means that accounts must be rendered to the king. This must not be confused with a similar parable in Luke 19 and the second parable in Matthew 25, in which a person left his goods (in the form of talents) with his servants while he travelled abroad, which is about the final judgment and the kingdom of God. We will discuss this later. The parable in Matthew 18, however, deals with our being accountable during our lives, which we acknowledge each time we pray the Lord's Prayer and ask for our debts to be forgiven.

What is this debt that the parable speaks of? When we enter into the kingdom of heaven, we become aware of what we owe its king. We also become aware of the judgment provoked by this debt. From our study of the book of Genesis, we learned that humanity was called to glorify God in his creation. We also saw that this has nothing whatsoever to do with singing hymns and participating in services of worship. Humanity glorifies God in his creation by revealing who God is. What this means is fully revealed in Jesus Christ, who alone is the fullness of the glory of God. Only he fully manifests the totality of God. In other words, what we owe God is to be his image. Instead, we have become alienated from the human condition. This is what alienation literally means: to be excluded from the human condition by not being the image of God and thus becoming dehumanized. It is much more than a question of economics and of exploitation. Hence, when we are called to the kingdom of heaven we are made aware of this situation and what we owe its king.

When we enter the kingdom of heaven, we become the servants of its king. We become accountable to the king and we become aware of our position of being unable to be his image in any way whatsoever, with the result that we cannot pay our debts. Justice demands that we are to be removed from our position of servant and to be sold. When we are sold we become slaves, which means we become alienated and excluded from the human condition. Up to this point, the king exercises a justice that is entirely comparable to human justice.

The condemned servant prostrates himself before the king and prays to be granted more time to pay the debt. In response to this prayer, the king completely transforms the situation by doing away with his judgment and totally abandoning his rights. This action is much more than what the condemned servant prayed for, namely, more time and the restoration of the king's confidence in him. What this means is that God does not necessarily grant us what we ask for in our prayers but always goes much further. In this case, a pardon removes the judgment that had been pronounced. This happens time and time again in our lives when, through prayer, we have a personal encounter with the king. Once again, there is no question of the final judgment here. After we discover the kingdom of heaven, we learn more about it throughout our entire lives and as we do, we also learn how far we are from being the image of its king and the judgment he has pronounced. However, all this happens within the ongoing discovery of this kingdom, which is God's love, pardon, and salvation. God's intervention restores us to our status of servants whose debts have been forgiven and who therefore no longer owe anything, thanks to the death and resurrection of Jesus Christ. Just as the condition of the servant in the parable has been transformed, so our condition is no longer one of alienation. I believe this is what the first theme of this parable reveals.

The second theme deals with the repercussions of the king's intervention for all his servants. Have we really grasped the implications of this intervention? According to the parable there appear to be two possible reactions. In the one case, we recognize that God's pardon transforms us by placing us in a condition of being truly human. What this means is that we glorify God by revealing to the world who this God of love is. The other reaction to God's pardon is to consider it as a good deal: 'I really got a very good deal and no longer owe anything.' This is a very common reaction within Christianity. Since we are forgiven we are out of trouble and no longer need to exert ourselves too much. This is one possible reaction to a theology of grace as set out by Luther, for example. To regard God's forgiveness as a terrific deal is not to have changed at all.

Both these reactions show that our understanding of what God has done for us will be expressed in our works and in the fruit these bear. The parable clearly shows this in the reaction of the servant to having his debt forgiven. He exercises his rights when one of his fellow servants cannot pay what he owes him. He does not do evil, but simply exercises justice by demanding what he is owed. The sum is non-trivial, even though it is much smaller than what was owed to the king. He therefore has a significant claim with his fellow servant, even though it is incommensurate with what he owed his master. The problem is that the servant has not really understood what the king has done, other than giving him a 'good deal.'

This second theme in the parable reveals the difficulty of spreading the kingdom of heaven by means of people. We have already seen that this kingdom grows in a way that is hidden, much like the mustard seed and the yeast, but here we have a glimpse of how it happens. It is the repercussions of God's action in a person's life on his or her fellow human beings, and requires the intermediary role of people. It is not God who comes into this world and who by himself builds the kingdom of heaven step by step. God gets the ball rolling, so to speak, which then touches other balls, and so on. However, this is only possible if people, on their own level and with their own means, reproduce what God has done. No more and no less is asked of us. We cannot take on the problems of humanity even if we wanted to. Only God can assume the burden of humanity and our history. We must work on our level and with our means together with the other people in our lives. The parable makes this very clear by the enormous difference in the size of the two debts. It is also clear that prayer is a fundamental part of what we are called to do. Here then we see what the parable reveals regarding the growth of the kingdom of heaven: it is our reproduction of what God has done for us.

What this implies is that the growth of the kingdom of heaven has an anti-juridical orientation. I would even go further and say that within the kingdom of heaven, justice and law represent the greatest injustice and, in a relative sense, evil itself. One commentator goes so far as to call the law demonic, and I would not disagree with that.[1] Of course, I do not mean that those who study or make laws are demonic. I have

---

1 Jacques Ellul's assessment is probably impossible to understand without the knowledge of his study of the role of law in human society and the necessities to which it responds. I have cited my summary of this study above.

already suggested that the law is purely utilitarian, and absolutely necessary to permit a society to function. No society can exist without it. However, the kingdom of heaven is not a society; and when we encounter the decision of its King we learn that biblical justice has nothing in common with the law and justice created by societies. In other words, because my debt has been forgiven, I forgive the debts owed to me. I will not deal with my neighbour according to the ways of justice and the law but instead according to the ways of love, of pardon, and of giving freely without recompense or charge. It turns everything upside down because in human affairs there can be nothing else but the rule of law, greed, and money. All this is so fundamental to a society that a radical proclamation of love and grace is far more threatening than any revolutionary movement; and I believe that Jesus' crucifixion had more to do with this than any political threat. I believe some of the leaders clearly sensed this deeper threat in his teachings.

I can only make everything gratis for others if I am totally confident that my debt has been forgiven. The parable makes this quite obvious. If I owe ten thousand talents and am at risk of being sold, I have no option other than collecting all the debts owed to me. Hence, if I believe that Jesus is merely an exemplary human being or some kind of ideal held out to us, then my conviction of having been pardoned has no substance whatsoever, and I will not be able to deal with others according to the ways of the kingdom. Jesus must have paid my entire debt so that being debt free, I have the freedom to forgive the debts of others. No person, no matter how good and exemplary, can do this, other than the king himself.

This brings me to the third theme in the parable, namely, the king's judgment. Thus far the parable has shown us that belonging to the kingdom of heaven means applying the law of that kingdom, namely, that everything must be gratis. We must also expect this from the church. An entirely new (and even abnormal) kind of relationship is being established between people, thereby creating what might be seen as an entirely new kind of society based on a complete forgiveness of all debts. It was envisaged by the king whose intervention made this possible. Hence, when we forgive others, cancel their debts, and make everything gratis, we constitute the kingdom. It is the very basis for answering the question of where the kingdom may be found and how it can be seen. It is that fundamental. Wherever there is a human act of pardon, or a giving that is completely gratis, that is where the kingdom is. The opposite is equally true. When I do not live by this law of grace, I do not belong to the kingdom of heaven.

What we are told in the beginning of this parable completely transforms our situation. The question is not whether I can pay the debt to God and whether I merit grace. It is now a question of what I have done with the gift of grace I have received. Has this gift transformed my life by having me adopt an approach to others based on forgiving and giving as a witness of the kingdom? As a result of this witness, others may come to understand the kingdom and enter into it. In this way, the kingdom of heaven grows. What this implies is that others become the witnesses to what I have done with the gift of grace. They will testify whether for them I was the bearer of love and pardon and the one who gave freely and generously. Before God they become my witnesses of whether I behaved this way toward them or not. The parable is very clear on this point, and it is in this light that we must understand other texts to the effect that we will be judged according to what we have said and done. If I have not brought love and pardon to others and given freely and generously, I have withheld all this from them; consequently, I have withheld all this from myself as well. In such a situation, it is I and not God who have withheld grace.

The king's judgment of me is a straightforward determination of what I have done. In this respect, God's approach is the same in the overall scheme of things. We are so used to thinking that God will bring an end to this world and will usher in the last judgment that we have forgotten that after the flood he promises never to do so. It is now becoming clear to us that in fact we have obtained the power to put an end to this world. The book of Revelation openly suggests that this is exactly what humanity will do. In this case also, God appears to limit himself to determining what is really going on. If we are no longer the bearers of love and grace, we bar others from that love and grace and judge ourselves. As Christians we are given a warning, and not a description of a final judgment or of a condemnation to hell. We are to bring grace to others, and are warned that if we return to the rule of law and money we re-enter an endless conflict that can only destroy us. The warning is analogous to others, such as that if you live by the sword you die by the sword. The choice is ours. Once again, there is no question of a hell. The parable deals with the kingdom of heaven and not the kingdom of God, and thus with history and not the end of history.

16 The Parable of the Labourers' Wages (Matthew 20:1–16)

I would like to begin with a few general remarks largely based on the commentary of Jeremias,[1] who provides an overview of some of the traditional interpretations of this parable. In the Roman Catholic tradition, this text was often used in the liturgy at the beginning of Lent, the period of repentance leading up to the passion and crucifixion of Jesus. The aim was to call people to service, which I believe is entirely appropriate and faithful.

Others have provided an allegorical interpretation based on the five times new workers were called in the parable, which were taken to correspond to the history of salvation since Adam. There were three such calls before Jesus, who was the fourth, with the Holy Spirit being the fifth, thus creating five periods in this history. Still others have seen a correspondence between the five calls and five stages in the spiritual development of becoming a full Christian. All this is somewhat amusing because it has nothing whatsoever to do with the central point of the parable, which deals with the distribution of the wages and everyone receiving the same amount.

Generally speaking, in the Protestant tradition there have been two major interpretations. Sermons of the sixteenth century frequently emphasized obedience to God and a warning not to compromise one's salvation by murmuring against his justice, while sermons in the nineteenth century tended to emphasize the equality of the grace extended to everyone. I believe these interpretations are equally incorrect, in the sense that it is not the fact that the wages were unequal which is at the heart of this parable but that those who worked less received the same amount as all the others.

---

1 Joachim Jeremias, *The Parables of Jesus* (New York: Scribner's Sons, 1955).

This parable may well represent an explanation and justification of what Jesus did, which was severely criticized by the Jews, especially because he called tax collectors, prostitutes, Galileans, strangers, and so on. In this parable Jesus replies that this is how God acts, and that he is not doing this on his own accord. When he calls these people who have not participated in the work of Israel until the eleventh hour, he does so because God acts this way. By implication, the people Jesus addresses with this parable are those who protest against and reject his work, namely, the Pharisees and scribes. Beginning with the early church, however, the parable has usually been interpreted as being addressed to Christians.

Let us now take a look at the text itself. The parable is a parallel of the parable of the talents, which we examined in Matthew 18. It also deals with the relationship between God's love and justice, but with one important difference. In the parable of Matthew 18 the teaching that God's love transcends his justice is put in the context of our relationships with others, while this parable puts it in the context of our relationship with God. After examining the story, I will turn to what I have previously referred to as the 'law' of the kingdom that emerges from this text.

Once again this parable likens the kingdom of heaven to a power at work. The kingdom is identified with the king. To belong to this kingdom is to have entered into his service, which is likened to the workers being called to labour in his vineyard. The story revolves around the landowner and not his labourers, as opposed to the frequently used title, 'The Parable of the Workers of the Eleventh Hour.' The subject clearly is the landowner and his love and goodness.

I believe that the service of the labourers is characterized by two elements. First, one is called to this work. It is not the workers who present themselves for God's work but God who calls them, each in his or her time. It is a question of grace. The implications are very important. We cannot enter this service when and where we want according to our ideas, aspirations, and desires that it is a true vocation (to use a word that has fallen from favour). In fact, I believe that it is only in this context that we can speak of a vocation at all, and that we cannot use it in the usual way, that is, the vocation of a professor, doctor, lawyer, and so on. The only real vocation is serving God in the work of bringing the gospel. Whenever and wherever a person is called, even at the eleventh hour, there is work to be done in the vineyard; and everyone waiting to work is called. In other words, God intervenes when he calls, and people must wait for this call with patience and endurance and in the knowledge that it will come and there will be work. It is very important not to identify a call to service with salvation, or to interpret the fact that not everyone is called as a limited salvation. Everyone who waits for a vocation will be called, even at the eleventh hour. God takes the initiative, and we must patiently wait for his call.

The second element is that this work may be paid. For some the pay is predetermined, but for others the landowner promises to pay what is reasonable. We are also told that when everyone is paid they all receive the same amount. In other words, the pay that God grants is not proportional to the work done.

To put this in perspective: it is crucial to remember that this work is unnecessary. It is a dimension that we easily forget when we read this parable, especially the part about the protest of the workers who were paid last. It is unnecessary work because the kingdom of heaven is a power that has the force to grow by itself without the aid of people. It is the power of God, who does not need people but calls them as an act of grace. What this means is that the servants have no usefulness, but they can only say this when they have finished their work. We cannot reason in advance that since the work serves no purpose there is no point doing it. When we have accomplished everything we must do, only then can we say: I am the unnecessary servant. Whether we accomplished a lot or a little, it is equally unnecessary and produces nothing of value, hence we are not owed anything in exchange. In other words, when God calls people he extends his grace to them. God could choose to accomplish his work in the world without calling anyone, and still bring about salvation, assure the future of humanity, and bring in the new Jerusalem, and so on. Instead, God takes people into account, calls some to his work, and thereby extends his grace in love. We need to understand that to do this work is a response to his love. It is not a duty imposed by God but an acceptance of the love addressed to us, hence we have no rights vis-à-vis God. By grace God draws us into his work, and it is he who gives that work its effectiveness. We cannot lay claim to anything.

The reward given by God does not so much correspond to the work done as to people's response to his call. I believe this is the key to understanding this part of the parable. The workers called by God have come, each one in his or her time, and God gives because they have come. It is this that may be called the justice of God. It also brings out two new elements regarding this justice. In the Old Testament, the justice of God refers to his accomplishing what he says. It strikes us as an alien concept because we have been so permeated by Greek notions of justice. Nevertheless, when the Old Testament speaks of God's justice it simply means that God does what he says. We might say that it is a measure of the extent to which what he accomplishes corresponds to his promises. Justice is done when the two match exactly. This parable provides a good example of it.

The Jews must have understood Jesus very well on this point. The landowner promises certain things, he does what he promised, and hence this is just. However, Jesus goes further, because the promise that the landowner will pay what is reasonable is somewhat uncertain and non-specific. Once again, we learn that God's love transcends his justice: he gives much more than what might be expected. He adds the grace of this gift to the grace of calling people.

God desires that those who were called first, those who served and understood his kingdom, also participate by rejoicing in his love and goodness. Instead, they judge the others, thereby revealing that under these circumstances they have not understood the kingdom of heaven. They have not understood that love and justice coincide there, and are judged accordingly. They are not, however, rejected or condemned by the king, who addresses them as friends and reminds them that he has done them no wrong.

A number of commentators have pointed out that, in the gospel of Matthew, being called a friend is always associated with being reproached for something. For example, in Matthew 22:12 we also see someone being addressed as a friend and then reproached for not wearing a wedding garment.

What begins to emerge from this parable is what might be called the law of the kingdom, which is the inverse of the law of this world. As a matter of fact, the actions God takes in this parable strike us as unjust because our conceptions of justice are based on equality and proportionality. In contrast, God's justice is based on his sovereign freedom and exercised in his love. If we are to understand the law of the kingdom, we must accept that it is the opposite of that of the world. This is particularly evident in the Sermon on the Mount, whose Beatitudes have been called the laws of the kingdom. For example: from the perspective of our world it is inconceivable to say that those who are crying and deeply distressed can be happy now because they will be comforted, and yet this is one of the laws of the kingdom.

A fundamental law of the kingdom is that of giving freely without charge. We need to be reminded of the fact that the work done in the kingdom is unnecessary and is not undertaken in view of compensation. It is a service rendered gratis. This takes us back to the fundamental question posed at the beginning of the book of Job, namely: do we serve God for free? The answer is in the affirmative. We serve God for nothing. God grants his grace as an act that is gratis, and we are to serve for free as well. We generally experience a great deal of difficulty in trying to understand this double gift – one that is entirely free and without strings attached.

One typical reaction is that because God extends his grace to us, we had better give something back by doing what we can in return. If we have truly entered into grace, our response to God and our neighbour is also for free. This doing everything for nothing is the most difficult thing for us to accept. The only virtue of those who came to work from the third hour on is their freely entrusting themselves to the grace of God. They were simply told that they would get something, and they went to work. In other words, they left God free to judge what would be reasonable. As a number of commentators have pointed out, this is exactly what Jesus does when he pardons the lame, the blind, the prostitutes, the tax collectors, the Canaanites, and so on. These are the people who come to him saying that they have no right to anything but entrust themselves to Jesus' free decision. They are ready to accept anything. They behave exactly as all the workers do who are hired after the first group.

In the end all are treated the same way. In order to understand this, we must pay attention to a small detail in the parable, namely, that the wage agreed upon for the first group of workers is a denarius. This not only represents the typical wage for a day's labour at that time but also the amount necessary to procure the necessities of life for one day; and this we know with a great deal of certainty from careful economic analyses of that period. In other words, to receive less than a denarius per day is to be condemned to starvation. What this sum represents is the gift of life much more than it represents a wage. It helps us to understand the profound significance of what the landowner replies to the workers who were called first. Literally translated: 'Do you see with an evil eye because I am good?' What this implies is: 'Do you want me to let these people die of hunger? They must also live.' The significance is clear. God promised life to the workers he called first, and to everyone else called afterwards he gave life as well. All are treated the same way because either you live or you don't. Life cannot be measured out in portions, nor can more than life be given. God grants life to everyone.

Some commentators have suggested that the conclusion that the last shall be first and the first shall be last doesn't fit the parable, and therefore may have been added later. I am not certain that this is the case. The people who were called first and promised a denarius knew all along that they would receive God's grace of resurrection and eternal life. All the time they worked, they had the assurance of that grace. They are the last because, during their entire lives, they were the ones who had that guarantee and assurance, which made them spiritually rich. I believe this is fundamental. The people in the church who firmly believe the word of God are the rich ones because they have an assurance and hope that others do not have. It helps us understand why the disciples wondered, 'Who then can be saved?' following Jesus' encounter with the rich young ruler and his comment about the camel passing through the eye of the needle. These disciples, who were not economically wealthy, had understood very well that Jesus was talking of them. Having been with Jesus, they had become rich. In a certain sense they had rights since they knew they belonged to the covenant, had been promised the resurrection, and so on.

The last to be hired are the poor. They have been unemployed for much of the time and have lived with uncertainty, in ignorance and darkness. These poor are placed first because they have been poor and thus are most in need of assurance and consolation. As the entire gospel shows, and the account of Jesus' birth in particular, the poor are the ones who are present before all the others. For this reason I believe that this parable is rather severe on this point. When you know you belong to the covenant, are a member of the body of believers, and work in the kingdom of heaven, you can never entirely avoid taking on the attitude of someone who has rights. You develop a certain familiarity with respect to God and have a great deal of trouble rejoicing when God extends his grace to everyone, especially when they pass before you. It is next to impossible to entirely avoid these attitudes of the rich and to be capable of rejoicing when God allows to pass ahead of us people we did not expect.

On this subject I would like to make three remarks. First, there is no room for a judgment of any kind on our part. We are unable to classify people as first or last. Whatever someone's behaviour or his or her estrangement from God, we can never come to any conclusion as to whether it is too late or whether everything is lost. Nor can we make any comparison between what I do and what someone else does. This parable completely rules out these kinds of attitudes and behaviours.

The parable equally rules out any kind of false calculations that have been all too common in the church, such as: You can do what you like during your life as long as you repent at the last moment. As long as I do this, I will be like the workers of the eleventh hour and everything will work out. To some extent the last confession of the dying is based on this attitude. As long as I die a good death, the rest of my life does not matter at all. I believe this to be a serious error, because everything does not depend on my decision to participate as of now in God's grace by accepting it, but instead depends on a vocation. Nothing guarantees a dying person that during his or her last fifteen minutes he or she will receive God's word and a vocation. It is not this person but God who decides. This is why it is a false calculation. Either God's call has come, is understood and hence cannot be postponed as we please, or if we make this calculation, it simply shows that we remain on the outside.

Finally, this poses the very difficult problem of Israel. Clearly, Israel as a people are the workers of the first hour who had a contract in the form of the covenant. With respect to Jesus Christ and the kingdom of heaven, however, Israel is not the first and may be considered as rejected. From this perspective, it is now the church (as the body of all believers) that does the work of the kingdom and bears all the difficulties that come with it. It is the church that is in the field and endures the problems of its time. Israel, who was the first, has been rejected and has become the last, in the sense that Israel is outside of that work. Because of this, Christians as the body of believers can expect that at the end of time Israel will be called first, and that she will pass before the church to receive more than what was said. Israel was called first with a particular promise, she was then rejected and left out of the work, and now another does the work, with all the difficulties that entails. However, the body of believers will be second because, during its entire history, it has known the fullness of God's grace. Israel comes first at the time of the last judgment, exactly as told in the book of Revelation. They are the 144,000, followed by the great multitude of the church. In other words, this parable of Jesus has a double meaning with regard to Israel.

I had forgotten one detail which wonderfully illustrates how the understanding of the kingdom held by the Jews was diametrically opposed to that held by Jesus. In the third century, essentially the same text of this parable was found in a Jewish collection. The parable had been transformed as follows. There was an excellent labourer in the field who did a lot of work. After two hours, the landowner sought out this labourer and spent the rest of the day talking to him. At the end of the day, he paid him the same as everyone else. The others protested, and the landowner asked them: 'Why do you protest? This worker has been a much better one than you, doing in two hours what you do in ten hours.' In this version, the element of grace has been completely eliminated, and this is characteristic. The labourer in question has been much more efficient, thus obtaining better results and meriting a higher pay. Jesus' parable clearly combats a fundamental Jewish orientation.

17   The Parable of the Wedding Feast (Matthew 22:1–14)

Most theologians have understood this parable as a kind of history of salvation, which goes roughly as follows. The wedding feast of the son is the salvation accomplished in Jesus Christ. The first guests to be invited are the Jewish people, followed by the church. Some people within the church are found to be unworthy, and these people are rejected. The church comes to an end with the last judgment, and those who are chosen are saved. Be this as it may, there is very little likelihood that Jesus gave a theological parable. It is we who have made it into something theological and dogmatic. As with all the other parables, Jesus makes a proclamation, and it is this orientation we need to rediscover.

The central point of this proclamation is that everything is ready, which implies a great joy. A little theology is helpful here in the form of a distinction between people who are very busy and do not have time, and those who do not recognize that the time of the wedding banquet has come (in the sense that everything is ready and the moment has arrived). From a theological perspective, this implies two notions of time. The Greek *kronos* refers to the time that passes and can be counted in the course of daily life, while *kairos* refers to a time that is favourable or exceptional – a kind of break in *kronos*. Examples of this latter time occur when, for example, Jesus says that his time has not yet come or when he says that his hour has come, thereby referring to an exceptional intervention that cuts through the normal passing of time. There is a clear opposition between these two kinds of time in the parable. The first guests have busy lives, demanding work schedules, and are immersed in *kronos*, to the point that they cannot recognize a disruption resulting from an event that changes everything. I believe that a proclamation of such an exceptional moment should urge us to take a position: Am I going to recognize that, yes or no, the moment has come?

In the gospel of Luke this parable is placed near our Palm Sunday, which marks Jesus' triumphant entry into Jerusalem. He weeps for the city and says, 'If only you had known the time you were visited.' That is the *kairos*. In other words, when the favourable moment came Jerusalem did not recognize it. In our lives as well there may be that presence, that bursting in of such a moment that shatters time but that we may not recognize. This is the central issue of this parable. When the Word is addressed to us, will we recognize it as a *kairos*, the moment that ruptures everything?

Some exegetes have pointed out that Jesus is using an earlier Jewish parable well known to everyone, but once again he gives it a completely different orientation. Originally, it was a story of a rich man who, when he died, was entitled to a funeral blessed by God because during his life he had done something truly exceptional. When he gave a big feast to which the important guests refused to come, he had all the poor people invited instead. Having thus fed the poor, he had accomplished a good work. The lesson of the Jewish parable was to encourage everyone to do similar good works so that they also could have a funeral blessed by God. Jesus borrows this story but gives it a completely different thrust.

Continuing my introductory remarks: During our Palm Sunday, when Jesus is welcomed by the Jewish people, he announces in two parables (namely, the one about the tenants of the vineyard and this one) that these very people are going to be rejected from the work of God and not retained as his people.

Once again, this parable compares the kingdom of heaven to a king, thus referring to God himself, his presence in the world, and his work among people. We encounter his sovereign power throughout the parable. He prepares, chooses, calls, sends messengers, gathers together, judges, and excludes, and does so not in heaven but right among people in this world. We also learn that the kingdom of heaven concerns a wedding feast for the king's son. It reflects what we have already been told, namely, that God is with people in his kingdom of heaven as a divine power working in history. Hence the image of a wedding feast. The kingdom is prepared for Jesus Christ and hence is not for our personal use – it finds its full expression in the communion.

After considering its general orientation, let us now turn to the text itself. There are three parts to the story: the preparation of the wedding feast and the first invitation, the second invitation to those who are on the outside, and the expulsion of the person who had failed to put on his wedding garment. Beginning with the first part (22:3–7), I do not think that the ones who are invited first are only the Jews. It is all the people who were called but refused. In other words: This parable is not a repetition of the story of the landowner who developed a vineyard and rented it to tenants before going abroad. That parable clearly regarded the Jewish people. This one addresses us, as will become evident from the warning we are given.

In anticipation of the wedding, God draws up a list of people he will invite to participate in the kingdom of heaven, that is, he chooses those he will call to undertake the work of that kingdom. The first invitation reveals God's will in the form of a choice of those who will be called to the wedding banquet. When everything is ready, a first group of servants calls those who were previously invited, but they will not come. A second group of servants is sent, with the same result. Of course, the traditional explanation holds that the first group of servants were the prophets and the second the apostles. Since the feast is ready, deferral is no longer possible, and the invited guests have to decide whether to come or not. Everyone refuses to come. What this means is that throughout human history, humanity has the freedom to refuse God's Word, his invitation to participate in his work, and so on. People have the choice of saying yes or no, which, once again, is not a question of their salvation but of their participation in the work of God.

What I believe this means is that humanity has other things to do, and it is a matter of priorities. They have bought land or oxen or have business to attend to, but God invites them to do something that appears less important and less serious. These are not bad people. They are simply busy with other work; hence, it is not a question of morality. There is a humorous rabbinical parable that gets at this point by telling a story of a king who invites people to a reception without specifying the time. According to this story, the wives prepare themselves so that they will be ready when they are called, while the fools go to work, thus making it impossible for them to be ready when the moment comes. I think this beautifully illustrates the point: the call comes when we are busy working and seeks to engage us in a different kind of work.

The refusal to come is very serious because it compels humanity to take a position before God. This is so serious, not because it is a question of our eternal salvation, but because it shows who we really are. It amounts to the same issue that I explained in terms of the difference between a *kronos* and a *kairos*. The entry of the kingdom of heaven is a kind of break in our lives, bringing as it does an unbearable conflict, driving some to even kill the servants who brought the invitation. I do not believe that this is merely an overreaction to a simple invitation. The people involved sense how unacceptable their refusal will be, and thereby reveal who they really are. The proclamation of the kingdom of heaven amounts to an unbearable upheaval of our affairs, which explains the violent reaction and even murder. Faced with the absolute commitment demanded by God, they show the equally absolute response of total rejection; and this response in turn leads to rejection by the king. To be sure, this latter rejection is temporary, occurring as it does in history. We can observe the same movement with respect to the city, whose spiritual significance is the attempt to create a place that excludes God.[1]

Next, the king sends out his servants to invite anyone they can find. No limit is placed on the number of people that can be invited. Nor does God have a predetermined list of guests, and there is no question of some kind of predestination. In Jesus everyone is chosen and everyone is called, without any discrimination. There are no moral qualifications: good people and bad people are equally invited, according to the text. People are simply not chosen because of their moral qualities. Only one person is finally rejected, but this is not because of moral considerations.

Concerning the originally invited guests who refused to come, the text tells us that they were not worthy. What is meant by this? It is not a question of the qualities or characteristics of these guests, such as their intelligence or good behaviour, but the fact that they refused to come. They were more deeply attached to their *khronos* than to the invitation that changed everything, and as a result they were unwilling to change their situation. Being worthy or not can therefore not be determined in advance. It is not until the invitation comes that we know if someone will enter the kingdom of heaven or not. The kingdom will be filled since its growth has no limits, as we have already seen in the other parables such as the seed becoming a gigantic tree.

There is an important detail that has caused endless trouble but that appears only in the version of this parable given in Luke 14:15–24, which otherwise is more or less the same. In verse 23 we read that after the second group of guests have been invited, the servants report to the king that they have carried out his wishes but there is still room for more people. He tells them to go to the highways and hedges and

---

1 Jacques Ellul, *The Meaning of the City*, trans. Dennis Pardee (Grand Rapids, MI: Eerdmans, 1970).

compel people to come: *compelle eos intrare*. It is these last few words that St Augustine interpreted during the conflict with the Donatists[2] as meaning that heretics should be compelled by force to enter the church. Calvin had the same perspective in believing that the church could use force to make people adhere to the Christian faith, and that the state could use violence to bring people to Christianity and have them enter the church. It is these three Latin words that have been used to justify the Crusades, religious wars, the Inquisition and so on. All this based on three words! It represents what I believe to be a very dangerous practice, against which I have warned so frequently: detaching a few words from their context in order to build a whole theology on it. For me it is the one real heresy.

In this particular case, there is a serious error of interpretation. First, in the gospel of Luke it is a question of the kingdom of God, which can never be identified with the church. Nowhere and not ever does the Bible equate the two. Second, the other unbelievable theological error becomes evident when we consider the identity of the servant asked to compel people to enter. If it is an earthly king who orders it, it is a question of material means such as the state, for example; but if it is God who speaks, the messenger is a spiritual envoy, namely an angel. This latter interpretation is not only the traditional one, it is unavoidable, given that it is about the kingdom of God. It is one thing for angels to compel you to enter; it is quite another for the state to use its armies to do so. The state has never been compared to an angel. Instead, it is a spiritual power, which is something entirely different. Since it speaks of the kingdom of God, the version of the parable in Luke does raise the question of eternal salvation. Here I would say that if grace obliges everyone to enter the kingdom, then so be it. The grace God accords will bring all of us into his kingdom. This is clearly what this text means, and it has nothing whatsoever to do with converting people by force. This historically disastrous heresy had its origin in the detachment of three words, followed by the building of a theology on them. Every biblical text must be interpreted in the context of the entire Bible.

The third part of the parable, beginning with verse 11, has the king join the banquet once it is well underway, in accordance with the customs of that time. He proceeds to a judgment and, following the traditional interpretation, this judgment falls on the church since it is the church

---

2 The Donatists believed that only people who led blameless lives could belong to the church.

that is assembled at the wedding. The judgment falls on the one who is not wearing a wedding garment. I will start with the explanation given by Jeremias,[3] which is completely positivistic and historicist but rather interesting. His thesis is that the text resulted from blending together two parables. One is the parable of the invited guests and the other of the wedding garment. The early church was pushed into mixing the two because of the following problem. If the church baptizes everyone who requests it, everybody, good and bad people alike, would be allowed to join. Does this mean that henceforth no judgment of the people of the church can be made? This would imply that once people are baptized everything should be fine, but this is clearly not the case. What is the church supposed to do about the people who have been baptized but who do not live a Christian life in conformity with the gospel? It is for these reasons, Jeremias argues, that the church added the last part about the wedding garment – to warn people that just because they had made it into the wedding banquet everything was not necessarily going to be all right.

It is quite possible that two texts were fused together, but I do not agree with the explanation of the motivation for doing so. If, as I believe, the central element of this parable is the joy that everything is ready, then the problem is not a moral one but one of joy. Will the guests who come because everything is ready participate in the joy of the wedding feast? Will they enter into the communion with Jesus Christ? I believe this communion is absolutely fundamental because without it a person does not belong at the banquet of the incarnation, as it may be called.

To another commentator this text appears scandalous. There is one person who is too poor to buy a wedding garment, and the result is his or her rejection at the banquet. This was written at a time when there was a great deal of concern about the poor being absent from the church. However, it is essential to recognize that a festive garment is not actually required. The garment becomes a wedding garment by virtue of participating in the wedding. In fact, the garment is provided by God himself, who will clothe us anew, as we are constantly told in the book of Revelation.

We then encounter the text that many are called but few are chosen. Once again, we encounter a situation where these words were separated from the remainder of the Bible and used to construct the doctrine of predestination. I believe that the overall orientation of the biblical

---

3 Joachim Jeremias, *The Parables of Jesus* (New York: Scribners Sons, 1955).

message is completely opposite to any idea that everyone will be invited but that once they are there, a few will be chosen to enter the kingdom of God (i.e., salvation). For example: Jesus says that he will call all people to him; Paul says in Timothy that Jesus desires to save all people; the letter to the Romans treats a calling and salvation as being identical; and the entire orientation of the book of Revelation supports this – it includes the particular description of only the powers being cast into hell.

Hence, I believe that the traditional explanation of this verse is impossible. I would like to point out that even Calvin, with his doctrine of predestination, has not interpreted this text in such a simple way. He notes that this verse says clearly that few are chosen but only a single person is rejected from the wedding feast. He goes on to say that Jesus is clearly not saying that a majority of people will be excluded. Hence, this cannot be a description of what will happen; instead, it must be a warning. To use Calvin's language: an outward profession of faith is not sufficient. What is required is a conversion of one's life. In other words, there can be a purely outward and verbal acknowledgment without any real change in a person's life.

I will conclude by summarizing the two principal remarks Karl Barth makes about this text. First, there are no specific numbers but simply a proportion of many and few. The real issue here is the belief that every human being has sufficient virtuous qualities to enter the kingdom of God. It is the belief that humanity can ascend to the heavens or that human nature has what is required to do so. The text, however, makes it clear that entrance into the kingdom of God is his decision alone. For Barth, this is the difference between being called and being chosen. There is no question of God's calling everyone to proceed to a 'sorting-out.'

Barth's second observation is that the will of God is the salvation of all of humanity. His power is sufficient to save everyone. God loves all people equally. However, we need to entrust ourselves to his will, which we cannot change. God's will remains his will and he alone decides, but he decides according to his mercy. In other words, to use Barth's favourite term, what we have here is 'the impossible possibility.' The possibility remains that God's will may be to reject us, and we must accept this. In one of the Psalms it says: 'If you condemn me, you will be without reproach in your judgment.' God would be right to condemn us. However, it is an 'impossible possibility' because God's love is without limits. As a result, this verse warns us (to use Calvin's idea) that we are subject to God's will (whatever that may be). What this means is that this text has nothing to do with the question of how many will be saved.

In response to your questions: If we consider human life from any kind of logical or rational perspective, it ends in death. If God extends grace and gives life, this happens whether we like it or not at first. This gift of life places us in the kingdom of God. It is his decision. The problem is that all this is very difficult to teach to someone. The church has never dared to do so openly out of fear of the moral consequences of telling people that, whatever they do, they will be saved in any case. All this is completely inconceivable for a community or society. It is also important to recognize that what is at stake here is not God's imposing some kind of obedience to him. God simply grants life; and throughout the entire Bible the central element of that life is freedom – a freedom that includes a relationship with the God who grants that life.

There is another issue here as well. The grace that God extends to every person is the grace of life and his love. However, when I hear this Word in the course of my life, I need to decide because of the *kairos*: at that moment I discover the will of God. I enter into a certain relationship with God in which I need to recognize that his will is good whatever happens. It is, so to speak, a second step on the path of faith and confidence. That is what this parable is all about. When you receive the invitation, are you going to get into a long discussion about the possibility that you may not like the cooking or are you going to trust that, whoever is in the kitchen and whatever they are going to cook, everything will be good? In a sense, that is what all this is about. Nevertheless, the situation is very difficult because the way we work and live excludes the possibility of this *kairos*. Even so, I believe that this is not so much a question of eternity bursting in, but of a moment of great joy despite the rupture in our lives.

I entirely agree that I could not have developed my commentary on this parable the way I did if it were based on the text in the gospel of Luke. As modern exegetes have pointed out, Luke has a social awareness that comes through in the different behaviour of the rich and the poor, for example. In the gospel of Luke, there is no opposition between the *kronos* and *kairos*, nor is there a distinction between the kingdom of God and the kingdom of heaven. Matthew and Luke represent two different perspectives on the same story.

18 The Parables of the Virgins and the Talents (Matthew 25:1–30)

There are three parables in this chapter, but I will omit the third one because its subject is the judgment of the nations and not the kingdom of heaven. The placement of these three parables in the gospel is rather significant. They are preceded by chapter 24 dealing with the end of the world with its wars and rumours of wars, earthquakes, famines, and the beginning of a great suffering, which is why this is often referred to as the apocalypse of the gospel of Matthew. The parables are followed by the beginning of the suffering of Jesus after the decision of the high priests to arrest and kill him. They may therefore be regarded as particularly important, since together they constitute roughly the equivalent of the last discussion of Jesus with his disciples in the gospel of John. They are placed in the same position, and represent the last warning Jesus gives to his disciples.

The parable of the ten virgins revisits the teaching of chapter 24:36–44, and the parable of the talents revisits the teaching of chapter 24:45–51. In other words, these parables take up the same two teachings that we find in the preceding verses of chapter 24, which follow Jesus' announcement regarding the end of the world. These teachings about the importance of being prudent, alert, and vigilant are so important that Matthew repeats them, first directly and then in the form of parables.

I would like to make several observations about these two parables. First, they revisit several things that we have already encountered. The kingdom of heaven is like ten virgins, or like a man who calls his servants to account. Again, we see that the kingdom of heaven is borne by and acts through people on earth. These people are not all alike, as some carry out their tasks and others do not; and the ones that do show varying levels of devotion and faithfulness. During the presence of the

kingdom of heaven in human history, they all participate in this waiting in darkness. This is exactly what we see in the church, with all its
infidelities and variations in the authenticity of its members. We are not
to judge this but to accept that these people are there. Again, there is the
passage of the kingdom of heaven into the kingdom of God, represented as a wedding in which Jesus encounters the church faithful and
as the return of a lord who brings to light everything they have done
and said, to reveal who they really are. Again, a judgment falls on only
one person.

Second, these two parables also have a unique teaching regarding the
role of the kingdom of heaven. A first new aspect of this role in history
is that of maintaining the light Jesus Christ brought to illuminate the
world while he is absent. This role was already announced in Matthew
5, which declares that 'you are the light of the world' and that a lamp
must not be put under a bushel. I believe that this light is the Word of
God, which must be borne in the world via the intermediary of people.
If people are silent, the stones may well cry out (as Jesus affirms) but the
Word will not be spoken. This is the central problem. We must not defer
our responsibility of speaking the Word of God to others. The church is
the lampholder that bears the light. It is not that light itself. People are
but the bearers of God's Word. It is a light because it permits people to
conduct their lives in the dark and illuminates the things of the world.
I believe this is the double role of the Word of God, which has often
been forgotten by shutting it up in a pietistic tradition where it speaks
to my heart, to my soul, to my emotions, and so on. On the contrary, it
is a guide to action, which is entirely different. Nor is the Word of God
an abstract or theological truth, because it concerns the reality of this
world by teaching us to see things differently. The maintenance of the
light in this way is the first task of the kingdom of heaven and of the
people called to it.

A second new aspect of the role of the kingdom of heaven is the preparation of the return of Jesus Christ. The Bridegroom is on the way and
we must be ready to meet him when he comes. This readiness must be
like that of John the Baptist, who recognized Jesus when he came for the
first time. I believe this presents the same difficulty as the one dealt
with in chapter 24. A traditional theological interpretation holds that
Jesus came incognito but will return in glory, but I am not convinced
this will be terribly obvious. For example, chapter 24 speaks of false
Christs and false prophets who will do great miracles; but Jesus warns
in advance that if someone says that he has come back in the desert or

some other place, you should not go there. Clearly, it will not be that obvious. The first time it happened, it took the insight of a John the Baptist to see in Jesus the one who was announced by the prophets.

The gospel of Matthew suggests that at the time of Jesus' coming there will be a great uncertainty. The five wise virgins are there to welcome the Lord because they are able to discern him. There has to be this ongoing ability to receive him. It is related to the all-important question of whether there will still be faith on this earth. This may in part explain the somewhat selfish response of the wise virgins refusing to share their oil. It would be disastrous for all concerned if they all ran out of oil, but even more so for Jesus Christ.

We encounter this problem in many forms. For example: a French priest recently said that if he had to choose between Jesus Christ and the revolution, he would choose the revolution. This is not possible, and not simply for ideological reasons but with regard to Jesus Christ: someone must be there when he returns. We must never give up our faith for the sake of solidarity with others.

A third new aspect of the role of the kingdom of heaven is to continue to develop what Jesus began on this earth. The second parable makes this clear. The talents Jesus has distributed by his work must be put to use and extended. The kingdom of heaven is the growth of what Jesus began. A variety of straightforward remarks can be made on this point. In the absence of Jesus Christ, this work is our responsibility. We must not expect God to do it for us or the Holy Spirit to act in our place. The work depends on our decisions and actions.

The means God provides are referred to in this parable as the talents. These are not merely the spiritual virtues. Nor are they whatever God places within us, as liberal Protestantism would have it. For example, intelligence is not a talent but simply a human quality resulting from genetic inheritance and culture. We can be thankful to God for such qualities but we must not make God into the good fairy that distributes them. Hence, there is a fundamental difference between the gifts that God grants and qualities that are entirely human. This distinction also applies to human activities. For example, when the wise virgins go and buy oil, this is a human activity, not a gift that is decided and distributed by God.

Another straightforward observation concerns the role played by the development and growth of human activities in this kingdom of heaven. We must not have any illusions about the importance of what we do since it is tiny in relation to what God does. Nevertheless, as we have seen, God's work would not be carried out without human participation.

By way of illustration, recall the miracle of the multiplication of the loaves of bread and the fish. Jesus did not do this from nothing. First, the disciples brought to him the bread and fish that was available. It was insufficient, but without this first step undertaken by people nothing would be done. This is exactly what Paul means when he says that we are co-workers with God. Even a theology as transcendental as that of Karl Barth, which I follow, in no way excludes human action.

According to these two parables, a fourth new aspect of the role of the kingdom of heaven is that it is a time of testing. How will people conduct their lives during this time of waiting while Jesus is absent? They are left alone, which tests their vigilance, effort, and dedication. The first parable appears somewhat pessimistic in this regard. All ten virgins fall asleep. In the larger biblical context, we also remember the disciples falling asleep in the garden of Gethsemane while Jesus prayed. At the same time, this is also extraordinarily comforting. We know that even when we fall asleep grace will continue, and this is very important. Hence, to belong to the kingdom of heaven and to participate in it is a testing of who we are and to what we are called.

Having considered what these two parables teach us regarding the role of the kingdom of heaven, I will next turn to the exhortations they present. Their character is a little different from the previous ones, which were more detached, as it were. They spoke of a merchant searching for a pearl or a person finding a treasure in a field, and so on. The present parables have a much more pronounced aspect of exhortation in that they deal with the kinds of qualities expected of those who are in the kingdom of heaven. We have already discussed a first quality and its importance, namely, vigilance. During the silence of God (presented as the bridegroom who is coming and the man who went abroad) it is night. It is up to us to watch, remain vigilant, and bear the light for the world. I believe this is particularly important for all the churches that are completely without direction at this time. We are tempted to speak in the ways of the world, to assimilate ourselves into that world, and hence to cease being a sign of who God is. We ourselves have no other reference point than that furnished by Jesus Christ from a distant past. We cannot claim that he is here or there manifesting himself in a bold miraculous way. All we have is that absurd perseverance which acknowledges that Jesus died and rose again two thousand years ago, and that this is as real as ever. Also, just because we have been waiting a very long time does not mean that there is only a little time left to wait. I hold this to be the central element of these two parables.

A second quality is wisdom, represented in the two parables by the wise virgins and the servants who worked well with the talents they had received. Such wisdom has nothing to do with exceptional intelligence or with what philosophers call wisdom, and certainly not with a moral orientation. In the Bible, wisdom has a very precise meaning, that being the discernment of God's will in terms of what He expects from us. There is nothing philosophical or moral about this. This will of God does not fall from the sky but must be discerned by us. The ten virgins knew that they had to keep their lamps burning, and the servants knew that they had to work with the money they received. What they had to discern may appear simple; but it is, of course, a parable.

What we face is much more complex. Yet I believe that it is ultimately simple to discern God's will. I am not talking about God's will *hic et nunc* at each moment in our lives. The difficulty stems perhaps not so much from discerning God's will as from living it. God has chosen a specific way, which is the revelation centred in Jesus Christ that we are invited to follow.

A third quality encountered in these two parables is the ability to put things into practice. It is not simply a question of knowing what to do but of actually doing it. In other words, it is a question of our works. The problem is that so often this has been made into something moralistic and trivial, but it is not when you think of it in terms of praxis (as in Hegelian or Marxist thinking). For example, when Jesus is asked how we can know that his words are from God, he replies that we should do what he says and then we will know that they are from God. It is by this practice that we can know this and not by some kind of intellectual mechanism or by some philosophy. Practice this and you will see.

There is much more involved than what was traditionally expressed as faith expressing itself in works. The letter of James suggests this very clearly when it says that there is no faith without works. The two cannot de dissociated, and this has led to serious theological errors. For example, the Catholic church taught that everything was tested by works, to which Luther replied that everything was a question of faith – and he was mistaken. Everything is not a question of faith, since there is no faith if there are no works. To some extent, the process may be likened to what used to be endlessly debated. Is there a prior thought that is subsequently expressed by language? It is now believed that there is a radical interpenetration of the two. I believe that the relationship between faith and works is similar. Faith cannot exist without works and vice versa. A practice without faith does not exist. These two parables reveal this fundamental relationship.

A fourth quality is hope. The second parable emphasizes that the lord of the servants came back only after a long time. This detail is frequently trivialized by explanations we have already encountered. Jesus supposedly thought that the end of the world was imminent, and when this turned out not to be the case, the early church added these kinds of details. I think this is a very bad exegesis. It implies that the first Christians were stupid enough to think that they could console themselves by adding such a phrase here and there. As far as this method of interpretation is concerned, I do not think that it is possible to base an exegesis on a single historical theory popular at the end of the nineteenth century, namely, that the delay in the return of Jesus Christ gave rise to an entire theology. I am not in the least convinced, because even if Jesus had believed this, he would have taken his precautions in case things worked out differently. In the case of the gospel of John, it is difficult to deny that the warning of Jesus, to the effect that I tell you these things so you will not be troubled, dates from very early on and is likely original. What Jesus says here is that you must continue to live in hope even if it takes a very long time. This quality of hope is fundamental. I am personally convinced that Jesus' warning that it could take a long time is from Jesus himself and not some addition, as suggested by a rather naïve hypothesis.

I believe that what we have just learned also clarifies the judgment of the five foolish virgins. They left, they are no longer present as bearers of light, and they remain outside. Hope is required to be able to wait a very long time.

All this is further reinforced by the judgment of the servant, who explains that he knew that his lord was a hard man who harvested where he had not sown. His master behaves exactly according to the judgment and words of this servant. It is not a question of the master really being a hard man. What it means is: 'You judged me as a hard master, hence I am such a master.' This response conforms to the entire Old Testament, where God is what people believe him to be. It is not that we impose something on God but, as the rabbis taught, that God makes himself for us. In other words, if you are convinced that God is good he will be good with you. If you are convinced that God is love, he loves. If, on the contrary, you believe God to be cruel and hard, then you will encounter him as such (but you have made him that way). We see this most clearly in the incarnation. God becomes a human being in the condition described by the gospels: as a weak, poor, suffering child of whom we can say that in these circumstances there is no God because he is not all-powerful. We may well ask: Does this mean that there is no objective God? We must pay attention to the wording. What would the existence of an objective God mean? It would mean that such a God would be limited, the way an object is limited. The God that we objectivize in this fashion is the kind of God we can represent as a triangle (possibly with a cross in the middle), as the kind father who rides the clouds, or as anything you like.

It is impossible to escape from all this unless we cease to treat him like an object by entering into a relationship with him. If you believe in a God who is love, you are in a relationship with him and he is love. It is no longer a question of how we think or imagine God; it is no longer a fiction or a phantom. The Bible reveals that God is love because he is what we expect him to be. If, instead, a servant judges his master to be hard, unjust, and without pity, he has no relationship of love with him. I think there is no other judgment than that. I believe that this is what Jesus meant when he said that you will be judged according to your *words*. He did not say according to your *works*. You will be judged according to what you say about God.

Finally, I will quickly touch on an explanation of these parables that is given by Jeremias. He makes an interesting distinction between what the original orientation of these parables was, and what this orientation became as a result of the history of the church. When Jesus told these parables, they were clearly aimed at the Jewish religious leaders and his adversaries, which is why they precede the account of his arrest and suffering at their hands. The parables thus announce the crisis that is about to happen. It will be a catastrophe, which is why Matthew 24 contains an apocalyptic description of it. The parables constitute an exhortation: the crisis is coming, and you have to take a stand. It is an appeal whether, yes or no, they are for Jesus. For Jeremias this is at the heart of these two parables.

According to Jeremias, this orientation evolved during the time of the early church (and I believe this is largely correct) – from being aimed at the leadership of the Jews and the people opposed to Jesus, to being aimed at the leaders of the church as well as the ordinary Christians because they had received the talents and were awaiting Jesus' return. As a result, the parables became an allegory of the return of Jesus Christ. (This largely corresponds to the interpretation I set out above). The exhortation is no longer to decide right now but to respond to a long period of waiting by watching and staying alert. There are thus two possible levels of interpretation of these two parables, and I believe both to be right. It shows once again that the content of these and other texts is never closed.

19 The Remaining References to the Kingdom of Heaven

In addition to the above parables, there are other references to the kingdom of heaven in the gospel of Matthew. These are found in chapter 5:3, 10, 19, and 20 (the Sermon on the Mount), chapter 7:21–7, and chapter 18:1 ff. I will begin with the verses in chapter 5. Jesus declares, 'Happy are the poor, for the kingdom of heaven belongs to them.' Clearly this is not because of some kind of natural truth but because Jesus declares it. We see this throughout the Sermon on the Mount. Thanks to the latest approaches to reading a text, we can better understand that a word is true because of the person who says it. Hence, these words cannot be detached from Jesus Christ. He is the king who rules his kingdom, with the result that what he declares is true even when things do not appear to work out that way in our experience.

Regarding the kingdom of heaven, we again encounter a number of things that we have already discussed. First, the kingdom of heaven is present now. The text clearly states (in the present tense) that it belongs to the poor in spirit and to those that are persecuted for righteousness' sake (5:3 and 5:10). The other texts are in the future tense: they shall be comforted, they shall inherit the earth, they shall see God, and so on. These all refer to a future encounter with God, when the promises will be fulfilled. In the case of the poor in spirit and those persecuted for the sake of justice, they are in the kingdom of heaven right now on this earth, even when they do not know it. They are the first to constitute this kingdom.

Another teaching about the kingdom of heaven, which we have already encountered, stems from the declaration that these people are happy. The kingdom is a living in joy and a moving forward with this joy. Finally, the kingdom of heaven is hidden and cannot be perceived by people. It is only as spoken by Jesus.

The poor in spirit are those who know that their main value or wealth in life is God's Spirit. They know they are poor because they do not have it, and they also know they must ask for it. They measure their poverty by what they lack in this regard. The kingdom of heaven is theirs because they have entered it by being in communion with its king, who is the one who is poor. Jesus is completely poor because he is at the same time totally humiliated and voluntarily humbled himself, as the text of the second chapter of Philippians 2 explains.

Those who are persecuted for the sake of justice are not those who seek human or social justice, but instead the justice of the kingdom of heaven. It is for the latter that they are persecuted. We have already encountered this kind of justice in the parable of the workers of the eleventh hour. It is the opposite of what the human communities create as justice. This justice is that of the king himself, as verse 11 makes clear. The people who pursue this justice are persecuted for his sake. In other words, being persecuted for the sake of this justice corresponds to being persecuted for the king. Jesus himself fully embodies that justice, and he is often called our justice. For this to be the case, there has to be complete communion between the servant who is persecuted and the lord, as is the case with the poor in spirit. Just as the king was persecuted, so are his servants.

It is worth recalling that, with regard to the kingdom of heaven, it is normal that Christians are persecuted. This is very clear in John 15:18–25, which shows that persecution is a part of the Christian life. As we have already seen, Christianity can only be that which calls into question what is most fundamental and central to the world. When we challenge this world in a manner that does not threaten it, there will be no persecution. The world is threatened only when the prince of this world or its spirit is called into question, not by a process of conquest and domination but by a presence of what is opposite to that world. In other words, what is important is the contradiction between the kingdom of heaven and the world. This kingdom is made up of those who are in communion with its king (the poor in spirit and those persecuted for his justice) and who therefore represent Jesus in the world by living in conformity to his example.

These two texts of chapter 5 also teach us that the means of action of the kingdom of heaven and its power to transform are opposite to the spirit of the world. These means involve humility, poverty, freely giving, and so on. It cannot be authority, spectacular conversions, breakthrough works, a strong organization of the church, miracles, or anything of this kind. The kingdom of heaven knows no efficient means, as we have seen in the parables. This kingdom grows differently from any power in the world, and certainly not by the way of efficiency.[1] The only means to the kingdom of the poor in spirit and of those who are persecuted for justice is their lives as lived in communion with Jesus Christ. There is an identity between who they are and the work of the kingdom itself. This kingdom is ourselves, which I believe is meant by its being 'in you and among you.' The kingdom is the lives of those who are in communion with Jesus Christ. It is who they are, and not any particular works, that constitutes the kingdom of heaven in action.

Jesus makes this very clear when he is asked who will be the greatest in his kingdom. He takes a child and says that if you do not become like one of these, you will not enter the kingdom of heaven. He is clearly not referring to something you do but to something you are, namely, to be humble and weak (in the sense of non-power). It is important to remind ourselves once more that belonging to the kingdom of heaven is not a question of salvation but of participating in God's work. Everything depends on who humanity is going to be. All this has nothing to do with accepting some people, rejecting others, or saving some and damning others. It is our participation in the humility of the kingdom that is its true greatness. Remember that when Jesus was crucified, the inscription on his cross read that he was Jesus of Nazareth, the king of the Jews. It is this final collapse that is its true greatness. There is none other.

All this is probably most difficult to accept. We are always looking for the most efficient means for ourselves or for the church. People organize big meetings like those of Billy Graham and use television networks, but anything like that amounts to nothing. We can do these things as long as we have no illusion that it has anything to do with the kingdom of heaven.

Turning to chapter 7, beginning with verse 21, we again see that those who are powerful are excluded. Entrance into the kingdom of heaven is equated in this text to doing the will of the Father. Also, entrance into the kingdom is not a reward for doing wonderful works.

---

1 The reader is referred to the many works of Jacques Ellul examining our civilization's dependence on the means of power and efficiency. See, for example, *The Technological Society*, trans. John Wilkinson (New York: Alfred A. Knopf, 1973); *The Technological System*, trans. Joachim Neugroschel (New York: Continuum, 1980); *Propaganda*, trans. Konrad Kellen and Jean Lerner (New York: Vintage Books, 1973); *The Political Illusion*, trans. Konrad Kellen (New York: Vintage Books, 1972); *The Technological Bluff*, trans. Geoffrey W. Bromiley (Grand Rapids, MI: Eerdmans, 1990); and others.

These words of Jesus are so commonly misinterpreted that we do well to ask why this is the case. One such misinterpretation argues that entrance into the kingdom of heaven is a recompense for good behaviour. Such an interpretation is impossible if this text is examined as being integral to the series of texts into which it is inserted. They are all related to behaviour: judge not, do not give what is holy to the dogs, do to others as you would like them to do to you, take the narrow road, beware of false prophets, you will know them by their fruits, entry into the kingdom of heaven is by doing the will of the father, and building a house is a symbol of living one's life. Since all these texts deal with life's practices, it is not possible that in the middle of this series there is a text dealing with eternal salvation and a recompense to be received. Like all the others, our text deals with living on this earth within and outside the kingdom of heaven. It has nothing to do with paradise but with conducting our lives on this earth.

This text also implies why it speaks of the kingdom of heaven. Those who do the will of the Father are in this kingdom. We come back to what we have already seen in the parables. The designation of this kingdom being from heaven as the dwelling place of God makes it other than the creation. It is the result of the stupendous event of the incarnation. Heaven (or the non-world) is now present on this earth on which we live. All the characteristics of the kingdom of heaven can be understood in relation to this event.

A second misinterpretation of this text is based on an opposition between words, which accomplish nothing, and deeds, which get things done. The typical sermon will argue that it is not sufficient to say 'lord, lord, …' but you must act. All this completely disregards verse 22, which does not talk about simply saying 'lord, lord, …' but about a whole series of extraordinary actions such as doing miracles or casting out demons, and doing these in the name of Jesus Christ. These Christians, and I believe we can call them that, manifest all the guarantees and yet they will not participate in the kingdom of heaven. The reason is entirely clear: they do not represent the will of the Father. Doing miracles and so on is not sufficient because Satan also performs miracles, and even good ones at that. It is not sufficient to use the name of Jesus Christ; and we must be reminded that we are not to take the name of our God in vain. In other words, what we have here is a warning that the name of Jesus Christ can endlessly be used in vain.

According to the text, Jesus reproaches the people engaged in the above kinds of actions of four things. First, these people contest the judgment of Jesus. He tells them that they will not enter into the kingdom of heaven, and they question this by saying that they have performed all these marvellous things. They are in fact implying that Jesus is not just because he is shutting them out even though they have done remarkable things in his name. We should remember the text of one of the prophets, to the effect that whatever you (God) decide, I know you will be just in your sentence and without reproach in your judgment. What we have here is another warning.

Second, the people Jesus is talking about pride themselves on their works. What this means is that they present their glory, which is the opposite of humility. It is the opposite of what Jesus speaks about when he brings out a little child in response to the question as to who is the greatest in the kingdom of heaven.

Third, the people in question have used spectacular means of power such as prophecy and miracles. They have forgotten that the kingdom of heaven does not come through power. Having said this, I would also caution us not to take texts like these to reassure ourselves about our lack of miracles. For example, if there are no healings in our midst it is not because we do not live with the Holy Spirit. What this text tells us is not to make healings or other miracles the keystone of everything else. To make them into more than means is a temptation to avoid.

Finally, the people Jesus is talking about lack an attitude of repentance and obedience. Instead, they regard themselves as having done many great works in the name of Jesus Christ. It is an attitude we are all familiar with because we are all tempted to use biblical texts to justify ourselves, for example. What is at stake here is obedience instead of seeking to do exemplary works. This obedience includes following the way of non-power and non-domination. The text is very clear on this point.

It also tells us that iniquity may be committed by people who, to all appearances, are devoted to Christian work in the church and in the world. Christians can end up doing something entirely other than the will of the Father. This is not a question of opposing words to deeds, nor of a moral evil. If you are possessed by a spirit of domination, power, or the spectacular, you are not participating in the work of the Lord and the kingdom of heaven. You are doing something else.

I think this text should be understood in relation to the ones about the Pharisees in Matthew 23:13, where we read that they close off the kingdom of heaven to the people. They will not enter into it themselves, and they bar others who wish to enter. When we read texts such as these, we must remind ourselves that the Pharisees and scribes were

very pious people who intimately knew the word of God and who scru-
pulously accomplished all possible works under the law. It is to these
very people that Jesus says that while they are accumulating good
works they shut the kingdom of heaven. Again, shutting the kingdom
of heaven is not a matter of salvation since that is related to the kingdom of God. What they are doing is preventing people from living out
of grace and of giving freely, which is the will of God.

I will close by considering Matthew 18:1, which deals with the question of being the greatest in the kingdom of heaven. Again, this kingdom is situated in the present. Jesus' answer is exceedingly clear: the
greatest is the smallest. In other words, it is the one who cannot claim
to be the greatest in any way whatsoever: not by faith, not by works,
not by human qualities, not by intelligence, not by spiritual qualities,
and so on. It is the condition of a small child. However, it is obviously
not a question of a psychological or moral disposition, because children
can be vain or boastful and not humble at all. It is a question of their
condition because even if they think they're strong, they are not. Even
if they are vain, they have no reason to be so. They are in the objective
condition of being humble; that is to say, they are weak. What Jesus tells
his disciples and us is not to make a virtue of being humble, but instead
to recognize the extent of our weakness – this is what it means to be
humble. It is the endless problem of pride. We know very well what
fighting back pride to become humble entails: each time we succeed
and do something exceptional, we marvel at how good we are; and this
leads us right back to pride. However, this is not what humility is about.
It is not a counter-pride but the recognition of our powerlessness. It
brings to mind the text in the seventh letter to the churches found in the
book of Revelation, in which the church at Laodicea is admonished because it thinks it is rich and in need of nothing, but according to the text,
it is really poor because this church does not know that it is unhappy,
miserable, poor, blind, and naked. Jesus Christ advises this church to
buy from him gold that has been refined by fire in order that it may
become rich. To be humble is to know the extent to which we are poor,
destitute in every way, and without any real strength regardless of the
means we employ. The recognition of this condition is livable only
when, at the same time, we are called to enter the kingdom of heaven.
This is what the text from the letter to the church in Laodicea makes
clear. Bringing someone to recognize their true condition is to lead them
towards suicide. Doing so may be done only in the context of the good
news: be humble because, as of this moment, you will participate in the

work of God in the kingdom of heaven. The two must be indissociably connected. Anything else would be catastrophic.

There is one more aspect to the question of who is the greatest in the kingdom of heaven. In a sense we have encountered this all along. The greatest is the one who is the closest to the humility of Jesus Christ. A structuralist reading of the text can help to bring this out. The disciples approach Jesus with this question. Jesus turns away from them to call a small child and brings forward this child, who is now the closest to him. Jesus then replies to his disciples that this child is great in the kingdom of heaven, being close to its king. Here we return to something we have already seen, namely, that to be great is to take the direction of imitating Jesus Christ. He is the servant who is entirely obedient, without violence, without power, and full of grace. These are the elements that enable the kingdom of heaven to be constituted.

PART FOUR

It Was All There in the Beginning
(John 1:1–2)

20 Love within the Beginning

I will begin this study of the opening two verses of the gospel of John with three introductory remarks. There is no doubt that this text is directly related to the one found in Genesis. The first Hebrew word in the Genesis text is better translated as '*Within* the beginning' than as '*In* the beginning.' The fundamental idea is that there is not a point zero followed by a beginning, but a long beginning within which various things happened. In the first verse of the gospel of John we find exactly the same expression in Greek: '*Within* the beginning of this history.' Such a literal translation from Hebrew means that this gospel relies on God's revelation to Israel. The text is also related to Genesis by the Word: 'Within this beginning God says …' God speaks, and this is what we learn about God right from the beginning of the book of Genesis. He is *Logos*, and of what went before he spoke there is nothing we need to know. As I have suggested earlier, the Bible is not there to satisfy our curiosity. There is no point asking what went before the Word was spoken – all we need to know is that this happened. In Genesis, as in the gospel of John, within the beginning there was the *Logos*, which for us marks the beginning of everything.

The translation of the Hebrew and Greek words as *logos* is inadequate. When Faust hears the church bells at Easter he is reminded of this text, and in a grand monologue he reasons that in the beginning there cannot be a Word because a word is of no importance. A better translation, he argues, would be that in the beginning there was the Meaning, but can the meaning of things create? This is clearly impossible. He then proposes that in the beginning there was the Power, but argues that this is also impossible because power has no value. Faust therefore concludes that in the beginning there was the Action; and this is the philosophy of Goethe, who reduces everything to the value of action.

I believe that this shows that *Logos* or the Word had none of these meanings, but refers to something much richer. If we translate *Logos* with 'the Word,' which is the only direct translation, it corresponds to the Hebrew word *dabar*. We do well to remind ourselves of the several meanings of *dabar*. It means the spoken word as well as the action involved – the event it produces. Consequently, when we read in the Bible that God said or God spoke, it is not merely a question of words but also an action. The Hebrew makes no distinction between speaking and doing: a word is an action, and this action is always included in the word. When God speaks he acts, and Genesis reveals to us, it is by his Word that he acts. All this is included in *Logos* (the event and the action) but in addition, the Hebrew word *dabar* has the same root as the Hebrew verb to create. When we say that God creates by means of his Word, this is literally what the Hebrew says. *Logos* implies this as well. Hence, when God speaks, he creates something new.

In addition, the Word is a bearer of meaning. What Faust says about this in his monologue is not wrong. To say that in the beginning there was the Word suggests a giving of meaning. For there to be a Word, he who speaks this Word must commit himself. In earlier times, when honour was still a value, this is what people meant when they said, 'I give you my word.' No oath was required because through that word they were totally committed. I will come back to this shortly.

Finally, a Word is necessarily addressed to someone in order to establish a communication. Hence, the affirmation that within the beginning there was the Word is at the same time an affirmation that there was someone to receive it. God does not speak to no one and nothing. I think that God, before bringing order to the *tohu wabohu*, creates an 'ear' to hear and receive his Word. However, more is required for a true Word. From the study of language we have learned that for a language to be understood there must be a metalanguage. We understand each other not simply because we share a vocabulary and a grammar. We also have in common a number of pre-established 'ideas,' as it were, that act as a pre-understanding shared by a speaker and a listener. This further reinforces the need for the speaker to be *within* the word.

We now begin to see the extent to which the two first verses of the gospel of John correspond to the first verses in Genesis. This does not mean that what we have here is a definition of God. It cannot be used as a point of departure for knowing everything about God. All we can know is what the *Logos* or Word reveals about him. We cannot go beyond this. This revelation tells us that we can receive and understand this Word of God and that he is with us.

Next, I would like to tackle the two difficult theological problems raised by these first two verses of the gospel of John. The first is that of the Trinity and the question of the divinity of Jesus, because this prologue is immediately followed by John bearing witness of Jesus. I believe that it is very important to understand the Trinity based on this text. We must recognize (and I can understand that this may offend some people) that the term 'monotheism' means absolutely nothing. I say this because in almost all religions regarded as polytheistic there is always a god above the others, of whom little is said but who is the one and only. For example, *Kronos* was such a god (before Zeus and the rest of the Greek pantheon). Moreover, the real question is not knowing whether there is one or several, but knowing who it is because there can be monotheisms that contradict each other. For example, I would claim that the monotheism of Islam is contradictory to that of Judaism. The term 'god' can be used for many things, such as Ramakrishna, Isis, or Thor. By itself the term has no meaning. I think, therefore, that the term monotheism is not helpful.

The answer given by the theologians of the Middle Ages was that there is one God in three persons, namely, God the Father, the Son, and the Holy Spirit. I must confess that this explanation never did much for me because I do not understand to what this personalization corresponds. I think that theological concepts such as person or substance (as in transubstantiation) belong to Medieval philosophy and are foreign to biblical thinking.

In the entire biblical revelation, the word for God is often a plural (Elohim). There are three elements. There is the name (the one used to avoid pronouncing the sacred tetragram), the Word, and wisdom. The three Hebrew words refer to what is integral to a one and only God; hence, there are no persons here. Karl Barth puts it well when he says that these are three expressions of God's being. In this sense, a person also has a word, wisdom, and intelligence, and yet it is one being. However, in the case of God each expression is entirely full and complete. Hence, Jesus as God's Word and God's Wisdom is not different from God. The *Logos* is God himself who speaks. This is confirmed in a rather astonishing manner by a text from the first century B.C. discovered in the archives of the Vatican library (where there exists a treasure of Hebrew manuscripts). It deals with the first three chapters of Genesis; and in it the Hebrew word for God (Elohim or YHWH) has been replaced by 'the Word.' We may conclude from this that for the Hebrews of that time God and the Word are one and the same. There is no plurality of different persons within God, but one God with different ways of expressing himself as Jesus or the Holy Spirit.

This brings me to the second theological problem, which is even thornier than the previous one. It has to do with the incarnation. We are in the habit of thinking about the incarnation as God's coming at the moment of Jesus' conception. God was in heaven, humanity was on the earth, and a union between the two took place through the Word at the moment of the incarnation. Especially in German sculptures of the eleventh and twelfth centuries, this is represented in an interesting manner. Another conception is that of the union between God and Jesus the man taking place at the time of Jesus' baptism as an adoption, recorded in the gospels as the declaration: 'This is my beloved Son.'

The text under discussion has led to a different thesis, which has been the subject of endless debate. The thesis is very old, dating back to the eleventh century, but it continually resurfaces, and most recently received theological support from Karl Barth. It holds that Jesus himself is the *Logos*. According to this view, there is not a divine Christ who is incarnated in a human Jesus, but a human Jesus who was himself in God.

This means that the prologue of the gospel of John speaks at the same time of the human Jesus and the eternal *Logos*. At a first glance, the second verse appears to repeat what has already been said in the first verse. However, the Greek word usually translated by the phrase 'the same' is also used in the seventh verse, where we read that John came to bear witness of 'the same.' Here the Greek word clearly refers to Jesus. In the fifteenth verse we encounter the same Greek word once more when we are told that John bore witness of 'the same.' Again this word refers to Jesus. Hence, this Greek word is repeated three times, of which two without question refer to Jesus, which may well suggest that the Greek word translated as 'the same' in the second verse also refers to Jesus. This verse now presents us with the astounding revelation that within the beginning Jesus was with God, and thus that before the creation of Adam, man was with God. The prologue would therefore tell us that within the beginning Jesus was the *Logos*, the *Logos* was with God, the *Logos* was God, Jesus was in the beginning with God. The second verse is now very different from the first.

This may explain two other things. When Pilate presents Jesus, he says, 'Here is the man,' in the fullest possible sense. It also corresponds to God creating Adam in his image, if that image was Jesus in God.

This interpretation presents us with a different view of the incarnation: Jesus being the *Logos* from all eternity. The incarnation is thus an integral part of God's creative work from the very beginning. All this is confirmed by many texts that we all know but tend to gloss over. In the letter of Paul to the Colossians 1:15 we read that in him (Jesus) all things were created. In verse 17 we read that he is before all things and in him everything was created. The second chapter of the first letter of John reveals that we have known him who was from the beginning (verse 13). These and other texts concern the reality of Jesus' humanity. An even more fundamental text is that of the second chapter in the letter to the Philippians beginning in verse 5, which tells us that although Jesus was in the form of God, he did not count equality with God a thing to be grasped but emptied himself, taking the form of a servant and that of a human being, and so on. Again, this text does not speak of *the* Christ but of Jesus Christ.

We thus encounter the monumental error of any attempt to separate the historical Jesus from the Christ of faith. This is absolutely impossible. It is the man Jesus who, from the beginning, was Christ in God. The fifth verse of Philippians 2 clearly speaks of Jesus Christ. We have here a unity of doctrine between the schools of thought of Paul and John.

All this affirms something radically different from what Greek philosophy had to say regarding the *Logos* and marks a complete break with it. The *Logos* is the man Jesus who existed before the creation. I think therefore that the prologue to the gospel of John speaks of Jesus the man and the eternal *Logos* at the same time. It is one of the ambiguities in this gospel. It also explains the surprising reference to John the Baptist within this encompassing prologue, only to return to him later: the significance of John the Baptist is interpreted entirely in relation to Jesus. All this is perfectly coherent if the prologue speaks at the same time of Jesus and the *Logos*. What appeared to be interjections now fit into the ensemble of this text.

I wish to emphasize once more that this revelation is extraordinarily difficult. Jesus the son is the Son for all eternity in God. Accordingly, God is the Father. It is not a superfluous detail: God being God and also the Father. God is Father because in him is the Son, who is none other than Jesus. No distinction can be made between the human Jesus and a divine Son. The two are the same. Because the *Logos* is the man in God, this *Logos* is necessarily the Word turned toward humanity as it is being created. The human Jesus in God is the expression of God's turning toward humanity. At the beginning of the world, there is God who is at the same time the Father, and man who is the *Logos* turned toward the creation to engage all life in a dialogue. It is clearly a very difficult theological issue. However, I believe that this prologue would be permeated by uncertain and incomprehensible elements were it not for this kind of explanation. I also recognize that such an explanation upsets many of our received ideas.

In reply to your questions, I would like to add the following remarks: My understanding of the Holy Spirit is its being the relationship between the Father and the Son. As such, it is the relationship between God and humanity.

As for the 'God is dead' theology: Its proponents hold that God died in Jesus Christ on the cross. When Jesus cries out to his Father, 'Why have you abandoned me?' there is no God, until Jesus says that everything is accomplished and that he places his spirit in God's hands. It is the one aspect of the 'God is dead' theology that is correct. Jesus knew everything was accomplished because all the catastrophes announced to the Jewish people as a consequence of evil were finished. God had paid with his own existence, so to speak. After this, God 'exists' anew because the entire Word has been accomplished. When Karl Barth was asked what he thought of the 'God is dead' theology, he answered that God died in Jesus Christ. When God is dead it is the disorder, the *tohu wabohu*, and the darkness that reappear.

As we struggle with these difficult issues, it is important to recognize that our faith does not depend on us. Our faith is constantly called into question, and it is in this way that it grows. A faith that does not encounter the threat of doubt is for me an impossibility.[1] In the course of our attempts to understand the Bible, this very Bible calls us into question, including our faith. However, this process of becoming aware of the limits of our faith must not be confused with losing it. It is the exact opposite because we are called to take another step and to go further. Remember the first commandment: to love God with our whole mind. I should also point out that I would not say these things to people who have not struggled with these issues and may not be able to deal with them. Here, I am simply struggling with what it means to love God with all your mind. In this respect, it is amazing how the Bible speaks to people of all kinds, including those who have little background and those who have studied a great deal. We must find our own understanding and nourishment. As that understanding grows, we will also come to a greater adoration. I can certainly affirm that in my own life the more I learn to understand, the more amazing this revelation becomes.

---

1 Jacques Ellul, *Living Faith: Belief and Doubt in a Perilous World*, trans. Peter Heinegg (San Francisco: Harper & Rowe, 1983).

Epilogue: History and Reconciliation

I cannot think of a more fitting conclusion to the previous four parts than Jacques Ellul's study of the book of Revelation.[1] For those readers who are not familiar with it, I propose a small foretaste of this remarkable work. This biblical text reveals the ultimate love story in five parts. Each one is characterized by a symbol that is repeated seven times to mark different aspects of what is being revealed. There are seven letters to the churches, seven seals that must be broken to reveal the contents of a scroll, seven trumpets heralding events of the greatest significance, seven bowls that are poured out, and a sevenfold affirmation of: '... and then I saw.' The number seven is very symbolic. It is the totality formed from the number of creation (four) and the number of God (three), which designates the subject of this revelation, namely, the reunification of God with his creation as the ultimate good news.

In the first part, the kingdom of heaven is (often inadequately) borne by the church as the community of all believers. Through it, the second part can be understood. The scroll represents the meaning of human history, whose major constituents are progressively revealed as each seal is broken. The first four components are represented by four horses with their riders. The first represents the Word of God, bearing the crown of victory and carrying a bow (symbolizing the rainbow) as the sign of the covenant. The colour of horse and rider is white, that of purity and sanctity. The given crown and the action of conquest represent the dialectic of the 'already' (the victory already won in eternity) and the 'not yet' (riding with the others in human history).

---

1 Jacques Ellul, *Apocalypse: The Book of Revelation*, trans. George W. Schreiner (New York: Seabury, 1977).

The breaking of the second seal reveals a red horse and rider. It represents political power which, in the form of the state, uses the sword for making war instead of promoting justice. However, this rider represents more than the immediate reality of the state: the historical manifestation of a deeper political power acting in that history.

The breaking of the third seal reveals a black horse and rider, who measures and weighs for the purpose of selling and rationing. Because the denarius was a worker's daily pay and a measure of wheat a person's necessary daily sustenance, the rider represents the power over the necessities of life. These are limited by excluding wine and oil. In other words, this rider represents economic power in human history.

The breaking of the fourth seal reveals a pale horse and rider, representing the active power of disease and death in human history. The powers of the last three riders are limited to one fourth of the earth.

Since the first rider has no limits, it signifies the presence of God revealed in Genesis, who delimits the powers of chaos and annihilation and who separates the light from the dark. The joint actions of the four riders affect everyone, both the just and the unjust. Jointly, these four riders weave the fabric of human history, which we tend to interpret as entirely under the control of God or of chance. Even when we believe that we understand the 'human cause' of historical events, we should recall this revelation that there is always something more that we do not understand. We may well believe that humanity makes its own history, but we must be prepared for things turning out very differently from what we intended. The good news is that all this is set in motion by the breaking of the first four seals brought about by Jesus Christ as the Lamb, crushed and condemned to death by the justice of his time. However, he has overcome these powers so that they can be revealed to us without causing fear and despair.

The breaking of the fifth seal reveals something that is bound to shock most of us. A decisive component of human history is the prayers of those who testify (as in a trial) to what is happening, even at the cost of their lives. Who still believes that prayer can have a major influence? It is because we have turned prayer into something else: the making of a spiritual shopping list sent up to the heavenly supermarket for home delivery. What this seal reveals is that prayer and testimony can accelerate the course of human history toward its fulfilment. The vengeance demanded is that of the triumph of the justice of God: the destruction of the powers, the judgment and separation of what is unto death and what is unto life, and the reconciliation between God and humanity in

the new creation. All this will become evident in what follows. The witnesses testify to the 'yeast' of the kingdom of heaven being present in
the 'dough' of human history. There can be no question of a kind of
vengeance falling on the unjust. The just are not so in themselves: they
receive their justice (symbolized as white robes) from the Lamb. They
must prepare for the Lamb's return, just as Elihu prepared the way for
God in the book of Job.

In the Roman Empire, the role of a witness in a trial was known by
everyone. The witnesses did not participate in the deliberations of justice: they intervened in the trial to testify to events outside of the court-
room, and then left. In the same way, the witnesses of the fifth seal
intervene in human history by testifying to events outside of history,
which can only be understood in faith. The witnesses introduce something that ruptures history in an unexpected way, and this will transform everything.

The breaking of the sixth seal reveals two aspects of the same thing.
It brings a series of disasters as well as the appearance of the people of
God. Without this revelation regarding human history, we see only the
terrible things that happen. However, there is also a great calm, which
nothing can disturb until all God's people have been liberated. It is a
'surgical' removal of everything that is unto death, with all the pain and
suffering this 'surgery' involves. It is the mysterious working of the
kingdom of heaven in human history, which liberates first the Jewish
people and then the body of believers. The symbolism could not be
more emphatic. The Jewish people are numbered as twelve times
twelve (a totality without any lack) taken to one thousand – a symbolic
totality of totality. Next comes the body of believers, for which no num-
bering is possible or useful. They come from all nations, including the
ones that are condemned because of the actions of their kings, generals,
or the rich. It must be remembered that this appearance of God's people
is a component of human history and not of the final judgment. It is
therefore the hidden working of the kingdom of heaven, for the accel-
eration of which the martyrs pray.

It is this kind of revelation that has always offended Jewish and
Christian religious institutions. We should remember that God's ways
are not our ways, and this is made very clear in the parables of the kingdom of heaven. However, we might say that the 'laws' of this kingdom
are not very practical for us. How can you run a religious denomination
without distinguishing between members and non-members? There are
those who are 'in' and those who are 'out.' The social necessity of making

such a distinction is then frequently extrapolated to the 'ins' being just and saved, and the 'outs' being unjust and damned. Such a radical separation of people must have an ultimate justification, which amounts to a self-justification. In this way, the revelation is transformed into a religion and a morality, even though the first few chapters of Genesis begin to reveal a God whose ways have nothing in common with religion and morality. His workers all receive the same wage of life, and his yeast transforms the entire dough, after which it ceases to exist. The extension of grace always exceeds the proliferation of sin. The flock of sheep is left by the shepherd so that he can search for a single lost one. We are told not to judge, but find it necessary to separate people in order to satisfy social and institutional necessities. In doing so we turn revelation into its opposite, and join the work of the great Divider.

These social necessities are frequently exploited by political powers. They reinforce the tendencies of traditional Christian communities to blame those who are poor and vulnerable for their predicament, because if they were rich like moral and hardworking believers, they would not be in this situation. In this way, they again reinforce the turning of the good news into a religion and morality and help bar the road to the kingdom of heaven. A Sunday morning in almost any church will likely convince most 'outsiders' that this is not for them.

All this is made clear in this revelation. God's people affirm that salvation comes from God and not from themselves. Humanity becomes aware of its true salvation and liberation. This salvation comes though Jesus Christ. They are then promised a resurrection and entrance into the kingdom of God at the end of time. This vision of God's people is both historical and prophetic and is lived in hope. As long as there is faith on the earth, human history can continue.

The breaking of the seventh seal does not reveal another component of human history. It ushers in the sounding of seven trumpets, which includes the revelation of the ultimate meaning of history. This brings us to the third and central part of this revelation.

This part deals with the birth, life, and death of Jesus Christ in general, and the incarnation and the crucifixion in particular. However, this is not another gospel. Jesus is not revealed as the Lord of the church (part 1) or of history (part 2). Here we find the Jesus of Philippians 2: the God who gives up being God, with the result that it is impossible to directly speak of him. There is a kind of absence of the son of God who sits on the throne and of his 'world' (the heavens). We are told that when the seventh trumpet is sounded, the mystery of God will be fulfilled. When this happens, we see the ark of the covenant, the woman, and the child. In other words, this part reveals what happens in heaven and on earth as the consequence of the incarnation and the crucifixion. Everything is disturbed as a consequence of these events, as signified by the terrible events on the earth and the upheaval of all of creation. It is the fulfilment of the mystery of God: that God ceases to be God in order to become a human being, that he dies in Jesus, that he is resurrected and overcomes death and the powers. When God is no longer there, when he no longer holds back the powers of destruction, the consequences are the reappearance of chaos and the abyss, and the undoing of creation (chapter 8). When God is no longer there to protect humanity, the cavalry of death is unleashed (chapter 9). There can be no greater trouble than the possible consequences of the incarnation and resurrection. These are the three great troubles of which the text speaks.

The first six seals on the scroll of human history can be broken only because of this incarnation, crucifixion, and resurrection. The other components of history take on their meaning in reference to these events. The half hour of silence that accompanies the opening of the seventh seal marks a great crisis. It has a double aspect. God's work of liberating humanity from the powers also threatens it because it is so closely associated with them. Hence, this work is perceived by humanity, not only as a disturbance of its history, but as an attack on itself. The other aspect (visible only in faith) is the liberation and salvation of humanity through these events. No salvation can take place without the painful removal and destruction of everything that is unto death. Nevertheless, both inside and outside the church we constantly hear the argument that if there is a God and if God is love, humanity would not have to suffer what it does; or: how can a God of love stand by as his creatures suffer? Once again, the analogy with a surgeon may be helpful. For people who have never experienced this form of medicine, the surgeon with the knife in his (or her) hand appears to be a murderer, while those who have confidence in surgery know otherwise. Similarly, a patient unfamiliar with this kind of treatment may wake up and feel only the pain and suffering caused by the surgery without realising that a deadly cancer has been removed. Of course, there is also a great deal of suffering that we bring on ourselves as we multiply disease and death, for example, by organizing work in the pursuit of productivity or by undermining the life-sustaining capacities of the biosphere.

The incarnation achieves the unthinkable: God has entered into humanity and is now inseparable from it. He has entered into a human culture and submitted himself to its laws, even unto death. The sounding of the trumpets reminds us that throughout these cosmic events there is the announcement, the coming, and the presence of an absolute majesty. Although he comes incognito, it is God nevertheless.

When God becomes a human being, the forces of destruction and the abyss are no longer kept at bay. This event must also be understood as the beginning of a new creation. It begins with this chaos, which reveals the disaster of what the original creation has become. That is why there appear the images reminiscent of the flood and the plagues of Egypt. It is no longer a question of destroying humanity to make a new world, nor of liberating a people from the land of the double anguish of life and death. What we find are signs of de-creation, such as the mixing of the characteristics of different species. Such mixing overwhelms what God had first separated in his act of creation. However, the power of the abyss is limited to five months (one year less the seven months of grace). The decision of God represents the seven months, and the rest the unchaining of the powers and chaos.

The two witnesses represent the duality of God incarnated in Jesus Christ. Their oneness is shown in their identical experiences, which are those of Jesus. However, there is more to this symbolism. This third part of Revelation joins the historical parts dealing with the church and history to the trans-historical parts dealing with the judgment and the new creation. One face of these two witnesses is thus turned towards the historical and the other to the transhistorical. The duality may also be related to the witnesses of Israel, who prophesied these events, and those of the church, who bore witness to them. In any case, the symbol of the two witnesses can readily be identified by the accounts of the gospels.

The incarnation fundamentally transforms the relationship between the Creator and his creation. The two have now become one and can no longer be separated. There is a whole new point of departure. The dragon clearly recognizes the implications of the incarnation and the possibility of chaos and death losing their place. It attempts to prevent all this by devouring the baby. Its very existence depends on it. Since the incarnation eliminates the distance between the Creator and the creation, there will no longer be any place for the powers and death. These include the dragon at the bottom of the sea, who represents the power of chaos; the serpent, who symbolizes the power of deception; the Devil, who symbolizes the power of dividing people against each other and against God (as the opposite of love); and the Accuser, representing the power of accusation among people and before God.

All this is very different from a battle between good and evil, found in many mythologies. God is creating a perfect union with humanity. As a result, the 'gap' between God and humanity, where these powers operate, is being eliminated. Soon there will be no place for the powers of chaos, misrepresentation, accusation, and separation. In the meantime, these powers are fighting for their very existence, but they have been stripped of the possibility of playing any decisive role during the last days between the incarnation and the coming of the kingdom of God. We should always remember that if God condemned humanity, he would do exactly what Satan demands and would destroy his creation. What God does instead is revealed in the next two parts: the elimination of everything that is unto death through the process of purification, and the gathering of what is unto life into his new creation. These are the closing parts of the ultimate love story.

The structure of this complex third part may be summed up as follows. The breaking of the seventh seal of the scroll makes it possible to read the ultimate meaning of human history. God enters into humanity, as symbolized by the sounding of the seven trumpets. The creation is shaken by its Creator's decision to be united with it, thus eliminating any distance between them (chapter 8:6–9 inclusive). Next, this good news (represented as the small book of the gospel) is given to the visionary, who thus becomes aware of God's decision (chapter 10). The content of this book is the two witnesses, who represent the life, crucifixion, death, resurrection, and glorification of Jesus Christ (chapter 11:1–14). The seventh trumpet reveals the perfect covenant of God through the incarnation (chapter 11:15–19). The birth is described following the death and resurrection, which reveals that the Christian story is not merely historical but part of God's plan for a total reunification with his creation (chapter 12:1–6). The place for the Devil between God and his creation is thus being eliminated, as represented by the Devil being thrown down (chapter 12:7–17). However, the end of time remains between the incarnation and the new creation. During this interval, the dispossessed powers attempt to destroy God's initiative (chapter 13). This part ends with the appearance of the slain but triumphant Lamb.

The fourth part is marked by the pouring out of the seven bowls. It begins with the prophetic announcement and preparation for the judgments (chapter 14:6–20). Next come the catastrophes, which represent the judgment of humanity (chapter 15:5–16:21). These are followed by the judgment and destruction of the powers that have dominated humanity throughout history (chapters 17–18). After a song of praise and prophecy, the powers that have acted in heaven are damned (chapter 19:17, 21 and chapter 20). This development makes the resurrection possible.

The prophetic announcement must reach all people. It begins with the proclamation of the victory of the Lamb and the salvation of his people. It is the very basis for the eternal good news, which means that it was before the creation and is realized beyond it. In other words, no event can spoil it. It is only then that the judgment can be announced without causing fear and despair. This gospel of the way of non-power has overcome Babylon. Ultimately, humanity is going to have to make the choice of communing either with Babylon or with the Lamb. However, this choice will not be made under duress, in the manner so often employed by the church. The people (those often confused with 'the damned') suffer in the presence of the Lamb, which means that they are becoming aware of who he is, who they are, and what they wish to be. In the light of God they begin to recognize what they have always refused to see, and this begins the judgment unto life.

The judgment is carried out by Jesus, the son of humanity, by order of his Father. The judgment unto wrath is not carried out by Jesus but by an angel, also according to God's orders. The angel who speaks to Jesus and who gives the order of the harvest of salvation comes from the temple, while the one who gives the order of the vintage of God's wrath comes from the altar where expiatory victims were sacrificed. There is a clear differentiation of two roles in the judgment. This also marks the double aspect of communion: the world killed Jesus Christ after he instituted the communion with his disciples. Jesus is the one who has borne the condemnation of all humanity, although it was humanity who killed the just and loving God. His blood shed on the cross is the absolute of the blood of humanity – it is without limits. It was on him and not on humanity that the wrath fell. There will be no other victim on the altar. It is not the son of humanity who collects the grapes and treads the wine, because he himself is the trampled grapes and the wine poured out for everyone. He was the condemned for all the condemned. Once this has been made abundantly clear, the revelation of the judgment can proceed.

The judgment is marked by the pouring out of seven bowls. The seven angels who do so leave from the temple, and they also receive their orders from it. The message could not be clearer: the temple is the place of the proclamation of the good news, of reconciliation, and of the love of God that sustains all life. How could this possibly signify a negative and destructive judgment? People do suffer, but nowhere is there any indication of killing or damning them. In chapters 17 and 18 it is never a question of human beings. They are subjected to suffering as they pass through the judgment; but what is rejected, destroyed, and annihilated is not people. While all members of humanity are passed through the fire no one can enter the temple, as it is being replaced by a new creation.

It should be noted that the plagues described here even more closely resemble those of Egypt than those found in chapters 8 and 9. In Egypt, they symbolized the beginning of the liberation, although at that point the oppressors refused to be converted. Furthermore, those who were liberated did not live up to God's calling either. The deeper underlying reality is the destruction of everything that enslaves, alienates, and reifies God's creatures. As God sovereignly carries out his plan for salvation, people constantly decide that God is unjust and evil, that the God of the Old Testament is a tyrant and that only the God of Jesus Christ is love, that God prevents humanity from growing up, that he is dead, and so on. Throughout the plagues humanity refuses to see that God is really attempting to liberate it, although this involves suffering. Instead, humanity constantly judges God, thereby revealing its dehumanization and enslavement. At best, God is deemed to be the hard master who reaps where he did not sow. All this simply means that humanity condemns itself and has no idea of what is really happening. The rupture seems to be even deeper than the one between Adam and God. For a time, God allows humanity to suffer the consequences of the way it has chosen to alienate and reify itself.

Beginning with the fifth bowl, there is no longer a judgment of humanity alone. Something new enters into the picture: the fifth bowl reveals the throne of the beast; the sixth the dragon, the beast, and the false prophet; and the seventh the great city of Babylon. In fact, the fifth bowl is poured out on the throne of the beast, whose kingdom is plunged into darkness, thereby causing great human suffering. Later, it becomes evident that this is the throne of political power and the state. This power has become so blind that it no longer knows what it does. It becomes incapable of providing leadership to groups and societies. Obviously, this plunges these groups and societies into great suffering. We have seen plenty of this in the twentieth century and are preparing for plenty more in the twenty-first century. Despite this, humanity continues to place its confidence in political power as the way to salvation. In other words, what is beginning to be revealed are the bonds between humanity and the powers. With the sixth bowl, the powers of humanity are added to the demonic powers in direct combat against God. With the seventh bowl, we see the bonds between humanity and the city as the centre of the rebellion against God. We then learn that these powers that alienate and reify humanity are destroyed; but this cannot be accomplished without tearing humanity away from these powers and causing enormous suffering. The cancer that is devouring humanity is removed, and this leaves a gaping wound and howls of suffering and protest. Humanity wanted to make the city its exclusive domain, and now people lament when they see its destruction. They still do not recognize that it is the locus of its alienation and reification.

In chapters 17 and 18 we are told about the condemnation and destruction of Babylon, the great prostitute. Babylon is much more than a historical city and the seat of a particular political empire. It represents the historical incarnation of political power, as well as the city and culture as the works of humanity. The woman is the great prostitute. Throughout the Bible this is never a question of the moral and the sexual. It represents the communication with religious and spiritual powers and their satanic sources. The accompanying immoralities are entirely secondary. It is also the sign of infidelity: the impossibility of trust, faith, and love. These have been withdrawn, redirected, and inserted into the domain of money, exchange, and power – the opposite of the ways of God. Love has been transformed into a diabolical parody of faithfulness to God. The prostitute is Babylon, which means the door to the gods, which are the pretenders, the seducers, the non-gods that penetrate into the human world to redirect it away from God. Babylon is also the place of the historical captivity of Israel, and as such, a symbol of the captivity of the revelation. It makes the world the negation of the Word of God. The prostitute holds a golden cup in imitation of what God does: the establishment of a communion; but in her case, it is communion with her corruption.

Rome appears next. It is founded on the political power of the beast, and its hills (representing its kings) seek to give over their powers to the beast and what it symbolizes. Rome represents political power and the state. The fact that Rome is a city has a deep spiritual significance, to which Jacques Ellul devoted an entire biblical study.[2] Within itself it concentrates economic power and all the other human works of a culture. This human world excludes God and his ways, leaving humanity alienated and dispossessed from itself.

---

2 Jacques Ellul, *The Meaning of the City*, trans. Dennis Pardee (Grand Rapids, MI: Eerdmans, 1970).

In the account of the destruction of Babylon, a clear distinction is made between the city (including everything it represents) and humanity, which watches and laments the spectacle from the outside. What happens to the powers it represents does not happen to the people. The communion with these powers is now broken: the kings have lost their power, the merchants their wealth, and the powerful their influence. However, as people they are outside the destruction, even though they lament their losses. What is being destroyed are the spiritual powers of human history: money, the state, the city, *technique*, and so on. What is left is humanity itself. Some understand what has happened, but others are still in mourning for what they have lost. Here we see the double meaning of the cup (bowl) of communion: it is the communion with God or with the non-gods and powers. The judgment will reveal the extent to which all people's lives are unto death and unto life. Everyone will come to the recognition that only God is the living One.

The judgment falls on everyone. It will be extremely painful to come to the realization that much or all of our lives has been in communion with the powers and hence unto death. We will recognize that much or all of our lives has been lived in vain, and that we have wasted much of this precious gift.

The destruction of the historical forms of the powers is followed by the damnation of the powers themselves. It is indeed a question of damnation, because these powers have pretended to abolish God. First, there is the destruction of the beasts (chapters 19–20), followed by the destruction of the dragon, Satan, and so on (chapter 20:10). Second, there is the destruction of death itself. The entire structure of the judgment is now apparent. First, humanity is judged and its works separated into 'wheat and tares.' This reveals an entanglement between these works and historical forms of powers (such as money, the city, and politics). In turn, this reveals that they are historical incarnations of 'deeper' powers (the beasts) and what has given power and authority to them (the dragon). It ends with the great agent of human life and history, which is their non-meaning, namely, death. It is in the name of this death that the dragon ruled, and it was in death that it had its origin. Since we are speaking of things historical and eternal, we should not interpret this structure as a temporal sequence. It has the didactic purpose of helping us understand what otherwise would be incomprehensible. We have all seen the distortions of these texts, which have been used to satisfy many fancies, including those of some political leaders and self-justifying sects. This revelation is not a kind of historical blueprint that we can use for our own purposes, no matter how tempting this may be. It is both historical and trans-historical.

I will restrict myself to a few details of these so often misused passages. All those who have the mark of the beast die. The text repeats six times that this death is carnal (the flesh). This must be interpreted in the sense this term has in the New Testament (in the gospels and by Paul), referring neither to the human body nor its matter. It designates people who are not only separated from God but who are also hostile to him, and whose works are unto death. It does not refer to the very being of these people, which is related to the spirit. Nowhere does it say in the Bible that human beings are nothing but flesh. What is taken away from people is everything that is flesh, revolt, and refusal of God and all that is attached to the world. It is the uprooting of the tares, and this is very different from death. It is the purification prior to the entrance into the kingdom. In passing, it is important to note that the birds are charged with the removal of this flesh, although they are among the weakest and most timid of all creatures.

In chapter 20 we learn that Satan is first chained up for a thousand years, then set free and finally destroyed. Much nonsense has been written about these texts, mostly based on the idea that it describes a specific historical period. Why should we suddenly interpret this text as being merely historical, when all along it has been symbolic and as much trans-historical as historical? These passages must be interpreted like all the others. A thousand years designates a very long time; and the enchainment of Satan is a placing before humanity of its responsibilities. This puts an end to the possibility of our saying that it was not I but someone or something else. This accusation already began in Genesis when Adam blamed Eve and Eve blamed the serpent as well as God, Who created it. All that is now impossible. Humanity must take responsibility for its works. These are much more than the fruits of people's labours because they constitute the whole of the individual and collective life of humanity. At the end of the thousand years, this work will be complete. At that point, the Accuser is unchained as a prelude to the final judgment. However, it is not people themselves who are thrown into a final combat but the nations, as described in Matthew 25. It is not a question of individual persons but of nations and cultures. Satan, as the great separator and divider, chooses and gathers together everything that is an expression of the revolt of humanity against God and hurls it against the One he wishes to destroy. This satanic separation of the works of humanity is the exact opposite of God's separations in creation and the separation of wheat from tares in the judgment, which were all unto life. Once again, there is no mention of the destruction or damning of people.

Before the destruction of death itself, all those who have been overcome by it must be withdrawn and raised in the image of Jesus. Once this has taken place, death and its abode can be destroyed. This is the second death: the death of death. Only life remains.

Everything in the total work of humanity (all the fruit it has borne) that was unto death has been eliminated in the destruction of the nations. In this way, each human being is judged on his or her works. In this context, there appear the books of the actions of human beings during the thousand years when Satan was chained up. These actions are now the full responsibility of humanity. We also encounter the book of life, showing the intermingling of two themes. On the one hand there is the resurrection and end of death, and on the other those who are not written in the book of life. This cannot refer to people whose works are found to be wanting, since everything unto death has been destroyed. Is God's love for his creatures limited after all? Is his ability to liberate humanity somehow impeded? Will he do to some people what Satan demands after all? Can the last few lost sheep not be found? Was Jesus mistaken when he told us not to fear this very revelation? Can the new creation as the triumph of love be compatible with the denial of that love to some? All these are hypothetical possibilities: it is God alone in his sovereignty who extends grace or who withholds it. Remember the parables of the workers of the eleventh hour, the pearl of great value, the yeast, the salt, and so on. Surely the teaching of the book of life is a pedagogical one. We had better not take God's love for granted by going about our business as usual, assuming everything will turn out all right in the end. All this reinforces what we have learned from the parables of the kingdom of heaven.

Can this revelation make any sense in our scientific and technical age? Is the personification of the powers not another instance of the age-old process of creating religious entities? I am tempted to argue the exact opposite: we are perhaps in a better position to understand these texts than people living in the nineteenth and early twentieth centuries, for example. As far as a person's individual life is concerned, near-death experiences have been mentioned in a previous part. The fact that people who have undergone such experiences talk about a reliving of their lives, but this time having the sense that they now really understand what they did to others and themselves is illustrative, although it proves absolutely nothing. As far as our collective life is concerned: psychology, the sociology of religion, cultural anthropology, and a variety of highly interdisciplinary studies have shown the dependence of any human culture on myths. There is every sign that this dependency continues in our age. All our knowing and doing, our institutions, values and beliefs, hopes and fears are anchored in myth; and when these anchors fail us our individual and collective lives are thrown into turmoil. Our relationship to myth is in some sense analogous to the relationship between fish and water. Knowing no other environment because it would mean instant death, fish live in a way that takes this water for granted. It is the same with human groups, societies, and civilizations. We are a symbolic species that makes sense of and lives in the world by means of a culture that is inseparable from myth. The rises and falls of societies and civilizations correspond to the ability of their cultures and myths to provide human life with an ultimate meaning, value, and direction.[3] Without this, *anomie* would take over.

Once again, I am not suggesting that these insights into the constant dialectical tension between order and chaos in human life and society prove anything. What I am suggesting is that these insights undermine the kinds of pre-judgments with which the book of Revelation has been so frequently judged. Personally, I have always been struck by the insight of the Jewish Bible into the tremendously destructive character of the creation of gods and the roles of religion and morality in a human community. Without these myths, individual and collective human life would be truly secular: freed from their bondage. As we already encountered in

---

3 Cultures, with their myths, have worked so effortlessly in the background of human life and society that they remained virtually unrecognized until the early twentieth century, when *technique* began to desymbolize them, and we could no longer take them for granted. I believe this insight is fundamental for understanding the writings of Jacques Ellul. The following anecdote may illustrate the point. Toward the end of my stay with him, I presented Ellul with the first draft of what would become *The Growth of Minds and Cultures* (Toronto: University of Toronto Press, 1985). After reading this manuscript, he thought he had already dealt with this subject in his own writings. Since I had not read all of these, I confessed (with some apprehension) that this was possible, and asked him to furnish me with the appropriate references. He agreed to do so; and a few days later we met again. He now said he had come to the conclusion that he had not developed this concept anywhere. Relieved, I thanked him, but acknowledged that my early intuitions about the importance of the role of culture in human life and society almost certainly came from attending his lectures and reading his writings. He agreed to write the introduction for my book, which explains his views.

the examination of the opening chapters of Genesis, the good news of liberation announces ways that are diametrically opposed to religion, morality, and magic. The latter are the social and cultural necessities that must be satisfied at the cost of our freedom. Until the contemporary church understands this, it will continue to misrepresent the good news.

I will close with a few brief remarks regarding the fifth part of the book of Revelation, which speaks of the new creation. As the culmination of the reunification of God with his creation, it has nothing to do with the usual descriptions of paradise found in religions. The judgment is a necessary step in the appearance of the new creation. God so much respects his creatures that he takes what is unto life of their works and incorporates it into the new creation, which is not a garden but a city. In this city God will be all in all, thus marking the completion of the ultimate love story. There is nothing more to be said other than amen.

Index

abandoned, 218
absolute majesty, 224
abyss, 20, 223, 224
accomplished, 218
according to its kind, 25
accumulating good works, 209
accusation, 224, 225
Accuser, 79, 97, 224, 230
action: Word of God as guide to
    human, 197–9; as Hebrew *dabar*,
    21, 213, 214
actions: of God, 107, 110, 116, 126,
    153, 156, 186; and those of
    humanity, 111, 155, 160, 231
active power, 174
Adam, 28–30, 35, 40, 43, 45, 48, 49,
    52–4, 58, 59
adultery, 54–6
afraid, 78, 91
age, come of, 86
alienate, 227, 228
alienation, 175, 176, 228
allegory, 157; allegorical explanation
    (of parables in Matthew), 160–3;
    allegorical interpretation (of Job
    by Rashi), 122–3
altar, 226

ambiguity of humanity, 31, 32
ambiguous beings, 28
analogical, 122, 123
'and then I saw,' 219
angel(s), 61, 85, 92, 95, 96, 108, 115,
    192, 226
animals, 27–9, 33
animate matter, 130
annihilated, 227
anomia, 163, 164
anomie, x, xii, xiii, 9n, 56n, 164, 232
answers, 140
anti-feminine, 144
anti-juridical, 177
anxiety, xiii
Apocalypse, 75, 137
ark of the covenant, 223
armour, 145
assimilate, 199
Augustine, St, 142, 192
authentic: Job as, 140; witness
    provided by Matthew, 161
authority, 161, 167, 168
autonomy, 70, 71

Babylon: city, 227; destruction of,
    228, 229; as great prostitute, 228;

mourning for loss represented by destruction of, 229; overcome by way of non-power of Lamb, 226; place of captivity of Israel, 228

Babylonian creation story, 14–15; as cosmogony, 18; and Egyptian creation story, 3, 14; and Genesis, 3, 14, 15, 16

baptized, 193

Barth, Karl, 62, 71, 73, 93, 94, 135–6, 194, 215, 216, 218

'bashing' (of science and technology), xiv

bearers of God's word, 197

beast of the abyss, 62, 130

Beatitudes, 183

beginning, 213

Behemoth, 129–32; mountains pay tribute to, 130

belief, 137

believers, 172

beloved Son, 216

bird(s), 112, 113, 166, 230

birth, 81, 83

black horse, 220

blessing, 27, 38, 39

body, 15, 16, 27; of believers, 221; of Christ, 154, 155

book of life, 231

bowls, 219, 225

brain-mind, organization of, xi, xiv

break with God, 34, 35, 39, 47, 48, 66, 70–2, 76, 77–98 passim

breath, and spirit (*ruach*), 20, 49, 105, 110; as fragile and ephemeral, 105; of life, 43; as opposed to 'vanity' (*hevel*), 105

calculation, 186

called, 190, 191, 193, 194, 197, 199; call(ed) into question, 128, 205, 218

Calvin, John, 192, 194

Canaanites, 13, 19, 184; religions of, 64–5

cancer, 228

canon, 102, 103

carnal, 230

catastrophes, 225

catechism, 6

Chaine, J., 8, 23, 44, 50, 54

Chaldeans, 112

chaos, 20, 130, 131–3, 223–5

Chesterton, G.K., 28

chosen, 188, 191, 193, 194

Chouraqui, André, 25

Christians, 170–3; Christian society, xii

Chronos. *See Khronos*

church: as body of believers, 186; disappears in kingdom of God, 167; early, 152, 181, 193, 201, 202; Ellul and, ix; and faith vs. works, 200; fathers, 45, 157, 160; and forceful conversion, 192; and history, 224; intolerance of institutional, xx; and judgment, 163, 172, 173, 178, 188, 192–3; and kingdom of heaven, 151, 152, 154–6, 169, 197, 219; as lampholder, 197; letters to (in Revelation), 209, 219; misrepresents good news, 133; without direction, 199

city, 189, 191, 228, 229, 233

clay, 132, 133

clothing, 77, 88–90, 92

comforted, 204

commandment(s), xvii, 32; as warning, 50

commitment to the text, 125
communication, 84, 85, 98
communion: break in, 78–80; double aspect of, 226; maintained in love, 78; meal of, 130, 143; lost, 89; sexual, 43, 50; and unity of man and woman, 84, 88; with corruption of prostitute, 228; with God, 46, 49, 50, 66, 72, 73, 86; with Jesus Christ, 193, 206; with king, 205; with powers, 229
compel to enter, 192
composition of the text, 12
condemn(ed), 115, 116, 194, 220, 225, 226
conflict, 190, 192
conquest, spirit of, 87
conservative (Christianity), xviii
constellation, 122
contradictions, 40, 45
contradictory accounts, 12
converting, 192
cosmogony, 18
covenant, 17, 79, 80, 88, 185, 186, 219, 223, 225
creation, 17, 18, 19, 83, 85, 86, 97, 98, 120–5, 223–5, 233
creationism, 25
Creator: and creation, 34, 36; discernment of in creation, 126; and his creatures, 120; kingship of, 151; name Elohim used for, 41–2; no longer separated from creation, 224, 225
crocodile, 127, 129–31
cross, 45, 90, 131–2, 135, 137, 206, 218, 226
crucifixion, 222, 223
Crusades, 192

cultivation, 51
cultural glasses, xii
culture, x–xv, 224, 228, 230, 232
cunning, 62, 63, 66
curse, 77, 79, 80, 83

daily sustenance, 220
damnation, 91, 156, 172, 173, 229
damned, 164, 172, 222, 226
Dante, 91, 95
day, 23, 24
dead (apart from God), 50, 52
death, 83, 84, 90, 91, 97, 176, 220, 223–5, 229–31
debt, 174–6
debtor, 174, 175
Decalogue, 70, 150
de-creation, 224
defend (ourselves), 114
delay, 152, 153
demonic, 96
demon(s), 62, 78, 96
denarius, 184, 185, 220
de Pury, Roland, 142, 143
desire, 66
d'Espagnat, Bernard, principle of inseparability of, 124
destiny, 32, 36
destruction of the powers, 220, 225
Devil, 47, 137, 224, 225
disasters, 221
discernment, 128
discipline, ix, x, xv, xvi, xviii
disease and death, 220, 223
disruption, 188
distortion of the text, xiii, xviii
divine paternalism, 85
doctrine of creation, 17
dogs, 207

d'Olivet, (Antoine) Fabre, 18, 19
domain of Satan, 162
dominate, 33, 34
domination, 82, 87, 88, 89, 205, 208
Donatists, 192
dough, 165–7, 221, 222
dragon, 61, 62, 130, 132, 224, 227, 229
dualism (impossibility of), 155
dualistic (Bible is not), 155
duality, 224
dust, 62, 80, 81, 83, 84, 90

eagles, 123
earth (*eretz*), 18, 20
east, 44
economic power, 220, 228
Eden: meaning of term, 43; symbolic
    associations with, 43–5. *See also*
    garden of Eden
efficient, 187
Egypt, 3, 14, 129, 130, 175, 224, 227
election, 156
eleventh hour, 181, 182
Elihu, 101–4, 105–8, 110, 115, 117
Elohim, 12, 13, 18–20, 22, 30, 41–3
Elohist tradition, 13
end: of time, 136, 137, 149, 151, 152,
    222, 225; of the world, 150, 152,
    196, 201
engagement, 173
enslaved, xii, xiv, xv, xviii
enslavement, to cultural myths, xiii,
    xiv, xv, xvii–xix
entirely other, xii
environmental crisis, 87
equality, 217
eternal, 216, 217; good news, 226
eternity, 41, 44, 151, 152
ethical (orientation), 173
Eve, 73, 74; name of, 88

evening, 23, 24, 36
evidence, 69, 75
evil, 45–51, 54, 61–3, 65, 66–71, 73,
    79, 93–5, 128, 130–3
exhortation, 199, 202, 203
existential questions, 118, 119
experience, xi
expression, 215, 217
expulsion, 189

fabric of human history, 220
faith, 119, 164, 168, 198, 200, 201, 218,
    221, 222, 228; and hope and love,
    164; without works, 200
fall, 61, 62, 70; view of as positive, 87
false prophet(s), 197, 227
Father, 217
fear, 220, 226, 231
fifth: bowl, 227; seal, 220, 221
final: cause, 111; judgment, 175, 179
finitude, 83–5
fire, 165, 172, 173
first: cause, 36; group of workers
    called, 183–4; Israel as, 186; vs.
    last, 185–6
fish and water (analogy for human
    relationship to myth), 232
flesh, 230
flexible, 128, 129
flood, 112, 224
food, 69
forgiven, 175, 176, 178
forgiveness, 175, 177, 178
form of God, 217
for nothing, 184
fragile, 105, 108, 116
freedom, ix, xiv–xviii, 22, 31, 35–7,
    48–50, 52, 53, 55, 56, 107, 114, 116,
    117, 170, 190, 195; of animals, 124
friend, 183

fruit, 177; from tree, 66
fruitful, 33
fulfilment, 151, 153
functionaries (of king), 175

gap, 225
garden of Eden, 121, 125; cross
    already present in, 45; ejection
    from, 88; location in 'east,' 44;
    return to not possible, 92; rivers
    of, 44–5; two trees in, 45; working
    and guarding of as worship, 51.
    See also Eden
generals, 221
gift(s): of grace, 179; of life, 184
glory, 44, 57; as opposite of humility,
    208; humanity called to glorify
    God, 175, 176
gnosis, 67
God: as 'all in all,' 156, 233; as
    all-powerful, 78, 107, 119, 144;
    analogy of totality of, 124; being
    of (three elements vs. three
    persons), 215; glory of, 117, 175; as
    hidden, 158; incarnation of as
    God-man, 132, 161; knowledge of,
    137; as love, 202, 223; as object,
    202; relationship with, 202;
    speaks, 119, 124; as triune, 22, 215;
    will of, 194, 200
god(s): Babylonian, 21, 24; as
    non-gods, 228, 229; term, 215
Goethe, 213
good, 43, 45, 46, 48, 49, 51, 54; and
    evil, 45–51, 91, 93, 225
good news, 170, 173, 225
gospel, 74, 163, 181; of liberation and
    love, xvii; of the way of non-
    power, 226; Revelation not
    another, 222

gospel of Mathew: differences from
    other gospels, 150–3
grace, 89, 90, 93, 108, 138, 174, 178,
    179, 181, 182, 192, 195, 209, 210
Graham, Billy, 206
grammar, 12
gratis, 184
great calm, 221
great prostitute, the, 228
greatest: in the kingdom of heaven,
    206, 208–10; is smallest, 209
greed, 178
Greek (language), 109, 112, 115
Greek philosophy: conception of
    Logos different from biblical, 217;
    influence on interpretations of
    Genesis, 8–9, 34; influence on
    Jerome's translation, 46
growth, 177
guilt, 83

Hagadah, 48
happy, 204
hearing, and seeing, 136
heavens, 151
Hebrew (language), 109
Heidegger, Martin, 74
hell, 91, 95, 157, 163, 164, 172, 173,
    179, 194
heresy, 192
hidden: dimension, 119; God, 158;
    kingdom, 149; working, 221
hierarchy, 89
hippopotamus, 127, 129–31
history, 5, 10, 22, 24, 31, 32, 36, 37, 39,
    62, 71, 72, 76, 77, 80, 86, 87, 95, 110,
    112, 162, 164–7, 172, 177, 179,
    219–29; historical event(s), 11, 220
holiness, 150
holy (God calls us to be), xii

240   Index

Holy Spirit, 4, 138, 153, 173, 180, 198,
    208, 215, 218
homosexuality, 54–6
honour, 214
hope, 222
horse(s), 219, 220
human: condition, 175, 176; history,
    36, 38, 39; Jesus, 216, 217; power,
    127; qualities, 198
humanity, 29–32, 220, 223, 225–31
humility, 205, 206, 208, 209; of Jesus
    Christ, 145, 205, 210; of Job, 137, 138
Husserl, Edmund, 74

idolatry, 96
idols, xii
image of God, 28, 29–31, 33, 57, 89,
    92, 93, 158
impossible: choice, 159; possibility,
    194
inanimate matter, 130
incarnation, 216, 223–5; Creator no
    longer separated from creation in,
    224; integral part of God's work
    from beginning, 216; of God, 132,
    161; historical incarnations of
    'deeper' powers, 229
incognito, 197
infallible inspiration, 4, 5, 13
infidelity, 228
inheritance, 144
inherit the earth, 204
injustice, 177
Inquisition, 192
inspiration, 3–5
integrality (of text), 8
integration propaganda, xix
intelligence, 144
intercede, 141

intercessor, 141, 144
interpretation, 107, 109
intervention, ix, xvi, xix, 112, 113,
    174, 176, 178
'in the beginning': better translated
    as 'within the beginning,' 23, 31,
    213, 214; Faust's understanding
    of, 213; Jesus was with God, 216;
    Jesus was with the Logos, 216;
    Word already present, 135
Israel, 186, 224
'it' is good, 54

Jeremias, Joachim, 180, 193, 202
Jerome, St, 46, 142
Jesus, 222, 223, 224, 226; and/as
    eternal Logos), 216, 217; humanity
    of, 216, 217
Jesus Christ, 188, 189, 193, 217, 224,
    225; as Lamb, 220–1, 225–6; name
    used in vain, 207; remarkable
    things done in name of, 208; as
    vehicle of salvation, 222
Jewish people, 188, 190, 221; as
    monogamous, 56–7; surrounded
    by polygamous societies, 57
Job: authenticity of, 140; confessions
    of, 135; end of, 142; friends of,
    140–3; as suffering servant figure,
    141; as prophet of Jesus Christ,
    132, 140; repentance of, 137–8
John the Baptist, 197, 198, 217
Jonah, miracle of, 137
joy, 169, 170, 188, 193, 195
Judaism, xiv, 215
Judges, 38, 111
judge(s), 110, 111, 207, 222, 227, 231
judgment, 150, 156, 172, 173, 174–6,
    178, 179, 197, 201, 224–7, 229, 233

justice, 110–15, 127, 128, 133, 140, 174,
    176–8, 180, 182, 183, 204–6, 220,
    221; of God, 110, 115, 127, 128, 220

Kabbala, 7, 8
kairos, 188, 189, 190, 195
keystone, 208
Kierkegaard, Søren, 172; definition
    of God given by, 137
kingdom of God, 73, 74, 75, 167, 225;
    distinguished from kingdom of
    heaven, viii, 149–56 passim; entry
    into is God's decision, 194, 195; no
    longer includes a church, 166–7,
    192; received as a promise, 168;
    and salvation, 192, 194, 209, 222
kingdom of heaven, 149–59, 219, 221,
    222; as combination of the actions
    of God and the actions of people,
    155; as domain, 162; as a force in
    action, 154, 155; as hidden in the
    world, 149; as justice and love,
    155; as kingdom of the Son, 151;
    as mystery, 156, 157; as opposition
    to laws of the world, 155
kings, 228, 229
knowing: and dealing with world;
    ix; discipline-based approach to,
    xvi; the good as communion with
    God, 73–4; good and evil, 45, 67,
    68, 93; science as human self-
    critical, xiii; scientific, and
    technological doing, xiv, 232; two
    ways of knowing God, 78
knowledge: of good and evil as
    separated from God, 93 (*see also
    under* good, and evil); of Hebrew
    language, 109; intellectual vs.
    love-based, 67, 78, 79; no objective,

    66; of serpent, 64, 68; true vs. exact,
    72, 75; vs. divine revelation, 95
kronos, 188, 190
Kronos/Chronos (god), 24, 215

labourer(s), 181, 186, 187
Lamb, 220, 221, 226
lament, 228, 229
land of Israel, 18
landowner, 181, 184, 187
Laodicea, church at, 209
last judgment, 137, 142, 150, 160, 163,
    166, 173, 174, 179, 186, 188
last (vs. first), 185, 186
Latin translation (St Jerome's), 109
law(s), 66, 69, 70, 79, 149, 150, 155,
    175, 177–9, 209; of the kingdom,
    181, 183, 226; and the prophets,
    149
letters (in Revelation), 219
Leviathan, 129–33
Levinas, Emmanuel, 57, 59
Leviticus, 132
liberal Christianity, xviii
life, 195, 231, 232
light, xvii–xix, 144
limits of life and death, 150
logical, 131
Logos, 213–16; corresponds to
    Hebrew *dabar*, 214; and Faust,
    213–14; Jesus as, 216, 217; transla-
    tion inadequate, 213; turned
    toward creation, 217; turned
    toward humanity, 217
Lord's Prayer, 175
lost sheep, 231
love, viii, ix, xiv, xvii–xix, 27, 30, 31,
    33–6, 38, 39, 65, 66, 70–4, 78, 79,
    87, 91–6, 125, 140, 141, 149, 150,

155, 158, 159, 171–3, 174, 176, 178, 179, 181–3, 194, 195, 223, 231, 233
love for nothing (forgiveness), 143
loving light, xvii
Lucifer, as foreign to Hebrew thinking, 47, 61, 62, 95
Luther, Martin, 200
lust, 69

magic, 64, 66, 69, 70, 233
Maillot, Alphonse, 135
male and female, 56, 57
Mammon, 170, 172
man, 216, 217; and woman, 53, 54, 57, 60
mark of the beast, 230
marriage, 36
masculine and feminine, 58
Maslow, Abraham, xiv
master, 53, 54, 201, 202
material and spiritual life, 84
material means, 134
matter, 129, 130–3
Matthew. *See* gospel of Matthew
meaning: Christocentric, 7; esoteric, 7; literal, 11, 19; literary, 11; meaning of, 11; spiritual, 6, 11; symbolic, 8; of the text, 6
meaninglessness, xii
meanings: of *dabar* as both spoken word and action, 214; distorted by translation, 46; double, 122; hidden or esoteric, 9; plurality of, 8, 19; seventy-seven plus the true one, 7, 109; and values and commitments, x, xi–xiii, xv
means, 168
measure(s): of flour, 166; of wheat, 220
mediation: between God and seekers, 138; by angels, 151;

required to access God, 13; work of Jesus Christ as, 75
mediator (within creation), 34; Job as, 141, 144
members, 154
memory, short-term loss of, xi
mercy, 174
messenger, 106, 107, 115
Messiah, 144
metalanguage, 214
metaphysics, 6
military leaders, 111
miracle(s), 133, 137, 138, 207, 208
mixing, 132, 224
monarchy, 38
money, 172, 178, 179, 228, 229
monogamy (of Jews), 56–7; as opposed to surrounding polygamous societies, 57
monotheism(s): as term, 215; can be contradictory, 215; of Islam, 215; of Jews/Judaism, 19, 215
monsters, 132
moral, 191, 193, 195, 200, 208, 209
morality, xii–xiv, 46–8, 54, 64, 66, 69, 70, 222, 232, 233
multiply, 'be fruitful and,' 32, 33, 35; fruits other than children, 33
mustard: seed, 160, 177; tree, 166
mutation, 166
mystery: of creation, 120; of God, 222, 223
myth(s): Assyrian and Babylonian, 90; as 'cultural DNA,' xii; and history, 71–2; human dependence on/enslavement to, xiii, xiv, xvii, 232; secular, xiv
mythical: meaning, 122; thinking, 157
mythology/-ies: Babylonian and Egyptian, 21; battle between good

and evil in, 225; celestial, 85; of
    Job's time, 121
naked, 63, 71, 75, 77
name(s): given to animals, 35, 52;
    knowing gives power, 42; of
    Adam, 30, 48–9, 72, 88; of Elihu,
    103; (of/used for God), 7, 12, 13,
    19, 40–3, 88, 119; of Satan, 79, 97;
    of woman, 53–4, 81, 88
nations, 221, 230, 231
nature: ability of to address God, 98;
    the Adam has animal, 48; cultural
    old, xii; diminished after break
    with God, 93; no gods in, 33;
    responsibility of man and woman
    for, 83
near-death experience(s), xvii, xviii,
    231
necessary evil, punishment as, 133
necessity/-ies, xiii, xiv; creation
    consisting of, 97; of life, 184, 220;
    social and cultural, 221–2, 233
neighbour, 113
neural and synaptic changes, xi
new creation, 85, 165, 221, 224, 227,
    231, 233
nomos, 163
non-power: of Jesus, 167, 168; and
    non-violence, 114; way of, viii,
    206, 208

objectivity, xv
oral tradition, 13
original sin, 70, 75, 87, 89, 94

pacifism, 114
pagan gods, 130
pagans, 172
pale horse, 220
parable(s): hell encountered in, 157;
    impossible to interpret as allegory,
157, 158, 161; make a single point,
    157; oriental thinking in, 167;
    simultaneously reveal and veil,
    158, 159; speak to faith, 153, 159
– of kingdom of heaven, viii, 150–207
    passim, 221, 231; of debtors, 174–9
    passim; of fishing net, 172; of grain
    of mustard seed, 160–8 passim, 177;
    of labourers' wages, 180–7 passim;
    of man sowing good seed, 160–8
    passim; of pearl of great value,
    169–73 passim, 199, 231; of prodigal
    son, 111; of talents, 196–203; of
    treasure hidden in field, 169–73
    passim; of virgins, 196–203 passim;
    of wedding feast, 188–95 passim; of
    wheat and tares, 110, 162; of
    workers of eleventh hour, 181–2,
    186, 205, 231; of yeast, 155, 160–8
    passim, 177
pardon, 108, 138
passes through the fire, 165
Passover, 141, 143
pay, 182
pearl. See under parable(s): of
    kingdom of heaven, of pearl of
    great value
people of God, 221
persecution, as part of Christian life,
    205; for righteousness' sake, 204–6
perseverance, 199
Pharisees, 48, 181, 208
pious, 209
plague(s), 133, 227; of Egypt, 224
politician, 114
polytheistic, 19, 215
poor, 185, 189, 193, 195, 204, 205;
    church as, 209; poor in spirit,
    204–6
poverty, 128, 205; gold along with,
    45, 47

power, 118–20, 123, 125, 205, 208,
210; of accusation, 79; of chaos
and the abyss, 133, 224; of God,
105, 107, 110, 111, 114–16; and
justice, 111, 115, 118; of language,
21; of matter, 129, 130, 133; and
non-power, 114, 208 (*see also*
non-power); as opposed to love,
33; political, 220, 222, 227, 228;
Satanic, 62; spectacular means of,
208; water as destructive, 21; will
to (*see* will to power); at work, 181
powerful, excluded, 206
powerlessness, recognition of our, 209
power(s): and death, 223, 224;
demonic, 96–8, 194, 220, 223–6,
228, 229; divine, 19; evil, 33, 144;
and principalities, 97, 151;
associated with serpent, 64
practices, 207
praxis, 200
prayer, 176, 177, 220
predestination, 191, 193, 194
pre-understanding, pre-established
ideas act as, 214
pride, 107, 112–15, 209
Priestly tradition, 12, 13, 16
prime mover, 36
prince of this world, 162, 170
principalities and powers, 97
principle of inseparability, 124
prison, 133
progress, 166
prophecy, 208
prophet, 106, 109, 116, 117, 207
prostitute, 228
protection, 63, 77, 89
providence, 37
purification, 225, 230
purpose, 121

quality/-ies (of those in kingdom of
heaven): ability to put things into
practice, 200; hope, 201; vigilance,
199; wisdom, 200
question(s): asked by God, 120, 131;
Bible as book of, 120; God's
answers to, 125; of Job, 118–20; not
asked of Father by Jesus, 137

Rabbinical tradition, 102, 104
radically other, xi, xiii
rainbow, 219
ransom, 108
Rashi, 122, 130
readiness, 197
reality, and truth: cannot be reconciled in our world, 136; fusion in
Apocalypse, 75–6
recompense (entrance into kingdom
of heaven as), 207
reconciliation, 143, 144, 220, 226
redemption, 171
red horse, 220
reference point, 199
Reformation, 70. *See also under*
theology
refusal: of call of God, 190; of
invitation to wedding feast,
189–91; to participate in kingdom
of heaven, 159
rejected power in history, 191
rejection: of God by people, 191; of
Israel, 186, 189; by king, 183, 191;
of one wedding guest, 191, 193; as
temporary, 191; of unworthy
members of church, 188
relativism, x
reliable (to the letter), 104
religion, xii, xiii, xiv, xvii, xix, 64, 65,
66, 68, 70, 222, 223, 233; and faith, 10

religious wars, 192

repentance, 208; advised by Job's friends, 142; averts condemnation by God, 116; insufficient to wait until last moment, 186; impossible to receive revelation without, 137; of Job, 115, 135, 137, 138, 143; Lent as period of, 180; suffering as call to, 107–8

reproduction, 177

responsibility, of humanity for its works, 230, 231

responsible (God makes people), 78, 79, 120

rest, 36–9

resurrection, 84, 85, 142, 143, 165, 167, 176, 222, 223, 226

return (of Jesus Christ), 150, 152, 153, 197, 198, 201, 202

reunification, 219, 225, 233

Revelation, book of, ix, 62, 75, 85, 90, 94, 164, 165, 193, 194, 219–33 passim. *See also* Apocalypse

revelation, xii, xvii–xix, 105, 106, 109, 115–17, 158, 159

reward, 165

rib, 58–60

rich, the, 185, 221, 222

Ricoeur, Paul, 11, 72, 75, 83, 86

right or wrong, 141, 143

river, 43–5

Roman Empire, 221

Rome, 228

rupture, 221, 227

sacrifice, 89, 90

salvation, 17, 19, 20, 27, 61, 62, 92, 94, 95, 141, 143, 156, 180, 182, 188, 192, 194, 222, 223, 226, 227

'same' (refers to Jesus in John), 216

Samuel, 38

Satan, 47, 79, 97, 171, 172, 225, 229, 230, 231, 207

saved, 156, 172

saying 'lord, lord,' not sufficient, 207

school, 13

science, viii, ix, xiii, xiv; and faith, 11

scribes, 181

sea, 121, 224

seal(s), 114, 219, 220, 223

second creation account, 40, 43, 46

second death, 231

secular, 232

security blanket, 145

seducers, non-gods of Babylon as, 228

seduction, by Crafty One, 71

seed, 171

seeing: and hearing, 136; reality the domain of, 75; refers to end of time, 136, 137

self-justification, xii, xiii, 208

separation, 66, 220, 225, 231; creation as act of, 23, 25, 224, 231; from garden, 91; from the good and from life, 46; of heavens from earth, 151; of historical Jesus from Christ, 217; of humanity from God, 17, 47, 63, 66, 80, 86, 91, 92, 93, 97, 230; of good from evil, 46, 172; from the good and from life, 46; of material from spiritual, 84; means death, 52; of saved from damned, 164, 222; of what is unto good from what is unto life, 220; of wheat from tares, xviii, 164, 229

Sermon on the Mount, 150, 204

serpent, 61–9, 77–81, 83–5, 94, 128, 224, 230; and magic, 64; and religion, 63–9

servant, 141, 144, 182, 205, 210

service, 48, 50, 51
seven, 17, 32, 36–9, 219; seventh bowl,
    228; seventh seal, 222, 223, 225
sexuality, 56
sheep, 222, 231
silence, 223
sin, xviii, 108, 110, 113
six, 28, 29, 32, 36; sixth bowl, 227;
    sixth seal, 221
slavery, 130
slave(s), xii, xiii, xiv, xv, xvii–xix, 176
small book, 225
smallest, is greatest, 209
social necessities, 222
son of God, 222
Son of man, 160, 161, 163
soul (*nefesh*), 27, 43, 49, 85, 197; Bible
    has no notion of immortal, 84;
    immortal soul a Greek invention, 85
speaks, 213–15
species, 25, 28, 29
spirit, 27, 50, 84, 85, 87, 97, 106, 110,
    218, 230; and breath (*ruach*), 20, 49,
    105; of domination, 205, 208; of
    the spectacular, 208; spiritual
    dimension, xii. *See also* Holy Spirit
Steinmann, Jean, 142
spiritual roots, viii, xii
state, xiv, xix, 192, 220, 227–9
status, 106
stoic philosophers, 164
strange, 173
structuralism, 11
submit, 35, 37
success, 167
suffering, viii, ix, 128, 131, 196, 221,
    223, 226, 227; and birth, 81–2; as
    call to repentance, 107, 108; of
    creation, 83; and work, 82–3; of
    Jesus, 196, 202; of Job, 112, 121,
    108, 140, 141, 143; servant, 141

suicide, 209
surgeon, 223
sword, 179, 220
symbol, 219

talents, 175, 178
Talmud, 59, 142, 144; Talmudic
    explanation, 104; Talmudists. *See*
    Levinas, Emmanuel; Rashi
tares, 162, 164, 229, 230
Targum, 138
technique, xvi, xix, 10n, 34, 55–6n, 63,
    77, 86, 87, 89, 133, 229, 232
temple, 226
temptation, 61, 62, 64–71, 73
Tertullian, 45
testimony, 220
testing, 199
tetragram, 41, 215; shares letters
    with name of Eve, 88
theogonies, Babylonian, 132
theologians, ix, xv, xvi
theological system, xii, xvii
theology, x, xv, xviii; 'God is dead,'
    218; natural, 123; Reformation, 123
thousand years, 230, 231
throne of the beast, 227
time, 23, 24; end of, 136, 137, 149,
    151, 152; and eternity, 44, 152; two
    notions of, 188–9. *See also khronos*;
    khairos
tohu wabohu, 20, 23, 94, 214, 218
totality (of God), 124
tower of Babel, 92
transhistorical, 224
transnational corporation, xiv
treasure, 169–71
tree: of life, 45, 50; of the knowledge
    of good and evil, 45, 49, 51
trial, 220, 221
Trinity, 215

troubles, 223
true, 204
trumpets, 224
trust, 228
truth, 67, 68, 70, 75, 76, 106, 107; as
    domain of Word, 75; and reality,
    9–10, 75
two witnesses, 224, 225
tyrant, 129, 131

ultimate love story, ix, 219, 225, 233
unconditional love, xiv, xvii
understanding: of the Bible, 218; of
    God, 126
unjust and damned (vs. just and
    saved), 222
unknown, xi
unliveable, 164
unto death, 220, 221, 223–5, 229–31
unto life, 220, 225, 226, 229, 233
unveiling and veiling (of revelation),
    158
unworthy, 188
upside down, 168
useless servants, 73
utility, 121

vanity, 105
victim, 226
vigilance, 162, 196, 199
violence, 192
virgins. See under parable(s), of
    virgins
Vischer, Wilhelm, 7
von Rad, Gerhard, 68
vocation, 181, 182, 186
void, 121
vowels, 109

wages, 180
waiting, 197, 199, 203
war, 220
warning, 172, 173, 207, 208
water, 19, 20, 21, 23, 25
ways of God, 228
weak, 206, 209
wedding: feast, 188, 189; garment,
    189, 193
wheat, 162; and tares, 162, 229. See
    also under parable(s): of kingdom
    of heaven, of wheat and tares
white: horse and rider, 219; robes
    (symbolizing justice), 221
wicked, 127, 128
will: of the Father, 206–8; of God, 68,
    70, 112, 113, 137, 194, 195; to
    power, 70, 87
wine, and oil, 220
wing of the ostrich (allegory in
    Calvin), 124
wisdom, 105, 106, 200
withdraw (from the world), 170, 171
witness, 221, 224
woman, 48, 53, 54, 57–60, 144
Word, 21–3, 213–15, 218
word of God, 69, 73, 219, 228
words and deeds, 207
work, 50, 51, 82, 83, 88, 94
works, 161, 163–6, 177, 200–2; of
    humanity, 228, 230
world of colour, xi
worship, 51
wrath, 226

Yahweh, 19, 41–3
Yahwist tradition, 12, 13
yeast, 160, 165–8, 171, 221, 222, 231